Manuals in Archaeological Method, Theory and Technique

Series Editors:

Charles E. Orser, Jr., *Vanderbilt University, Nashville, TN, USA*
Michael B. Schiffer, *University of Arizona, Tucson, AZ, USA*

For further volumes:
http://www.springer.com/series/6256

João Manuel Marreiros
Juan F. Gibaja Bao • Nuno Ferreira Bicho
Editors

Use-Wear and Residue Analysis in Archaeology

Editors
João Manuel Marreiros
Universidade do Algarve
Faro
Portugal

Nuno Ferreira Bicho
Universidade do Algarve
Faro
Portugal

Juan F. Gibaja Bao
Institución Milà i Fontanals
Barcelona
Spain

ISSN 1571-5752
ISBN 978-3-319-08256-1   ISBN 978-3-319-08257-8 (eBook)
DOI 10.1007/978-3-319-08257-8
Springer Cham Heidelberg New York Dordrecht London

Library of Congress Control Number: 2014950062

© Springer International Publishing Switzerland 2015

This work is subject to copyright. All rights are reserved by the Publisher, whether the whole or part of the material is concerned, specifically the rights of translation, reprinting, reuse of illustrations, recitation, broadcasting, reproduction on microfilms or in any other physical way, and transmission or information storage and retrieval, electronic adaptation, computer software, or by similar or dissimilar methodology now known or hereafter developed. Exempted from this legal reservation are brief excerpts in connection with reviews or scholarly analysis or material supplied specifically for the purpose of being entered and executed on a computer system, for exclusive use by the purchaser of the work. Duplication of this publication or parts thereof is permitted only under the provisions of the Copyright Law of the Publisher's location, in its current version, and permission for use must always be obtained from Springer. Permissions for use may be obtained through RightsLink at the Copyright Clearance Center. Violations are liable to prosecution under the respective Copyright Law.

The use of general descriptive names, registered names, trademarks, service marks, etc. in this publication does not imply, even in the absence of a specific statement, that such names are exempt from the relevant protective laws and regulations and therefore free for general use.

While the advice and information in this book are believed to be true and accurate at the date of publication, neither the authors nor the editors nor the publisher can accept any legal responsibility for any errors or omissions that may be made. The publisher makes no warranty, express or implied, with respect to the material contained herein.

Printed on acid-free paper

Springer is part of Springer Science+Business Media (www.springer.com)

Contents

1 **Use–Wear and Residue Analysis in Archeology** 1
  Nuno Bicho, João Marreiros and Juan F. Gibaja

2 **Macro and Micro Evidences from the Past: The State
  of the Art of Archeological Use-Wear Studies** 5
  João Marreiros, Niccollò Mazzucco, Juan F. Gibaja and Nuno Bicho

3 **Ethnoarchaeology and Functional Analysis** 27
  J. González-Urquijo, S. Beyries and J.J. Ibáñez

4 **Use-Wear Analysis on Flint Tools. Beyond
  the Methodological Issues** 41
  Juan F. Gibaja and Bernard Gassin

5 **Use-wear Analysis of Nonflint Lithic Raw Materials:
  The Cases of Quartz/Quartzite and Obsidian** 59
  I. Clemente Conte, T. Lazuén Fernández, L. Astruc
  and A. C. Rodríguez Rodríguez

6 **Keys to the Identification of Prehension and Hafting Traces** 83
  Veerle Rots

7 **Current Analytical Frameworks for Studies of Use–Wear
  on Ground Stone Tools** 105
  Laure Dubreuil, Daniel Savage, Selina Delgado-Raack, Hugues Plisson,
  Birgitta Stephenson and Ignacio de la Torre

8 **Use-Wear Methodology on the Analysis of Osseous Industries** 159
  Marina Almeida Évora

9 Traceology on Metal. Use-Wear Marks on Copper-Based
   Tools and Weapons 171
   Carmen Gutiérrez Sáez and Ignacio Martín Lerma

10 Pottery Use-Alteration Analysis 189
   James M. Skibo

11 About Small Things and Bigger Pictures: An Introduction to
   the Morphological Identification of Micro-residues
   on Stone Tools 199
   Geeske H. J. Langejans and Marlize Lombard

Index 221

Acknowledgments

At the time of the organization of the International conference on Use-Wear analysis 2012, held in Faro (Portugal), due to the participation of papers from all different research topics, we realize that Use-Wear and residue analysis required a solid handbook covering all multidisciplinary methods and techniques. Thus, we approached several researchers to contribute with a chapter on their research topic in order to provide a methodological framework for different materials and techniques. Therefore, we would like to thank all colleagues that kindly accepted our invitation to participate in this handbook, with interesting papers covering a range of diverse topics and techniques recently used on usewear and residue analysis. We also would like to acknowledge Springer for accepting this handbook and Teresa Krauss and Hana Nagdimov for the consistent support and contribution, adding fundamental suggestions and adjustments during the submission process of this volume.

Contributors

L. Astruc CNRS/ArScan, Nanterre, France

S. Beyries CEPAM—UMR 7264, C.N.R.S./Université Nice Sophia Antipolis, Pôle Universitaire Saint Jean d'Angély, Nice, France

Nuno Bicho Interdisciplinary Center for Archaeology and Human Behavior, FCHS—Universidade do Algarve, Campus de Gambelas, Faro, Portugal

I. Clemente Conte Dpto. de Arqueología y Antropología, IMF-CSIC, Barcelona, Spain

Ignacio de la Torre Institute of Archaeology, University College London, London, UK

Selina Delgado-Raack Human Development in Landscapes, Christian-Albrechts Universität Kiel, Kiel, Germany

Laure Dubreuil Department of Anthropology, Trent University, Peterborough, ON, Canada

Marina Almeida Évora Interdisciplinary Center for Archaeology and Evolution of Human Behaviour, FCHS—Universidade do Algarve, Faro, Portugal

Bernard Gassin TRACES, Toulouse Cedex 9, France

Juan F. Gibaja Departamento de Arqueología y Antropología, Investigador contratado por el Ministerio de Economía y Competitividad—Subprograma Ramón y Cajal, Institución Milá y Fontanals, Consejo Superior de Investigaciones Científicas (IMF-CSIC), Barcelona, C/Egipciàques, 15, Spain

CSIC—Institución Milà y Fontanals, Barcelona, Spain

J. González-Urquijo Instituto de Prehistoria (IIIPC)/Departamento de Ciencias Históricas, Universidad de Cantabria, Santander, Spain

J.J. Ibáñez Institució Milà i Fontanals, C.S.I.C., Barcelona, Spain

Geeske H. J. Langejans Centre for Anthropological Research, University of Johannesburg, Auckland Park, 2006, South Africa

T. Lazuén Fernández PACEA, UMR 5199, CNRS-Université Bordeaux, Pessac Cedex, France

Ignacio Martín Lerma Dpt. de Prehistoria y Arqueología. FFLL, Universidad Autónoma, Madrid, Spain

Marlize Lombard Department of Anthropology and Development Studies, University of Johannesburg, Auckland Park, South Africa

João Marreiros Interdisciplinary Center for Archaeology and Human Behavior, FCHS—Universidade do Algarve, Campus de Gambelas, Faro, Portugal

Departamento de Arqueología y Antropología, Institución Milá y Fontanals, Consejo Superior de Investigaciones Científicas (IMF-CSIC), Barcelona, C/Egipciàques, 15, Spain

Niccollò Mazzucco CSIC—Institución Milà y Fontanals, Barcelona, Spain

Hugues Plisson UMR 5199 PACEA, PPP Bâtiment B18, Université Bordeaux 1, Talence cedex, France

A. C. Rodríguez Rodríguez Dpto. Ciencias Históricas, Universidad de Las Palmas de Gran Canaria, Las Palmas de Gran Canaria, Spain

Veerle Rots Service de Préhistoire, University of Liège, Liège, Belgium

Carmen Gutiérrez Sáez Dpt. Prehistoria, Arqueología, Hª Antigua, H ª Medieval y CCTT Historiográficas, Campus de la Merced Universidad de Murcia, Murcia, Spain

Daniel Savage Department of Anthropology, Trent University, Peterborough, ON, Canada

James M. Skibo 4640 Anthropology, Illinois State University, Normal, IL, USA

Birgitta Stephenson In the Groove Analysis Pty, Ltd., Brisbane, QLD, Australia

About the Editors

João Marreiros is an archaeologist working as a post-doctoral researcher (FCT-grant) in the Interdisciplinary Center of Archaeology and Evolution of Human Behaviour (ICArEHB), Universidade do Algarve (Portugal) and in the Departamento de Arqueología y Antropología de la Instituición Milà I Fontanals, del Consejo Superior de Investigacionres CIentíficas (CSIC, Catalonia). His research focuses on stone tools technology and functionality from the Early Upper Paleolithic in Western Europe, particularly on techno-typological and use-wear analysis of lithic tools from the Early Upper Paleolithic industries from Iberian Peninsula with special interest in human ecological behavior and the first evidences of Anatomical Modern Humans industries in this region. He, in collaboration with the other two editors, organized the International Conference on Use-Wear analysis 2012, held in Faro (Portugal).

Juan F. Gibaja received his PhD in Archaeology & Prehistory from Universidad Autónoma de Barcelona in 2002. From 2006–2011 he worked as a post-doctoral fellow at the Universidade do Algarve (Portugal) funded by Fundação para a CIência e Tecnologia (FCT). Currently, since 2011, he is an Ramón y Cajal researcher at the Departamento de Arqueología y Antropología de la Instituición Milà I Fontanals, del Consejo Superior de Investigacionres CIentíficas (CSIC). During the last decade, he headed several research projects focus on lithic use-wear analysis. His research focuses on the key transition phases from Late and Early Prehistory: the transition between the last Neanderthals and anatomically modern humans and the transition from the last hunter-gatherers from the Mesolithic to the first farmers of the Neolithic in the Occidental Mediterranean.

Nuno Bicho received his Ph.D. in Anthropology from Southern Methodist University in 1992. He is currently an Associate Professor of Archaeology at the Universidade do Algarve, Portugal. He was Dean between 1998 and 2001 and 2005–2007. In addition, Bicho is the Director of the Interdisciplinary Center of Archaeology and Evolution of Human Behaviour at the University of Algarve. He specializes in Paleolithic ecodynamics and his research focused on prehistoric coastal hunter-gatherers of southern Iberia for the last two decades. More recently he has also developed research on the Mesolithic of the Tagus Valley and on Middle Stone Age of Mozambique.

Chapter 1
Use–Wear and Residue Analysis in Archeology

Nuno Bicho, João Marreiros and Juan F. Gibaja

1.1 Introduction

In October 2012, the University of Algarve organized the *International Conference on Use–Wear Analysis—USE–WEAR 2012*. To our surprise, over 100 researchers from all continents traveled to Faro and presented an incredible array of papers, now in press (Marreiros et al. in press). One main aspect became clear during the meeting: the field was growing at a very high rate, seen by the large number of very young researchers, many working in their MA or Ph.D.s, and thus attesting the clear and unequivocal increasing interest in use-wear and residue analysis. The consequence of this fact was bipolar:

1. A new scientific institution was constituted during the meeting—the Association of Archaeological Wear and Residue Analysts (AWRANA) aiming to bring together experts in the research dealing with the analyses of functional and modification of all archeological artefacts, including lithics, faunal remains, metals, and ceramics among others. One of the responsibilities of this new association is to organize a periodical conference following the general lines of that of Faro;
2. The need of a handbook on use–wear and residue analysis, since those published volumes on the topic are mostly geared for presenting research results

N. Bicho (✉) · J. Marreiros
Interdisciplinary Center for Archaeology and Human Behavior, FCHS—Universidade do Algarve, Campus de Gambelas, 8005–139 Faro, Portugal
e-mail: nbicho@ualg.pt

J. Marreiros
Departamento de Arqueología y Antropología, Institución Milá y Fontanals, Consejo Superior de Investigaciones Científicas (IMF-CSIC), C/Egipciàques, 15, 08001 Barcelona, Spain
e-mail: jmmarreiros@ualg.pt

J. F. Gibaja
Departamento de Arqueología y Antropología, Investigador contratado por el Ministerio de Economía y Competitividad—Subprograma Ramón y Cajal, Institución Milá y Fontanals, Consejo Superior de Investigaciones Científicas (IMF-CSIC), C/Egipciàques, 15, 08001 Barcelona, Spain
e-mail: jfgibaja@imf.csic.es

© Springer International Publishing Switzerland 2015
J. M. Marreiros et al. (eds.), *Use-Wear and Residue Analysis in Archaeology*, Manuals in Archaeological Method, Theory and Technique, DOI 10.1007/978-3-319-08257-8_1

or, more rarely, to publish new technological or methodological developments in the field. The young researchers present in the Faro meeting, in general, felt that there was a need for a manual with basic information on many aspects of theory and method and, if possible, with specific information on how to analyze, a hands-on approach, so young students could either alone or supervised by their professors, start use–wear and residue analysis.

Following our own feelings and to fulfill this gap, we contacted a series of researchers, both at the meeting and outside, and started to put together the present Handbook of Use–Wear and Residue Analysis in Archeology, that Springer swiftly accepted to publish after the traditional formal review process.

1.2 The Setting

The success of this volume (hopefully to take place …) will most likely due to the fact that prehistoric tools and implements are one of the most important and most common types of evidence for the study of ancient populations. Historically, the function of objects has been of high interest within archeological research in spite of the fact that only in the last couple of decades, use-wear studies became increasingly prevalent in the field. Actually, they became an emergent approach in archeological studies, as mentioned above.

Use-wear analyses have been focusing on different approaches to the study of archeological data. Despite the technological and functional perspective on use-wear studies, archeologists use these types of data to infer about and discuss broad topics of prehistoric living activities. Thus, these sources of diverse information are used necessary to solve local, regional, and global issues, from the simple identification of functions of individual tools up to the reconstruction of prehistoric economic systems and, therefore, of socio-cultural transformations within and between communities.

Since Semenov's pioneering work on functional interpretation in mid twentieth century, during the last decade experimental tests, macro- and microwear, and residue analyses have grown to become used as important methods to recognize diagnostic evidence of prehistoric human technology. Functional analysis is based on the study and observations of physical alterations made on the active areas and edges of tools made and used by human populations. It is based on methodological principles that are in turn based on experimental observations. From functional analyses, different types of use-wear evidences can be identified and recorded from tool surfaces (e.g., hunting projectiles, domestic tools, or residue traces). Thus, the initial development of use-wear studies was characterized mainly by methodological questions. During that phase, three main avenues were present: (1) the studies were carried on different raw materials and activities based on experimental replications and ethnographic data, (2) the uses of different types of macro- and microscopic approaches, and (3) the development of terminology. Such diversity of data had from very early received full attention on and thought to have great potential for archeology data gathering and interpretation.

On this onset, methodological approaches led to the development of new and different methods and techniques in this archaeological discipline. The major emphasis was on the identification of diagnostic wear traces for tool functionality. This perspective led to the use of experimental activities, based mostly on experimental analogy as a proxy for tool functionality. At the same time, during the methodological development, the use of use-wear studies became more common and different chronologies and materials, such as different lithic and osseous raw materials were included under the larger umbrella of use-wear studies.

It has been said by various experts that use-wear literature, aiming at different methods and techniques, has three main problems: (1) It is very scarce, mainly focusing on one specific type of tool, worked raw material, or chronological context, (2) It is highly disperse, and (3) It is outdated, with questions concerning methods and techniques in use-wear analysis used in the initial phase of the discipline and, therefore, focuses on preliminary and incipient approaches.

As mentioned above, the initial great expectation on functional analysis led specialists to apply those methods to their research, and methodological consolidation was sometimes overlooked. With time, use-wear studies became more common and started to be applied to general aspects of general past human behavior.

This effort led to the development of new, complex, and specific methods and techniques in order to solve specific problems facing different types of tools and worked materials. Thus, the aim of this volume is to present new methodological references on the topic, and highlight and describe the important role of methodological and technological approaches within use-wear studies. Therefore, the focus is placed on presenting an updated compilation of the most important methods (e.g., experimental and ethnographic tests), techniques (e.g., microscope and photograph techniques, and modern quantitative methods in use-wear analysis), tools (e.g., siliceous and nonsiliceous materials, and osseous materials), and materials (e.g., residue analysis) developed and improved during the recent years by use-wear experts. This handbook, thus, is intended to be a methodological reference for use-wear analysis researchers, students, and forthcoming specialists.

1.3 The Organization of the Volume

The volume is organized in 11 chapters (the present introduction and 10 chapters on various topics). Marreiros et al. focus on the history of use–wear and residue analysis. They detail the aspects of the origin and development of specific methodology for use-wear and residue analysis, give a few examples, and set the pace for the following chapters.

Gonzalez et al. describe the importance that Ethnoarchaeology has in functional analysis, from the theory to the method, based on various ethnographic examples from many regions around the world, including, North America, Asia, and Africa. They focus on three main aspects: tool production and use, technical processes, and production contexts.

Chapter 4 deals with the use-wear in chert materials. Gibaja and Gassin give a wide narrative with many examples on how to analyze flint tools, the method, and possible interpretations, using examples from the Paleolithic to the late Neolithic of Europe and Africa. Clemente-Conte et al. follow on the same path in Chap. 5, but focusing on non-flint raw materials.

Veerle Rots, in Chap. 6, describes in great detail the issue of prehension and hafting in stone tools and how to detect those functions through the use-wear. The difficulties are clearly discussed as well as the problems related to data interpretation.

In Chap. 7, Laure Debreuil and colleagues describe the techniques for analyzing use-wear on Ground Stone tools. This topic is still in its beginning, but with the continuous expansion in recovery of early materials, will be one of the most important areas of use-wear and residue analysis for prehistoric settings. These tools frequently present different traces than those found in other types of materials (i.e., flint stone tools), but when analyzed properly, they can be very informative about early subsistence strategies.

The following three chapters discuss the use–wear found on less common materials: bone (Marina Évora), metal (Carmen Gutiérrez Sáez and Ignacio Martín Lerma), and ceramic (James Skibo). The study of these materials is relatively recent compared to the analysis of stone raw materials and these chapters describe the methodological possibilities, with various practical examples, of extending traceology to other materials other than the traditional stone tools.

The final chapter (Chap. 11) by Langejans and Lombard focuses on the analysis of microresidues. This method is also relatively new and some researchers agree that it is best practice to combine it with use-wear. The authors describe various methodological applications as well as some results from various practical examples.

Many other topics could have been included in this volume. We hope, however, that the present set of chapters, giving detailed information on methods, equipment, observations, use-wear characteristics and, finally, on critical analyses on data and on interpretation make an interesting and suitable volume for those interested in use-wear and residue analysis.

Chapter 2
Macro and Micro Evidences from the Past: The State of the Art of Archeological Use-Wear Studies

João Marreiros, Niccollò Mazzucco, Juan F. Gibaja and Nuno Bicho

2.1 Introduction

Since very early, functional interpretations on prehistoric tools revealed large interest and investment, becoming an emergent method in the archaeological research. In fact, the first reference to functional interpretations on archeological lithic tools was made during the late nineteenth century and beginning of the twentieth by research of John Evans (1897), John Spurrell and Morse Pfeiffer (1912), Cecil Curwew (1930), and Denis Peyrony (Peyrony 1949), mostly focusing on the analysis of macro-wear traces and fractures identified in the surface of lithic prehistoric tools.

Following these initial efforts, during the 1930s, Sergei Semenov research focused on the observation of physical alterations on the active areas of lithic and bone tools made and used by prehistoric human populations. Starting with the pioneering work of Semenov, (Semenov, S. 1957) resulting in his Ph.D. dissertation "Pervobitnoya Tekhnika" (i.e., prehistoric technology), new methods were introduced in functional studies. Based on experimental observations, use-wear analysis became an important proxy to identify and classify wear traces that allow functional interpretations. From a theoretical

---

J. Marreiros (✉) · N. Bicho
Interdisciplinary Center for Archaeology and Evolution of Human Behavior,
FCHS—Universidade do Algarve, Campus Gambelas, Faro 8005–139, Portugal
e-mail: jmmarreiros@ualg.pt

N. Bicho
e-mail: nbicho@ualg.pt

J. Marreiros · N. Mazzucco · J. F. Gibaja
CSIC—Institución Milà y Fontanals, Barcelona, Spain

N. Mazzucco
e-mail: nicomazzucco@imf.csic.es

J. F. Gibaja
e-mail: jfgibaja@imf.csic.es

© Springer International Publishing Switzerland 2015
J. M. Marreiros et al. (eds.), *Use-Wear and Residue Analysis in Archaeology,* Manuals in Archaeological Method, Theory and Technique, DOI 10.1007/978-3-319-08257-8_2

point of view, Semenov's work follows the Marxist perspective that characterized the Russian archeology during the twentieth century (Trigger 1984, 2006). According to this theoretical agenda, the technological characterization of archeological artifacts was seen as a fundamental proxy to understand the economic and social organization of the past populations. This techno-functional approach shows no distinction between the history of tool production and the human record, from which the main goal was to understand the origin and function of the first tools used by humans, allowing the reconstruction of human technological evolution (Childe 1936, 1942; Clemente et al. 2002; Klejn 1982; Longo et al. 2005; Phillips 1988).

Semenov's research, first published in Russian, was translated and presented to the Western Europe during the 1960s (Semenov 1964). The introduction of Semenov's methods in the Western world is associated with the emergence of the New Archeology (e.g., Binford 1962). Following this idea, the New Archeology agenda, emergent from the American anthropological school, placed emphasis on the use of a tool as a result of a specific task made by humans (Schiffer 1975), resulting from an environmental and cultural stimulation (Hayden and Kamminga 1979; Shiffer 1976). Thus, according to this interdisciplinary approach, the archeologist is seen as a social scientist, whose main concern is to infer about human technological, economic, and social behavior and organization reflected on the *function* and *use* of tools. Therefore, use-wear analysis was seen as one of the keys to interpret the archeological record as a clear indicator of human behavior (Sterud 1978), and an essential proxy for the reconstruction of social and cultural human behavior and organizatiomn (Redman 1973).

During the initial phase, use-wear studies were developed from Semenov's work and characterized mainly by methodological questions, with three main concerns:

1. The studies were carried out on different raw materials and activities, testing distinct variables used on experimental replications, blind tests and ethnographic data (e.g., Bamforth 1986; Keeley and Newcomer 1977; Odell and Odell-Vereecken 1980; Shea 1988)
2. The use of low power magnifications, mainly focused on macro traces (i.e., edge damage) and fractures resulting from tool use kinematics (Brink 1978; Broadbent 1979; Kamminga 1982; Nilsen and Dittemore 1974; Hester and Heizer 1973; Hester and Shafer 1975; Rosenfelid 1971; Sonnenfeld 1962), although some studies start introducing micro approaches (Hayden 1979)
3. The review of the terminology of the discipline and its methods. Since Semenov's work, use-wear studies have developed new analytic methods, improving the accuracy in the identification and record of use-wear traces on archeological tools and functional interpretations.

In this scenario during the last decades, use-wear disciplines were characterized by the development of numerous methodological agendas, mainly focusing on experimental studies (Anderson 1999; Buc 2011; Fischer et al. 1984; Hodgskiss 2010; Odell and Cowan 1986; Pétillon et al. 2011; Shea et al. 2001), blind tests (Álvarez et al. 2011; Evans and Donahue 2005; Odell and Odell-Vereecken 1980; Wadley and Lombard 2007), identification and quantification (e.g., Grace et al. 1985; Gonzalez-Urquijo and Ibáñez-Estevez 2003; Vardi et al. 2010; Stevens et al. 2010) of all different kinds of use-wear traces and residue remains on different materials such as lithics, bone, shell and ceramic, among others (e.g., Hardy 1998; Langejans 2010; Lombard 2005; Lombard and Wadley 2009; Wadley et al. 2004). Such multi-approach of use-wear and residue analysis led to the development of specific and complementary techniques in order to improve a clear and solid background to the interpretation of technology, resource exploitation and settlement patterns from different chronological and geographical contexts that characterized human prehistoric behavior.

2.2 Functional Studies vs. Typology and the Beginning of the Use-Wear Studies in Western Europe

Experimental and ethnographic data allow the use of analogy between the observed artifacts and archeological tools. The French ethnographic approach, led by Leroi-Gourhan (1964), had a significant contribution to lithic studies. Lithic tools, such as endscrapers, sidescrapers and burins were categorized due to their morphological similitude with observed tools, as indirect evidence (e.g., Vila 2002). In this debate, the relation between typology and functionality was early explored, during the construction of the so-called descriptive lithic typology, whose classification is based on the technological and morphological attributes, from which functional interpretations were made, assuming that only the retouched pieces were used as tools (Sonneville-Bordes 1954; Sonneville-Bordes and Perrot 1953, 1954, 1955, 1956).

As mentioned above, during the first decades, functional interpretation of lithic tools was marked by an exciting discussion and criticism to Semenov's work. François Bordes and Semenov themselves played one of the main debates focusing on the methodological aspects of how to analyze functionality and the evolution and reconstruction of human technology from lithic assemblages (Bordes 1969; Bordes and Sonneville-Bordes 1970; Semenov 1970).

Refusing the classical typological classification, Semenov's perspective was that the functional attribution based in a simple analytical description with no direct evidences of use was erroneous (Semenov 1970). On the other hand, according to Bordes, the so-called functional types should not be only based on use-wear analysis. However, Semenov argued that "[…] typology assumes an important role in archeology […], however, Paleolithic studies should not be limited by typological classification. Researchers show enquiry about function and use of human old stone tools. Thus, Paleolithic studies need a paleoethnographic and paleotechnological reconstruction of the past human societies" (Semenov 1970, p. 123). Therefore, according to Semenov, functional studies, combined with typological categories, allow a broad and complete interpretation of the lithic technology, reflecting prehistoric human socio-economic patterns.

From a functional perspective, the definition of lithic tool refers to a lithic artifact that was used to modify other material, independently from the raw material, morphology and presence or absence of retouch, and, therefore, according to

Semenov's perspective, this can only be directly tested using use-wear analysis. Due to these debates, during the last decade functional studies have focused on this dichotomy between retouched tools and functional interpretations: (1) the presence of retouched is not diagnostic to tool use, since tools without retouch show wear traces, (2) the used edge is not always the tool active area but the handle edge, (3) several tools had multi-functions, showing different active areas associated with different uses. This approach focusing on several topics on lithic technological studies led to a new interpretation on different lithic morph-types and technological strategies (e.g., Bicho and Gibaja 2006; Gassin 1996; Gibaja and Palomo 2004; Ibáñez and González 1996; Igreja 2005; Moss 1983; Plisson 1985).

2.3 The Definition

Use-wear and residue analysis refers to the study of wear traces on the edges and/or surfaces of objects caused by use (e.g., Fullagar and Matherson 2013; Odell 2004). Although with some initial skepticism, use-wear studies revealed to be one of the most important disciplines to interpret site and artifacts function in the archeological research (Grace 1996; Stafford and Stafford 1983). As mentioned above, the initial phase of use-wear research was marked by several methodological and theoretical debates including the methods, terminology, and its definition. In fact, the terms traceology, *functional analysis* or *use-wear and residue analysis*, commonly used today, were adopted only in the last decades. Associated with the emergence of the Marxist agenda, the term *traceology* or *traceological analysis* (e.g., Levitt 1979), praises the concept of *wear traces* and characterizes the *mechanical* character responsible for the formation and modification of tool edges and surfaces, as main indicator of the tools' function (Semenov 1964). Thus, during the 1970s of the twentieth century the terms *use-wear analysis* and *functional analysis* were introduced and globally embraced during the "Conference on lithic use-wear analysis" held in Vancouver (1977).

Since the 1990s the use-wear research has brought in new methods characterized by new technological techniques, microscopic systems and software, and include the investigation of different materials such as residues (e.g., Christensen et al. 1992; Fullagar 1993; Thomas 1993). In this scenario, parallel to the technological novelties, different types of archeological contexts, chronologies, and raw materials were analyzed, such as lithic (e.g., chert, quartzite, quartz, obsidian), organic (e.g., bone, ivory, antler and shells), ceramic, and metallic tools (e.g., Anderson-Gerfaud 1980, 1981, 1983; Barton and White 1993; Bertrand 1999; d'Errico and Giacobini 1985; d'Errico 1993; Évora 2007; Donahue 1988; González and Ibáñez 1994; González and Ibáñez 1993; Lemorini et al. 2005; Lammers-Keijsers 2008; Moss 1983; Plisson 1985; Sidéra and Legrand 2006; Semenov 1964, 1981; Unger-Hamilton 1988; Villa and d'Errico 2001).

Recently, this multidisciplinary approach in use-wear studies was expressed during the International conference on use-wear analysis 2012 held in Faro, Portugal.

The meeting was marked by contributions from all different use-wear topics, such as theory and methodology, archeological artifacts, and residues analysis (Marreiros et al. in press). As a consequence of this approach the Association of Archeological Wear and Residue Analysts (AWRANA) was established. Aiming to bring together specialists in archeological research who deal with the analysis of artifacts to study function and modification, the association extends to all aspects of wear, modifications, and residue in different artifact materials (Fullagar and Matherson 2013).

2.4 Methods and Techniques

As mentioned above after the introduction of Semenov's contribution, the first use-wear studies were mainly characterized by low power magnifications simply replying Semenov's methodology using a stereomicroscopy (low-power approach, 5× to 60×, generically <100×). These observations focused mainly on attributes such as edge angle and profile, edge damage, and diagnostic fractures (Brodbent and Knutsson 1979, 1981; Kamminga 1982). According to the classification and distribution of these attributes on artifact edges and surface, the observations using low-power method revealed a huge difficulty to identify in detail some traces, since this approach makes possible only the preliminary identification of the nature and hardness of the worked materials and type of movement (Grace 1996; Keeley and Newcomer 1977; Odell and Odell-Vereecken 1980). This procedure led to a strong criticism on Semenov's methods, and many authors considered the methodology inappropriate to clearly identify diagnostic wear traces associated with a specific worked material. Today we know that these assumptions were likely related to: (1) the use of reduced focus microscopes and (2) the absence of an experimental program. After all, according to Semenov observations, functional studies should identify different types of diagnostic stigmas using both low and high magnifications using an experimental background reference (Semenov 1964).

The high-power approach was introduced by Lawrence Keeley (1980) that initially used a reflected light microscope (10× to 400×). According to Keeley, the high-power method, allows, not only to distinguish the degree of hardness of the worked material, but at the same time identify and classify different types of material (e.g., hide, wood, bone, antler, etc.; Keeley and Newcomer 1977). In the 1970s, the publication of *"Technique and methodology in microwear studies: a critical review"* (Keeley 1974), shows that use-wear analysis requires a quantification method of the diversity development and distribution of micro-wear traces, of which one of the most important is the polish formation (Vaughan 1985).

According to this new methodological protocol, the high degree of observation on high magnification almost eclipsed the low power approach, claiming that diagnostic polishes rendered macro observations of surface and edge fractures. However, the polish formation was not clear and its analysis shows some difficulties associated with: (1) distinct materials producing distinct polishes and (2) how to quantify those distinctive polishes.

Nevertheless, the debate between low and high power microscopy continued over the last decades, mainly considering the advantages and limitations of both approaches. As a result of this debate, during the Uppsala conference in 1989 (Graslund et al. 1990), several papers focused on the low and high magnification, consensually showed that both methods were complementary and not alternative for clear functional interpretations (Odell 2001; Olausson 1993). These two approaches and their proposes were categorized: (1) macroscopic observation (low magnifications), using a stereoscopic microscope, allows the identification of macro-wear traces (e.g., edge damage and diagnostic impact fractures) and detect the area that should be analyzed using microscopic observations (high magnifications); and (2) microscopic method, that allows a detailed observation, identification, and record of micro-wear traces in the tool edges and surfaces, not visible using only macroscopic approach (e.g., striations and polish formation).

In sum, the combination of both approaches marked the beginning of a new integrated methodology, although the debate on standardized criteria and quantification methods for all different micro-wear traces is still today one of the main methodological debates in use-wear studies. Therefore, during the last decades the effort has been to develop standardized criteria (i.e., methods and terminology) for an objective use-wear analysis. This became even more relevant during the 1980 and 1990s, since one of the main goals of use-wear studies was to identify and quantify different wear traces associated with all possible different processes (i.e., use, fractures and postdepositional; Grace 1996) and raw materials (e.g., different types of lithic rocks: chert, quartz, quartzite, and obsidian; Yamada 1986). These studies show that the configuration of distinct categories of wear traces, such as formation, distribution, extension, and morphology, were influenced by a large range of variables (Akoshima 1987), for which the experimental tests became the main reference for testing hypotheses (e.g., Anderson-Gerfaud 1988; Josht 2006; Odell 2001).

Initially, the polish formation was described based on simple visual characterization. However, this method had several problems, since the identification of different polishes were subjective and not clearly quantified (Mansur 1983; Vaughan 1985).

One of the main debated topics during the last decades within use-wear studies is to create standardized criteria of quantification for wear traces. At the same time Yamada (1986) and Bradley and Clayton (1987), using the macroscopic analysis of chert microtopography argued that different raw material compositions influence the wear-traces formation. Akoshima (1987) argued that wear-traces analysis should record and measure shape and distribution of different macro- and micro-traces (number, shape, distribution, extension, and termination). Experimental tests and the creation of quantification methods must play an important role in use-wear studies. According to this idea the creation of a recording method built a quantifying basis for functional interpretation, grounded on recording differences during the formation of wear traces, material hardiness, and movement.

Thus, during the last decades use-wear studies focused on developing several quantification methods and specific software, from which the main goal was to identify the origin, classification, and agents responsible for the polish formation process on the micro-topography of tool surface. Following these questions, the meetings "Technical aspect of micro-wear studies on stone tools" (Ungrath et al. 1986) and "Le geste retrouve" (Anderson et al. 1993) marked the impulse on the interpretation and quantification of polish formation. This debate was followed by several projects such as the "Fast expert system" and "Image processing software" (Grace 1996; Grace et al. 1985; van den Dries 1994), interferometry (Dumont 1982), image analysis (Grace et al. 1987; Vila and Gallart 1993; González-Urquijo and Ibáñez-Estevez 2003) or atomic force microscopy (Kimball et al. 1995), and recently scanning electron microscopy (SEM; Debert & Sherriff 2007; Mansur 1983) and lase scanning confocal microscope (LSCM; Evans and Donahue 2008; Evans and Macdonald 2011).

At this moment, the methods used in use-wear and residue analysis follow four main observation techniques: optical microscope, that includes (1) macroscopic (low power) and (2) microscopic (high power) magnifications, (3) scanning electron microscope (SEM), and (4) laser scanning confocal microscope (LSCM).

2.4.1 Optical Microscope

As mentioned above, the most common technique used on use-wear and residue analysis is the light-sensitive optical microscope method, including macroscopic (low power) and microscopic (high power) magnifications. Low power use-wear analysis is usually referred as stereomicroscope analysis using magnifications between 4–10×. In this apparatus, the artifact is illuminated by reflective light that could be placed in different angles, enabling shadow effect. In this procedure, all edges and surfaces of the artifact are systematically analyzed, in order to analyze and record small fractures and features, as well as to select the areas for microscope observation (e.g., Kamminga 1982; Odell and Odell-Vereecken 1980, 1981, 2004; Tringham et al. 1974). On the other hand, the high power technique consists the use of a metallurgical microscope at higher magnification with incident light perpendicular (90°) to the material surface. In order to distinguish, classify, and record different wear traces, such as polish, the high power magnification (50–400×) is the most successful technique. As mentioned above, the combination of both magnifications allow a more complete analysis, and during the last decades researches have used both techniques in order to improve methodological approaches (e.g., Grace 1996; Clemente and Gibaja 1998; van Gijn 1998; Rots 2002).

2.4.2 Scanning Electron Microscope (SEM)

The SEM uses a stream of electrons controlled by magnetic or electric fields instead of light illumination projection. This lightning method allows SEM to produce an image at higher magnification, resolution, and depth of field than a traditional metallographic microscope (Del Bene 1979; d'Errico and Moucadel-Espinet 1986;

Hay 1977). However, the use of the SEM technique when applied to archeological analysis has several limitations, mainly regarding to (1) price, since it is an expensive technique, whether buying or renting SEM apparatus, (2) sampling, the SEM analysis is limited to the object volume, and (3) time, due to the necessary time required for sample preparation, when using acetate peels, and analysis. Thus, SEM technique, even being very efficient, is most of the times limited to specific questions and small sample sizes.

2.4.3 Laser Scanning Confocal Microscope

The laser scanning confocal microscope technique consists on an image formed by the conjugation of images of reflected light from distinct focal planes. In other words, this technique creates an image multifocus image in real time. LSCM allows observations ranging between 25–800× magnification (e.g., Debert and Sherriff 2007; Derndarsky and Ocklind 2001; Evans and Donahue 2008; Mansur 1983; Shanks et al. 2001; Scott et al. 2005, 2006). The LSCM florescent technique developed for biomedical research during the 1980s, have been used in the archeological research to illustrate and model (topography) the texture of the analyzed object surface, allowing to a more detailed wear quantification. Contrary to the SEM technique, the LSCM, although expensive, is similar to the traditional metallurgical microscope, with no limitations regarding to sample size and time of use (Evans and Donahue 2008).

2.5 Methods

As previously shown, during the last decades use-wear and residue analysis have developed different and complementary methodological approaches and techniques to a more detailed and complete analysis of all type of wear traces. This section consists on a brief description of wear traces commonly recognized on lithic tools. Traditionally use-wear analysis is organized in two main categories: macroscopic, including edge damage and diagnostic impact fractures, and microscopic traces, referring to striations, polish, hafting traces, and residue remains.

2.5.1 Macroanalysis

2.5.1.1 Fractures

As mentioned above, macro wear analysis focuses on the identification and classification of fractures. The origin and formation of fractures is the results of edge retouched or edge damage resultant from a use of a tool in a specific task. Attributes such as distribution, quantity, and classification are assumed as reflex of various sources responsible for their origin and formation: raw material (e.g., chert, quartzite, quartz), hardness, resistance, and nature of the worked material (e.g., bone, antler, wood), edge angle of the tool, angle of tool to the material, period of time of use, and direction and/or movement of use (e.g., scraping or cutting; Adams 1989; Broadbent 1979, 1981; Grace 1996; Hayden 1979; Hubercome 1992; Kamming 1982; Odell 1981, 2001; Odell-Vereecken 1980; Risch 1995; Semenov 1964; Tringham 1975).

Experimental tests and macro observation show that nature and formation processes of such fractures might be related to various natures and variables. Such complexity and unpredictability indicate that different macro traces were not clearly diagnostic of a specific material and/or use. Nevertheless, experimental work has shown that specific uses and/movements are responsible for a specific origin and distribution of fractures in tools. As an example, regarding to lithic tools, longitudinal movements (e.g., cutting) result in macro and micro fractures in the ventral and dorsal surface of the tool. From transversal movements (e.g., scrapping), macro and micro fractures are concentrated in the surface of contact between the tool and the worked material, and the formation of these stigmas occur normally in the opposite surface to this contact. The distribution is perpendicular to the used edge and show low variability regarding to shape and extension than the cutting movement (e.g., Odell and Odell-Vereecken 1980; Trigham et al. 1974). Also, circular or semicircular movements (drilling or incision), produce fractures in all the edges of the contact surfaces.

2.5.1.2 Classification

The classification of edge damage commonly used in use-wear studies is organized according to the morphology, distribution, position, and termination of the small fractures along the edges (Anderson-Gerfaud 1981; Akoshima 1987; Grace 1989; Gutiérrez 1990; González and Ibáñez 1994; Hayden 1979; Kamminga 1982; Keeley 1980; Odell 1975; Odell and Odell-Vereecken 1980; Tringham et al. 1974; Unger-Hamilton 1988). Morphology is organized by semicircular, circular (half-moon), triangular, quadrangular, trapezoidal, and irregular forms. The continuity or discontinuity between the micro fractures characterized the distribution of the edge damage, while the position refers to the formation of small fractures, which is typed as isolated, aligned, or superimposed. The termination categories indicate the distal end morphology of the micro fractures, described as regular, reflected, stepped, and oblique (90°).

Experimental tests have shown that such morphologies are likely related to type of movement and the resistance/hardiness of the worked material. Thus, for example, it is generally accepted that working soft material (butchering or fresh vegetal material) creates semicircular shapes, and hard materials triangular and trapezoidal (bone or antler). Although some researchers argue that the duration of the work, rather than the worked material, led to the formation of triangular or trapezoidal shapes (Akoshima 1987). Experimental studies and functional analysis, macro and micro wear, allow the identification of diagnostic impact fractures associated with projectile activities (Bergmann and Newcomer 1983; Bradley 1982; Bradley and Frison 1987; Frison and Bradley 1980; Fischer et al. 1984; Geneste and Plisson 1986, 1990, 1993; Lombard 2005; Lombard et al. 2004; Odell and Cowan 1986; O'Farrell 1996, 2004; Shea et al. 2002; Villa and Lenoir 2006). These fractures are categorized in two main groups: (1) macro impact marks, diagnostic fractures, and striations, and (2) micro hafting and prehension traces, polish and organic residues (i.e., resin or mastic).

2.5.2 Microanalysis

2.5.2.1 Striations

Striations consist linear grooves present in the tool surface resulting from the abrasive contact between the tool and the worked material or abrasive materials on one or both surfaces (Semenov 1964, 1981). The distribution and intensity (depth) of the striations were classified in different categories: (1) dark background, as an observed thin dark line, (2) smooth background, characterized by a bright line, and (3) grooves, that consists on a series of parallel grooves and perpendiculars to orientation of the striation (Keeley 1980; Mansur 1983). This classification has been seen as a reflex of different shapes and resistance of the tool and/or worked material. Following this idea, d'Errico (1985) suggests three different types of striations: (1) protuberant, (2) *comet-like*, and (3) stretch.

Vaughan in "*Use-wear analysis of flaked stone tools*" (1985) suggests a third type of classification: deep, superficial, and direction indicator. Deep striations are continuous grooves in the tool surface; superficial grooves are characterized by a succession of punctual linear striations present in a small area that have not deep penetrated in the surface; the direction indicator striations clearly indicates a direction of a certain movement. Although, the data from striation analysis do not present enough data, mainly because striation might be caused by postdepositional disturbance, and the interpretation of tool functional rarely are exclusively based on the striation analysis.

2.5.2.2 Polish Description and Formation

The origin and formation of polish has been one of the most complex and debated topics in the methodological agenda of use-wear studies. From early on, the paper "Technique and methodology in microwear studies: a critical review" from Keeley (1974) states that the main focus of the use-wear studies was the quantification of the development of wear polish formation.

It was commonly assumed among researchers, that distinctive polishes are associated with specific worked materials, and hence the classification and quantification of the polish formation became one of the fundamental questions to be addressed in functional analysis (e.g., Dumont 1982). However, according to some authors the definition and origin of the polish formation had never been precise and objective, and huge criticism was expressed by Grace et al. (1985, 1987). In fact, the formation and distribution of polish is influenced by several variables, some of them not related to its use, including different postdepositional processes such as water, temperature, and other abrasive agents might influence the formation of micro-wear traces and polish (van Gijn 1990; Moss 1983; Vaughan 1985). On the other hand, polish reflects tool's natural characteristics, such as surface micro topography and hardness, and/or raw material texture (Bradley and Clayton 1987; Grace et al. 1993; Keeley 1978, 1980). Other important variable that influences the development of micro-wear traces is the duration and pressure of each action, according to Grace the polish made by the same material but that took different durations and pressure may show significant differences (Grace et al. 1993).

Following that critical view, many researchers developed a matrix analysis based on the different polish characteristics and classifications that were identified during its formation stages (Hubercome 1997; Vaughan 1985). However these attempts were confused and offered many details and low objectivity, making such characterization more difficult.

Types such as smooth-pitted polish, terraced-bumpy polish, stuccolike or gently undulating glow and pit-depression valleys, were not that accurate, and therefore some researchers argued that this typology introduced by Keeley needed to be reviewed and refreshed.

In fact those researchers argued that the analysis of polish is associated with the analyst experience of archeological and experimental materials. Distinguish polish from different materials and movements are easier than make a complete description. Thus, it is important that all researchers have a comparative reference assemblage, experimental materials, and a photographic collection. New technologies, such as image editing software and GIS software started playing an important role to quantify and describe micro-wear traces, making possible the comparison of data from different sources. One of these specific polishes results from the hafting of a tool with a handle. Prehensile wear or hafting traces is still a debated topic in use wear studies (Collin and Jardon-Giner 1993; Keeley 1982; Moss 1983). Many points of this debate are related with all the variables within this process: handle material, used tool and type of adhesive materials, resin, and other organic materials. According to Grace (1993), some of those supposed hafting traces are the result of the tool production process and therefore misclassified. Frequently, hafting is recognized by indirect evidences, such as tool morphometry, functionality, other wear traces, and mainly its distribution on the tool surface. The hafting process is associated with different types of wear traces: polish, striations, edge rounding, and micro striations. However such observation and identification is difficult since much of these traces may be attributed to other factors including technological process, trampling, and postdepositional processes.

This debate was expressed during the meeting "*Technical aspect of microwear studies on stone tools*" in 1985 (Owen and Unrath 1986), with the introduction of methodological approaches as the silica-gel theory, deposition model and abrasive theory, as proxy to impulse the research on the polish formation process (Anderson-Gerfaud 1980; Grace 1990; Kamminga 1979; Meeks et al. 1982; Levi-Sala 1993; Witthoft 1967; Yamada 1993; Yamada and Sawada 1993). The main aim was to determine the origin and formation of distinctive polishes and its association with different various materials. Using image-editing software, Grace (1996; van der Dries 1994) created the "Fast expert system" that could identify and use 33 variables during the polish formation and therefore identify the material worked and its movement.

Thus, it is clearly important that the analysis should focus on all available data, through the different analyzing methods, and not be based only on one single type of wear trace.

2.5.2.3 Hafting Traces

From the early Semenov's work, those archeologists mentioned that morphology and wear traces indicate that many lithic tools were possibly hafted (Keeley 1982; Odell and Odell-Vereecken 1980, 1981, 1994; Owen and Unrath 1989; Semenov 1964; Stordeur 1987), however, hafting and prehension were never intensely explored, and researchers focused on the thought to be working edge. The main argument was that, even if hafting produce wear traces, the contact would be minimal and traces associated with this movement would be not clearly diagnostic to a reliable interpretation, easily confused to any type of minimal result of use of postdeposition modification. Recently, thanks to the experimental works of Rots (2003, 2010), new data has been acquainted, that realized systematically and relying both on microscopic evidences and residues analysis, as well including ethnographic sources.

2.5.2.4 Residue Analysis

During the first phase of use-wear studies, the residue analysis was a separated approach from functional interpretations (Grace 1996). While use-wear analysis concerns the use of the tool, residue studies consists the identification of organic or inorganic residues present on the artifact (Fullagar 1993; Fullagar and Matherson 2013; Haslam 2006). The preservation of such organic results from: (1) heating processes caused by the intense contact and friction between the tool and the worked material; (2) water in the worked material; (3) high percentage of silica in chert tools; (4) the acidity and abrasive particles in some organic materials (Hardy and Garufi 1998; Hardy 2004; Levi-Sala 1986; Lombard 2008; Loy 1983, 1993; Thomas 1993; Fullagar 1998; Shanks et al. 2001). The identification of residues, under favorable conditions of preservation is possible with the analysis of embedded remains in micro fractures, cracks, and micro-striations, or stuck (adherent) to the surface (Haslam 2006; Langejans 2010; Longo et al. 2005; Wedley et al. 2004; Wedley and Lombard 2007). Thus, it focuses mainly on blood and muscular tissue (Gernaey et al. 2001; Hohberg et al. 2009; Tuross et al. 1996), amid (Barton 2007; Lu 2003, 2006), lipids and fat acids (Evershed et al. 2001), animal (bone, scales, collagen or hair) remains (Jans et al. 2004), plant remains and microfossils (phytoliths, pollens, etc.), and pigments (Blanchette 2000).

From the methodological perspective the residue analysis is organized in three techniques: (1) optical incident light macro, (2) microscopic observation, and (3) the observed residue remain is removed for detailed analysis. The identification of the residue remain is made using polarized light microscopy and analysis, depending on the type of remain, may include different techniques, such as a simple biochemical or a spectroscopic analysis.

In residue analysis there are many problems regarding postdepositional contamination from surrounding sediments, organic remains not related to the use of the artifact, and excavation or postexcavation handling of the artifact (Evans and Donahue 2005; Grace 1989, 1996). Furthermore, residue analysis has been used as a complementary method to use-wear studies and functional interpretations in order to interpret the function of archeological tools. Its potential replies properly in the integration and confirmation of macro- and micro-wear data, with the possibility of further specifying the type—or included the species—of the worked material. However, functional interpretations based exclusively on residue observation should be avoided, as extremely dangerous and still unreliable.

2.6 Postdepositional, Collecting, and Sampling Artifacts

One of the main issues of use-wear analysis is the preservation and alterations of wear traces in archeological tools resulting from the postdepositional processes during the formation of the archeological record. From early on, John Evans and George Escol Sellers recognized that several natural processes could produce fractures on lithics tools similar to those generate by human handling (Baesemann 1986; Kamisnka et al. 1993; Levi-Sala 1986, 1993; Mazzucco et al. 2013; Geneste and Plisson 1986; Plisson and Mauger 1988). From this assumption, during the first decades of the development of use-wear studies, several studies show the existence of similarities in wear traces from natural postdepositional processes and human use (Keeley and Newcomer 1977). Factors such as postdepositional alterations and trampling among others might cause significant alterations on tools edge and/or surface such as edge damage, fractures and surface polish, and striations.

During the last decades, experimental tests have tried to replicate postdeposition processes (soil deposition, movement and transport, erosion and trampling) and identification and classification of associated wear traces (e.g., Burroni et al. 2002; Evans and Donahue 2005; Levi-Sala 1986). From these essays, even for similar to use wear traces (macro observation), the stigma resulting from the action of these processes show a random distribution, resulting on isolated and disperse marks (micro observations), that may modify or destroy the use wear evidences (Vaughan 1985).

Resulting from postdepositional processes, the *colored* or *gloss patina*, consists in the deposition of various minerals present in the surrounding soil, water and/or rocks, resulting in the oxidation and corrosion of the tools surface (Anderson-Gerfaud 1980). Other type of postdepositional alteration is the so-called *luster* or *miscellaneous luster* (Gijn 1990). Caused by various natural and mechanical postdepositional processes, this process consists of luminous and lustrous effect distributed in all directions and all over the tool surface (Longo et al. 2001).

Likewise, one of the most important issues in use-wear analysis is the state of preservation of the archeological materials. Besides all the postdepositional processes during the archeological site formation, the recovery (e.g., contact with metal trowels, *metal polish*), cleaning (abrasive cleaning materials or acids), storage (frequent contact between materials), and analysis of archeological assemblages (e.g., metal caliper) may cause surface and edge alterations and therefore interfere with the use wear analysis.

Thus, the use of correct methods and conditions (including the appropriate equipment) after recovering the archeological materials is fundamental to preserve all data available. As a result, during the past years many researchers have held to this methodological process in use-wear studies as follows:

1. Wash and rub the archeological materials must be done with the use of soap and water with hands avoiding any abrasive material.
2. When necessary, due to the presence of concretion or soil remains, the tools should be emerged in a solution of water and hydrochloric acid (5–10%) for not more than 1 or 2 min, or emerged only in water using an ultrasonic cleaner. Finally, during the macro and microscopic analysis, in order to remove wear grease from handling, the artifact surface is cleaned using cotton imbued with petroleum.

2.7 Final Remarks

This chapter focuses on the historical background of the theory and methodological background of functional studies. Since Semenov's systematic research, use-wear and residue studies had focus on the observation, identification, and interpretation of different evidences of use in archeological tools in order to understand human technological and socio-cultural behavior.

One of the main statements in use-wear and residue analysis is that different variables (i.e., raw materials, worked material, movement) are responsible for different kinds of relict macro- and micro-wear traces, requiring occasionally specific analyzing methods.

Although as discussed above, functional studies are complex, wear traces undoubtedly associated with numerous variables, requiring a constant methodological and technological improvement. This has been clear from the last decades of research, during which functional analysis have focused on different research topics. Therefore, during the last decades, functional analysis was marked by the development of theory, method, and techniques in order to infer prehistoric tools functionality. This methodological agenda effort to improve systematic criteria to clear identify, classify, and interpret all different wear traces, while the development of specific techniques, such as several macro and microscopic approaches (e.g., SEM and LSCM) focuses on specific question related to specific variables.

References

Adams, J. (1989). Methods for improving ground stone analysis: Experiments in mano wear patterns. In D. Amick & R. Mauldin (Eds.), *Experiments in lithic technology. BAR International Series 528* (pp. 259–276). Oxford: British Archaeological Reports.

Akoshima, K. (1987). Micro-flaking quantification. In G. Sieveking & M. Newcomer (Eds.), *The human uses of flint and chert: Papers from the Fourth International Flint Symposium* (pp. 71–79). Cambridge: University of Cambridge Press.

Anderson-Gerfaud, P. (1980). A testimony of prehistoric tasks: Diagnostic residues on stone tools working edges. *World Archaeology, 12*(2), 181–194.

Anderson-Gerfaud, P. (1981). Contribution méthodologique Ã l'analyse des microtraces d'utilisation sur les outils préhistoriques. Ph. D. Thesis, Université de Bordeaux.

Anderson-Gerfaud, P. C. (1983). A consideration of the uses of certain backed and ''lustered'' stone tools from late Mesolithic and Natufian levels of Abu Hureyra and Mureybet (Syria). In (M.-C. Cauvin, Ed.) Traces d"Utilization sur les Outils Neolithiques du Proche Orient. Lyon: GIS-Maison de l"Orient, *5,* pp. 77–101.

Anderson-Gerfaud, P. C. (1988). Using prehistoric stone tools to harvest cultivated wild cereals: preliminary observations of traces and impact. In (S. Beyries, Ed.) Industries Lithiques: Traceologie et Technologie, BAR International Series *411*(i), 175–195.

Anderson-Gerfaud, P. (1999). Experimental cultivation, harvest and threshing of wild cereals: Their relevance for interpreting the use of Epi-Paleolithic and Neolithic artifacts. In P. C. Anderson (Ed.), *Prehistory of agriculture: New experimental and geographic approaches* (pp. 118–145). Los Angeles: University of California Press.

Anderson-Gerfaud, P., Beyries, S., Otte, M., & Plisson, H. (Eds.). (1993). Traces et fonction: les gestes retrouves. Actes du colloque international de Liège (Liège, 1990), ERAUL 50 (1/2), Liège.

Baesemann, R. (1986). Natural alterations of stone artefact materials. In Technical aspects of microwear studies on stone tools. L.-R. Owen, G. Unrath (Eds.), Actes de la conférence de Tübingen février 1985. Early Man News 9.10.11: 97–102.

Bamforth, D. (1986). Technological efficiency and tool curation. *American Antiquity, 51,* 38–50.

Barton, H. (2007). Starch residues on museum artefacts: Implications for determining tool use. *Journal of Archaeological Science, 34,* 1752–1762.

Barton, H., & White J. P. (1993). Use of stone and shell artifacts at Balof 2, New Ireland, Papua New Guinea. *Asian Perspectives, 32*(2),169–181

Bergmann, C., & Newcomer, M. (1983). Flint arrowhead breakage: Examples from Ksar Akil, Lebanon. *Journal of Field Archaeology, 10,* 239–243.

Bicho, N., & Gibaja, J. (2006). Le site de Vale Boi (Algarve, Portugal): Production d'un outillage expédient au Paléolithique supérieur. In Normes techniques et practices sociales: de la simplicité des outillages pré- et protohistoriques. XXVIe Rencontres Internationales d'Archéologie et d'histoire d'Antibes. Antibes, pp. 129–134.

Binford, L. (1962). Archaeology as anthropology. *American Antiquity, 28*, 217–225.
Blanchette, R., (2000). A review of microbial deterioration found in archaeological wood from different environments. *International Biodeterioration & Biodegradation, 46*, 189–204
Bordes, F. (1969). Reflections on typology and techniques in the Paleolithic. *Arctic Anthropology, 6*, 1–29.
Bordes, F., & Sonneville-Bordes, D. (1970). The significance of variability in Palaeolithic assemblages. *World Archaeology, 2*, 61–73.
Bradley, B. (1982). Flaked stone technology and typology. In Frison, G. & Stanford, D. (Eds.), *The Agate Basin Site: A record of the Paleoindian occupation of the Northwestern High Plains* (pp. 181–208). New York: Academic.
Bradley, R., & Clayton, C. (1987). The influence of flint microstructure on the formation of microwear polishes. In Sieveking, G. & Newcomer, M. (Eds.), *The human uses of flint and chert* (pp. 81–89). Cambridge: Cambridge University Press.
Bradley, B., & Frison, G. (1987). Projectile points and specialized bifaces from the Horner site. In Frison, G. & Todd, L. (Eds.), *The horner site: The type site of the Cody Cultural Complex* (pp. 199–232). New York: Academic.
Brink, J. (1978). Notes on the occurrence of spontaneous retouch. *Lithic Technology, 7*, 31–33.
Broadbent, N. (1979). *Coastal resources and settlement stability. A critical study of a Mesolithic site complex in northern Sweden.* Uppsala: Aun 3.
Buc, N. (2011). Experimental series and use-wear in bone tools. *Journal of Archaeological Science, 38*, 546–557.
Burroni, D., Donahue, R. E., Pollard, A. M., & Mussi, M. (2002). The surface alteration features of flint artefacts as a record of environmental processes. *Journal of Archaeological Science, 29*(11), 1277–1287.
Childe, V. G. (1936). *Man makes himself.* London: Watts.
Childe, V. G. (1942). *What happened in history.* Harmondsworth: Penguin.
Christensen, M., Walter, P., & Menu, M. (1992). Usewear characterisation of prehistoric flints with IBA. *Nuclear Instruments and Methods in Physics Research B, 64*, 488–493.
Clemente, I., & Gibaja, J. (1998). Working processes on cereals: An approach through microwear analysis. *Journal of Archaeological Science, 25*, 457–464.
Clemente, I., Risch, R., & Gibaja, J. (Eds.). (2002). Análisis funcional. Su aplicación al estudio de sociedades prehistóricas. British Archaeological Reports (International series), 1073, Oxford: Hadrian Books Ltd.
Collin, F., & Jardon-Giner, P. (1993). Travail de la peau avec des grattoirs emmanchés. Réflexions sur des bases expérimentales et ethnographiques. In Anderson P., Beyries S., Otte, M., & Plisson H., (Eds.), Traces et fonction: les gestes retrouvés. Actes du Colloque international de Liège 8–10 Décembre, 1990. ERAUL 50/2, pp. 105–117.
Curvew, E. (1930). Prehistoric flint sickles. *Antiquity, 4*, 179–186.
Debert, J., & Sherriff, B. L., (2007). Raspadita: A new lithic tool from the Isthmus of Rivas, Nicaragua. *Journal of Archaeological Science, 34*, 1889–1901.
Del Bene, T. A. (1979). Once upon a striation: Current models of striation and polish formation. In B. Hayden, (Ed.), *Lithic use-wear analysis* (pp. 167–178). New York: Academic.
Derndarsky, M., & Ocklind, G. (2001). Some preliminary observations on subsurface damage on experimental and archaeological quartz tools using CLSM and dye. *Journal of Archaeological Science, 28*(11), 1149–1158.
d'Errico, F. (1985) Meccanica di formazione delle usure e funzione dei micrograttatoi mesolitici. *Preistoria Alpina, 27*, 85–87.
d'Errico, F., & Giacobino, G. (1985). Approche methodologique de l'analyse de l'outillage osseaux: un exemple d'étude. *L'Anthropologie, 89*(4), 457–472. Paris.
d'Errico, F., & Mouncadel-Espinet, P. (1986). L'emploi du micro- scope électronique Ã balayage pour l'étude expérimentale de traces d'usure: reclage sur du bois de cervidé. *Bulletin de la Société Préhistorique Française, 83*, 91–96
Donahue, R. (1988). Microwear analysis and site function of Paglicci Cave, Level 4A. *World Archaeology, 19*, 357–375.

Dries, M. van den. (1994). WAVES: An expert system for the analysis of use-wear on flint artifacts, in methods in the mountains. In *Proceedings of UISPP Commission IV meeting Mount Victoria*, Australia: Sydney University Archaeological Methods.

Dumont, J. (1982). The quantification of microwear traces: A new use for interferometry. *World Archaeology, 14*(2), 206–217.

Evans, S. (1897). *The ancient stone implements, weapons and ornaments, of Great Britain*. London: Longmans, Green and Co.

Evans, A., & Donahue, R. (2005). The elemental chemistry of lithic microwear: an experiment. *Journal of Archaeological Science 32* (12), 1733–1740.

Evans, A., & Donahue, R. (2008). Laser scanning confocal microscopy: A potential technique for the study of lithic microwear. *Journal of Archaeological Science, 35*, 2223–2230.

Evans, A., & Macdonald, D. (2011). Using metrology in early prehistoric stone tool research: Further work and a brief instrument comparison. *Scanning, 33*, 294–303.

Evershed, R. P., Dudd, S. N., Lockheart, M. J., & Jim, S. (2001). Lipids in archaeology. In D.R. Brothwell & A.M. Pollard (Eds.), *Handbook of archaeological sciences* (pp. 331–349). Chichester: John Wiley and Sons.

Évora, M. (2007). Utensilagem Óssea do Paleolítico Superior Português. Unpublished M.A. thesis, Universidade do Algarve, Faro, Portugal.

Fischer, A., Vemming Hansen, P., & Rasmussen, P. (1984). Macro and micro wear traces on lithic projectile points: Experimental results and prehistoric examples. *Journal of Danish Archaeology, 3*, 19–46.

Fullagar, R. (1993) Flaked stone tools and plant food production: A preliminary report on obsidian tools from Talasea, West New Britain, PNG. In P. Anderson, S. Beyries, M. Otte, & H. Plisson (Eds.), *Traces et fonction: Les gestes retrouvés* (pp. 331–337). Liège: ERAUL

Frison, G.C., Bradley, B.A. (1980). Folsom Tools and Technology at the Hanson Site. Academic Press, New York.

Fullagar, R., & Matherson, M. (2013). Traceology: A summary. In C. Smith (Ed.), *Encyclopedia of global archaeology* (pp. 73–85). New York: Springer.

Gassin, B. (1996). *Évolution socio-économique dans le Chasséen de la grotte de l'Église supérieure (Var). Apport de l'analyse fonctionnelle des industries lithiques* (326 p). Paris: CNRS Editions. (Monographies du CRA, 17).

Geneste, J.-M., & Plisson, H. (1990). Technologie fonctionnelle des pointes Ã cran solutréennes: l'apport des nouvelles données de la Grotte de Combe Saunière (Dordogne). In J. K. Kozlowski (Ed.), *Feuilles de Pierre. Les Industries Ã Pointes Foliacées du Paléolithique Supérieur Européen* (pp. 293–320). Liège, ERAUL 42, Université de Liège.

Geneste, J.-M., & Plisson, H. (1986). Le Solutréen de la grotte de Combe Saunière 1 (Dordogne). *Gallia Préhistoire 29*, 9–27.

Geneste, J.-M., & Plisson, H. (1993). Hunting technologies and human behavior: Lithic analysis of Solutrean shouldered points. In H. Knecht, A. Pike-Tay, & R. White (Eds.), *Before Lascaux: The complex Record of the early Upper Paleolithic* (pp. 117–135). New York: Telford Press.

Gernaey, A. M., Waite, E. R., Collins, M. J., Craig, O. E., & Sokol, R. J. (2001). Survival and interpretation of archaeological proteins. In D. R. Brothwell & A. M. Pollard (Eds.), *Handbook of archaeological sciences* (pp. 323–329). Chichester: John Wiley & Sons.

Gibaja J., & Palomo A. (2004). Geométricos usados como proyectiles. Implicaciones económicas, sociales e ideológicas en sociedades neolíticas del VI-IV milenio CAL BC en el Noroeste de la Península Ibérica. *Trabajos de Prehistoria, 61*(1), p. 81–98.

Gonzalez-Urquijo, J.E., & Ibanez-Estévez, J.J. (1993). Utilización del instrumental lítico y funcionalidad del asentamiento en el yacimiento de Berniollo (Alava, España). In: Anderseon, P.C., Beyries, S., Otte, M., Plisson, H. (Eds.), Traces et Fonction: Les Gestes Retrouvés. Université de Liège, Service de Préhistoire (ERAUL, 50), pp. 97–104.

González-Urquijo, J.; & Ibanez-Estévez, J. (1994). Metodología de análisis funcional de instrumentos tallados en sílex. Universidad de Deusto.

Gonzalez-Urquijo, J., & Ibanez-Estevez, J. (2003). The quantification of use-wear polish using image analysis: First results. *Journal of Archaeological Science, 30*, 481–489.

Grace, R., (1989). Interpreting the Function of Stone Tools: The quantification and computerisation of microwear analysis. In: B.A.R. International Series 474. Oxford.

Gräslund, B., Knutsson, H., Knutsson, K., & Taffinder, J. (1990). The Interpretive Possi- bilities of Microwear Studies. In: Aun 14. Uppsala.

Grace, R., (1990). The limitations and applications of use-wear analysis. Proceedings of the International Conference on Lithic Use-Wear Analysis, AUN 14, 9–14.

Grace, R., (1996). Use-wear analysis: The state of the art. *Archaeometry, 38,* 209–229.

Grace, R., Graham, I., & Newcomer, M. (1985). The quantification of microwear polishes. *World Archaeology, 17*(1), 112–120.

Hardy, B. (2004). Neanderthal behaviour and stone tool function at the Middle Palaeolithic site of La Quina, France. *Antiquity, 78,* 547–565.

Hardy, B., & Garufi, G., (1998). Identification of woodworking on stone tools through residue and use-wear analyses: Experimental results. *Journal of Archaeological Science, 25,* 177–184.

Haslam, M. (2006). Potential misidentification of in situ archaeological tool-residues: Starch and conidia. *Journal of Archaeological Science, 33,* 114–121.

Hay, C. (1977) Use-scratch morphology: A functionally significant aspect of edge damage on obsidian tools. *Journal of Field Archaeology, 4,* 491–494

Hayden, B. (1979). *Palaeolithic Reflections. Lithic Technology and Ethnographic Excavation among the Australian Aborigines.* Australian Institute of Aboriginal studies 5. New Jersey: Humanities Press Inc.

Hayden, B., & Kamminga, J. (1979). An introduction to use-wear: The first CLUW. In B. Hayden (Ed.), *Lithic use-wear analysis* (pp. 1–14). New York: Academic Press.

Hester, T., & Heizer, R. (1973). Arrow points or knives? Comments on the proposed function of 'Stockton Points'. *American Antiquity, 38,* 220–1.

Hester, T., & Shafer, H. (1975). An initial study of blade technology on the Central and Southern Texas coastal plain. *La Tierra, 5*(3), 22–25

Hodgskiss, T. (2010). Identifying grinding, scoring and rubbing use-wear on experimental ochre pieces. *Journal of Archaeological Science, 37,* 3344–3358.

Ibáñez, J., & Gonzalez, J. (1996). *From tool use to site function, use wear analysis in some final upper Paleolithic sites in the Basque country. British Archaeological Reports international series, 658.* Oxford: Archaeopress.

Igreja, M. (2005). Étude fonctionnelle de l'industrie lithique d'un grand habitat gravettien en France: les unités OP10 et KL19 de La Vigne Brun . Ph. D. Thesis, Aix-en-Provence: Université Aix-Marseille I, Loire.

Jans, M. M. E., Nielsen-Marsh, C. M., Smith, C. I., Collins, M. J., & Kars, H. (2004). Characterisation of microbial attack on archaeological bone. *Journal of Archaeological Science, 31,* 87–95.

Kamminga, J. (1979). The nature of use-polish and abrasive smoothing on stone tools. In. B. Hayden, (Ed.), *Lithic use-wear analysis* (pp. 143–157). New York: Academic Press.

Kamminga, J. (1982). Over the Edge: Functional Analysis of Australian Stone Tools. Anthropology Museum, University of Queensland.

Keeley L. (1974). Techniques and methodology in microwear studies: A critical review. *World Archaeology, 5*(3), 323–336

Keeley L. (1980). *Experimental determination of stone tool uses: A microwear analysis.* Chicago: University of Chicago Press.

Keeley, L. (1982). Hafting and retooling: Effects on the archaeological record. *American Antiquity, 47,* 798–809.

Keeley, L., & Newcomer, M. (1977). Micro-wear analysis of experimental flint tools: A test case. *Journal of Archaeological Science, 4,* 29–62.

Klejn, L. (1982). *Archaeological Typology. British Archaeological Reports International Series 153.* Oxford: Archaeopress.

Lammers-Keijsers, Y. (2008). Tropical choices: A study of wear traces on the toolkit of the pre-Columbian inhabitants of Morel and Anse Ã la Gourde, Guadeloupe, FWI. In Prehistoric Technology 40 years later: Functional studies and the Russian Legacy. Longo, L. (dir.). Actes du Colloque de Vérone 20–23 Avril 2005. BAR International Series 1783: 365–368.

Langejans, G. H. J., (2010). Remains of the day-preservation of organic micro-residues on stone tools. *Journal of Archaeological Science, 37,* 971–985.
Lemorini, C., Peresani, M., Rossetti, P., Malerba, G., & Giacobini, G. (2005). Techno-morphological and use-wear functional analysis: An integrated approach to the study of a Discoid industry. In M Peresani (Eds.), *Discoid lithic technology: Advances and implications. British Archaeological Reports, International Series 1120* (pp. 257–275). Oxford: Archeopress.
Leroi-Gourhan, A. (1964). *Evolution et technique I: l'homme et la matière.* Paris: Albin Michel.
Levi-Sala, I. (1986). Use wear and post-depositional surface modification: a word of caution. *Journal of Archaeological Science, 13,* 229–244.
Levi-Sala, I. (1993). Use-wear traces: Processes of development and post-depositional alterations. In P. Anderson, S. Beyries, M. Ottte, & H. Plisson (Eds.), Traces et fonction: les gestes retrouvés. Actes du Colloque international de Liège, Vol. 50/2, pp. 401–416, 8–10 Dec 1990, ERAUL, Liège.
Levitt, J. (1979). *A review of experimental traceological research in the USSR. Lithic Use-wear analysis.* In: Hayden, B. (Ed.), Proceedings of the Conference held at Department of Archaeology, pp. 27–38, Burnaby, Canada, 16–20 March 1977, New York, Academic Press.
Lombard, M. (2005). Evidence of hunting and hafting during the Middle Stone Age at Sibudu Cave, KwaZulu-Natal: A multi analytical approach. *Journal of Human Evolution, 48,* 279–300.
Lombard, M. (2008). Finding resolution for the Howiesons Poort through the microscope: Microresidue analysis of segments from Sibudu Cave, South Africa. *Journal of Archaeological Science, 35,* 26–41.
Lombard, M., & Wadley, L. (2009). The impact of micro-residue studies on South African Middle Stone Age research. In M. Haslam et al. (Eds.), *Archaeological science under a microscope: Studies in residue and ancient DNA analysis in honour to Thomas H. Loy. Terra australis 30* (pp. 11–28). Canberra: ANU E Press.
Lombard, M., Parsons, I., & van der Ryst, M. (2004). Moddle Stone Age lithic experimentation for macro-fracture and residue analyses: The process and preliminary results with reference to the Sibudu Cave points. *South African Journal of Science, 100,* 159–166.
Longo, L., Skakun, N., Anderson, P., & Plisson, H. (2005). *The roots of use-wear analysis: Selected papers of S. A. Semenov.* Verona: Museo Civico di Storia Naturale di Verona.
Loy, T. H. (1983). Prehistoric blood residues: Detection on tool surfaces and identification of species of origin. *Science, 220,* 1269–1271.
Loy, T. H. (1993). The artifact as site: An example of the bio- molecular analysis of organic residues on prehistoric tools. *World Archaeology, 25*(1), 44–63
Lu, T. (2003). The survival of starch residue in a subtropical environment. In: D. M. Hart & L. A. Wallis (Eds.), *Phytolith and Starch Research in the Australian-Pacific-Asian Regions: The State of the Art* (pp. 119–126). Canberra: Pandus Books.
Lu, T. (2006). The survival of starch residues in a subtropical environment. In R. Tor- rence & H. Barton (Eds.), *Ancient starch research* (pp. 80–81). Walnut Creek: Left Coast Press.
Mansur, M. (1983). Traces d'utilisation et technologie lithique: exemples de la Patagonie. Ph.D. Thesis, Université de Bordeaux.
Marreiros, J., Gibaja, J., & Bicho, N. (In press) *Lithic use-wear analysis from the Early Gravettian of Vale Boi (Southwestern Iberia).* In J. Marreiros, J. Gibaja, N. Bicho (Eds.), Proceedings of the International conference on Use-Wear analysis, Use-Wear 2012, Cambridge Scholars Publishing, Cambridge.
Mazzucco, N., Trenti F., Gibaja F., & Clemente I. (2013). Chert taphonomical alterations: Preliminary experiments. In P. A. Estudio, R. Piqué, & X. Terradas (Eds.), *Experimentación en arqueología. Sèrie Monogràfica del MAC* (pp. 255–263). Girona: Academia.
Meeks, N., Sieveking, G., Tite, M., & Cook, J. (1982). Gloss and use-wear traces on flint sickles and similar phenomena. *Journal of Archaeological Science, 9,* 317–340.
Moss, E. (1983). *The functional analysis of flint implements: Pincevent and Pont D'Ambon, two case studies from the French final Palaeolithic 117. British Archaeological Reports.* Oxford: Archeopress.
Odell, G. (2004). *Lithic analysis.* New York: Kluwer.

Odell, G., & Cowan, F. (1986). Experiments with spears and arrows on animal targets. *Journal of Field Archaeology, 13,* 195–212.
Odell, G., & Odell-Vereecken, F. (1980). Verifying the reliability of lithic use-wear analysis by "Blind Tests": The low magnification approach. *Journal of Field Archaeology, 7,* (1), 87–120.
Odell, G. (1981). The mechanics of use-breakage of stone tools: some testable hypotheses. *Journal of Field Archaeology 8* (2), 197–209.
Odell, G. (2001). Stone tool research at the end of the millennium: classification, function, and behavior. *Journal of Archaeological Research 9* (1), 45–100.
O'Farrell, M. (1996). Approche technologique et fonctionnelle des pointes de La Gravette. Dipomes d'Etudes Approfondies, Universite Ì Bordeaux 1.
O'Farrell, M. (2004). Les pointes de La Gravette de Corbiac (Dordogne) et considérations sur la chasse au Paléolithique supérieur ancien. In P. Bodu & C. Constantin (Eds.), *Approches Fonctionnelles en Préhistoire. XXV Congrès Préhistorique de France* (pp. 121–128), Nanterre 2000. Société Préhistorique Française.
Owen, L. R., & Unrath, G. (eds.), (1986). Technical aspects of microwear studies on stone tools, Tiibingen, Early Man News, 9-11, 69–81.
Pétillon, J.-M., Olivier, B., Pierre, B., Pierre, C., Grégory, D., Mathieu, L., Véronique, L., Hugues, P., & Boris, V. (2011). Hard core and cutting edge: experimental manufacture and use of Magdalenian composite projectile tips. *Journal of Archaeological Science 38* (6), 1266–1283.
Peyrony, D. (1949). *Le Périgord préhistorique.* Périgueux: Société Historique et Archéologique du Périgord.
Pfeiffer, L. (1912). *Die Steinzeitliche Technik und ihre Beziehungen zur Gegenwart: Ein Beitrag zur Gaschichte der Arbeit.* In Festschrift zur XLIII algemeinen Versammlung der deutschen anthropologischen Gesellshaft. (Vol. 1). Jena: Gustav Fischer.
Phillips, P. (1988). Traceology (microwear) studies in the USSR. *World archaeology, 19,* 349–356.
Plisson, H. (1985). Etude founctionelle d'outillages lithiques prehistoriques par l'analyse des micro-usures: recherché metodologique et archeologique. Ph.D. Thesis. Universidad de Paris, Paris.
Plisson, H., & Mauger, M. (1988). Chemical and mechanical alteration of microwear polishes: An experimental approach. *Helinium, XXVIII*(1), 3–16.
Redman, C. L. (1973). multistage fieldwork and analytical techniques. *American Antiquity, 38,* 61–79.
Risch, R. (1995). Recursos naturales y sistemas de producción en el Sudeste de la Península Ibérica entre 3000 y 1000 ane. Ph.D. Thesis Universidad Autónoma de Barcelona, Ed. Microfotográfica, Bellaterra.
Rosenfelid, A. (1971). The examination of use marks on some Magalenian endscrapers. *British Museum Quarterly, XXXV,* 176–182.
Rots, V. (2002). Are tangs morphological adaptations in view of hafting? Macro- and microscopic wear analysis on a selection of tanged burins from Maisières-Canal. *Notae Praehistoricae, 114,* 61–9.
Rots, V. (2010). *Prehension and hafting traces on flint tools: A methodology.* Leuven: Leuven University Press.
Schiffer, M. (1975). Archaeology as behavioral science. *American Anthropologist, 77,* 836–848.
Schiffer, M. (1976). *Behavioral archeology.* New York: Academic Press.
Scott, R. S., Ungar, P. S., Bergstrom, T. S., Brown, C. A., Grine, F. E., Teaford, M. F., & Walker, A. (2005). Dental microwear texture analysis shows within-species diet variability in fossil hominins. *Nature, 436*(7051), 693–695.
Scott, R. S., Ungar, P. S., Bergstrom, T. S., Brown, C. A., Childs, B. E., Teaford, M. F., & Walker, A. (2006). Dental micro-wear texture analysis: Technical considerations. *Journal of Human Evolution, 51*(4), 339–349.
Semenov, S. (1957). *Pervobytnaja technika. Materialy i Issledovania po Archeologii SSSR 54.* Moskva—Leningrad: Nauka.
Semenov, S. A. (1964). *Prehistoric technology: An experimental study of the oldest tools and artefacts from traces of manufacture and wear.* London: Cory, Adams e Mackay.

Shanks, O.C., Bonnichsen, R., Vella, A.T., & Ream, W. (2001). Recovery of protein and DNA trapped in stone tool microcracks. *Journal of Archaeological Science, 28*, 965–972.

Shea, J. J. (1988) Methodological considerations meeting the choice of analytical techniques in lithic use-wear analysis: Tests, results, and application. In S. Beyries (Ed.), *Industries lithiques: Traceologie et technologie, Vol. 11. BAR international series 411(ii)* (pp. 65–81). Oxford: Archeopress.

Shea, J., Davis, Z., Brown, K. (2001). Experimental tests of Middle Palaeolithic spear points using a calibrated crossbow. *J. Archaeol. Sci. 28*, 807–816.

Shea, J., Brown, K., & Davis, Z. (2002). Controlled experiments with Middle Palaeolithic spear points: Levallois points. In: J. R. Mathieu (Ed*.), Experimental archaeology: replicating past objects, behaviours and processes. BAR International Series 1035* (pp. 55–72). Oxford: Archeopress.

Sidéra, I., & Legrand, A. (2006). Tracéologie fonctionnelle des matières osseuses: une méthode. *Bull. Soc. Préhist. Française, 103*(2), 291–304.

Sterud, E. L. (1978) Changing aims of American archaeology: A citations analysis of Americon Antiquity 1964–1975. *American Antiquity, 43*, 294–302.

Stevens, N.E., Harro, D.R., & Hicklin, A. (2010). Practical quantitative lithic use-wear analysis using multiple classifiers. *J. Archaeol. Sci. 30*, 2671–2678.

Sonnenfeld, J. (1962). Interpreting the function of primitive implements. *American Antiquity, 28*, 56–65.

Sonneville-Bordes, D., & Perrot, J. (1953). Essai d'adaptation des méthodes statistiques au Paléolithique supérieur. Premiers résultats. *Bulletin de la Socie'te' Pre'historique Francaise, 50*, 323–333.

Sonneville-Bordes, D., & Perrot, J. (1954). Lexique typologique du Paléolothique supérieur. *Bulletin de la Socie'te' Pre'historique Francaise, 51*, 327–335.

Sonneville-Bordes, D., & Perrot, J. (1955). Lexique typologique du Paléolithique supérieur. *Bulletin de la Socie'te' Pre'historique Francaise, 52*, 76–79.

Sonneville-Bordes, D., & Perrot, J. (1956). Lexique typologique du Paleolithique supérieur. *Bulletin de la Socie'te' Pre'historique Francaise, 53*, 408–412.

Stafford, C. R., & Stafford, B. D. (1983). The functional hypothesis: A formal approach to use-wear experiments and settlement-subsistence. *Journal of Anthropological Research, 39*(4), 351–375

Stordeur, D. (1987). Manches et Emmanchements Pre İhistoriques: Quelques Propositions Pre İliminaires. In D. Stordeur (Ed.), *La Main et L'outil: Manches et Emmanchements Préhistoriques* (pp. 11–35). Lyon: CNRS.

Thomas, K. D. (1993). Molecular biology and archaeology: A prospectus for interdisciplinary research. *World Archaeology, 25*(I), 1–17.

Trigger, B. (1984). Alternative archaeologies: Nationalist, colonialist, imperialist. *Man, 19*(3), 5–70.

Trigger, B. (2006). *A history of archaeological thought*, 2nd ed. Cambridge: Cambridge University Press.

Tringham, R., Cooper, G., Odell, G., Voytek, B., & Whitman, A. (1974). Experimentation in the formation of edge damage: A new approach to lithic analysis. *Journal of Field Archaeology, 1*(2), 171–196.

Tuross, N., Barnes, I., & Potts, R. (1996). Protein identification of blood residues on experimental stone tools. *Journal of Archaeological Science, 23*, 289–296.

Unger-Hamilton, R. (1988). *Method in microwear analysis: Prehistoric sickles and other stone tools from Arjoune, Syria. BAR international Series 435*, Oxford: Archaeopress.

Ungrath, G., Owen, L. R., Gijn, A. Van., Moss, E. H., Plisson, H., & Vaughan, P. (1986). An evaluation of use-wear studies: A multi-analyst approach. *Early Man News, 9/10/11*, 117–75.

Van Gijn, A. (1998). A closer look: A realistic attempt to 'squeeze blood from stones. In R. Fullagar (Ed.), *A closer look: Recent Australian studies of stone tools* (pp. 189–194). Sydney: University of Sydney.

Vardi, J., Golan, A., Levy, D., & Gilead, I. (2010). Tracing sickle blade levels of wear and discard patterns: a new sickle gloss quantification method. *J. Archaeol. Sci. 37*, 1716–1724.

Vaughan, P. C. (1985). Use-wear analysis of flaked stone tools. Arizona: University of Arizona Press.

Vila, A., & Gallart, F. (1993). Caracterizacion de los Micropulidos de Uso: Ejemplo de Aplicacion del Analisis de Imagenes Digitalizadas. In P. Anderson, S. Beyries, M. Otte, & H. Plisson (Eds.), *Traces et Fonction: Les Gestes Retrouvés*. Liege: University de Liege.

Villa, P., & Lenoir, M. (2006). Hunting weapons of the Middle Stone Age and the Middle Palaeolithic: Spear points from Sibudu, Rose Cottage and Bouheben. *South African Humanities, 18*, 89–122.

Wadley, L., & Lombard, M. (2007). Small things in perspective: The contribution of our blind tests to micro-residue studies on archaeological stone tools. *Journal of Archaeological Science, 34*, 1001–1010.

Wadley, L., Lombard, M., & Williamson, B. (2004). The first residue analysis blind tests: Results and lessons learnt. *Journal of Archaeological Science, 31*, 1491–1501.

Witthoft, J. (1967). Glazed polish on flint tools. *American Antiquity, 32*(3), 383–388.

Yamada, S. (1986). The formation process of use-wear polishes. *Archaeology and Natural Science, 19*, 101–123.

Yamada S., & Sawada, A. (1993). The method of description for polished surfaces. In P. Anderson, S. Beyries, M. Ottte, & H. Plisson (Eds.), Traces et fonction: les gestes retrouvés. Actes du Colloque international de Liège, pp. 447–457, 8–10 Dec 1990. ERAUL 50(2), Liège.

Chapter 3
Ethnoarchaeology and Functional Analysis

J. González-Urquijo, S. Beyries and J.J. Ibáñez

3.1 Introduction

Actualist approaches including experimentation and analogies from ethnographic sources are the two main ways to generate rules of inference in the study of prehistoric tools. Ethnographic sources have been used since the beginning of the discipline in the nineteenth century. Comparisons with contemporary technology or ethnographic references lie at the base of the names applied to most types of prehistoric stone tools in typological classifications; names like scrapers, burins, borers and so on (Brézillon 1971; Trigger 1989). Deductions about tool use were made through the formal resemblances between ethnographic and archaeological implements.

In the mid-twentieth century, archaeological research strongly rejected the use of analogies. This attitude was due to the excesses of some arbitrary comparisons made out of context and mistrust towards historicist approaches to parallels between modern primitive societies and prehistoric communities.

After the 1960s, the use of ethnoanalogies returned, through the means of ethnoarchaeology. In this new framework, greater trust was placed in the pertinence of comparisons between past and present groups who displayed common elements in their ecological conditions, level of technological development or socio-economic organisation. In the widely cited (Ascher 1961; Spriggs 1977; Wylie 1985) words of Clark (1953) it would be possible to compare the cases of populations 'at a common level of subsistence (…) existing under ecological conditions which approximate those reconstructed for the prehistoric people under reconstruction'. In addition, critical criteria for a more pertinent use of analogies have improved, in terms of their validity and relevance. They are now based on structural comparisons (relational analogies, *sensu* Wylie 1985) rather than formal analogies. The consensus on the risk of direct analogies is widely accepted and also a consensus exists on the limitations of transcultural rules, which are judged to be better used as sources of hypotheses than as interpretative keys.

The use of ethnoarchaeological references in connection with functional analysis began with the pioneering work of Semenov (1964), who in the very introduction of his work noted the importance of ethnographic information and, at the same time, its limited and biased nature. Ethnoarchaeological information can be used both to create the rules of inference and to interpret the results of archaeological functional analysis (Owen and Porr 1999; Beyries and Petrequin 2001; Terradas 2005). In reality, as Owen pointed out (1999), analogies from ethnographic sources form the basis of most of the experimental programmes, and therefore, they also lie at the base of the resulting reconstructions of use. When an experimental programme is being planned, the tasks to be performed must be defined. To do this, in the first place, the archaeological record should be taken into account as this may suggest the kind of tasks that might have been carried out at the archaeological site being studied. Thus, for example, the finding of bones with butchery marks indicates that this work was carried out at the site. However, many tasks involving perishable substances leave few evident signs in the deposit, such as working wood, hide or plants. Ethnographic examples not only suggest ideas about what kind of tasks were performed but also about how they were done (such as hand movements made and types of hafting).

In certain cases, ethnoarchaeology itself can act as a form of experimentation. The work performed in ethnographic contexts can be observed and documented, and the tools used can be collected in order to study the use-wear marks. This has been done, for example, for hide-crafts in Siberia and Canada, or for the use of pebbles to work with ceramics in the Canary Islands (Beyries 1999; Rodríguez et al. 2006).

In fact, the comparison between evidence from experimentation and ethnographic sources in general—or ethnoarchaeology in particular—is quite common. Although the importance of having experienced workers reproduce the tasks involved in the experiments has been noted—as this may change the characteristics of the marks (Beyries 1993)—few studies have combined both approaches (Altinbilek et al. 2001; Anderson 2007).

In general terms, experimentation is able to deal with and monitor tool characteristics (raw material, weight, dimensions, shape) and the variables defining the activity (movement, kind of substance worked, duration).

By the observation of ethnographic contexts we are able to study the same aspects, although it is often impossible to monitor the variables. However, ethnographic observation can explain a vast array of other questions. These aspects include the sequence and duration of the work, the working area, tool management, the know-how used, the gender, age and skill of the user, seasonality and socioeconomic background (Owen 1999; Beyries et al. 2001; Beyries 2008). These also include other significant points, like production objectives, product management, the existence of other tasks or stages involved and/or avoided in the production, access to or ownership of tools, the reasons for the distribution of labour, the social condition of the workers, the ideological, symbolic and narrative context of the technical work, just to cite some of the most obvious.

In reality, this is the potential framework because the ethnographic record is, in fact, limited and often imprecise (Owen 1999). Ethnographic data to which we normally have access have not been provided by ethnographers interested in the techniques, but by social anthropologists interested in aspects of the social and ideological organisation of the populations they are studying. Consequently, very rarely is information recorded with details of the working process or the substances worked. This limits the use of the information by archaeologists in general and by functional analysts in particular. Similarly, the ethnographic collections held by museums tend to be poorly or incorrectly documented (Terradas et al. 1999). Ethnohistorical sources, about ancient contacts or classical sources (Rodríguez 1999; Barris and Totelin 2000), are equally of limited use and restricted application. In contrast, ethnoarchaeological data is of a better quality as it specifically records aspects that derive in immediate interpretations. However, for the case studied here, the information is limited or partial because few modern or sub-modern human groups still knap and use chipped stone tools (cf. Brandt 1996; Beyries 1999).

3.2 Information from Ethnographic Sources

3.2.1 Tools

Ethnographic sources have provided a great deal of information about tool types and the relationship between tools and particular tasks. We have referred to the role this information has played even in giving names to the tools. Important details have been obtained about substantial aspects of tool functions and methods of hafting (Albasini-Roulin 1987; Mansur-Franchomme 1987; Weedman 2006), the conservation of residues (Kimura et al. 2001; Rots and Williamson 2004) and the use of specific implements like cobble-stones and mortars (Rodríguez et al. 2006). The abundance of this information does not mean that it should not be handled with care as seen in some cases.

One of the problems derives from the number of different functions or functioning which can be carried out by tools that are at least apparently very similar. The seminal study by Sigaut (1991) about the variable functions that knives can be put to is just one example. The same study highlights how the morphology of the objects or tools, seen out of context, does not provide any clues to the functions they were given. In Sigaut's words, they are the riddle objects filling the back rooms

Fig. 3.1 Einkorn (*Triticum monococcum*) harvesting directly by hand in northern Morocco

of ethnographic museums when they become separated from the documentation explaining their context.

Ethnographic observations of tools clearly show the limits of analogical inferences (Owen 1999) which mistaken references sometimes lead to. The analogies should not only be morphological because formal resemblances are rarely enough to deduce functional similarities. A clear example is that of the bitter manioc graters in the low Tropics of South America. Modern ethnographic sources show the use of quartz microliths inserted in wooden shafts for processing these edible roots. The findings of similar microliths in ancient archaeological contexts has suggested the deduction that these were used for similar tasks. This deduction is highly significant because manioc is a cultivated plant and can therefore be used to interpret the presence and expansion of early agriculture in these regions. However, the study of the residue on the archaeological artefacts has consistently shown that the archaeological quartz microliths found at sites in the Orinoco Valley were used to process a large number of plants, but not manioc (Walker and Wilk 1998; Perry 2005).

Ethnographic references, however, are able to give access to invisible technologies: tasks performed with perishable implements that are rarely found in archaeological deposits, or which are performed without any kind of implement. One of these is cereal harvesting. Despite being always associated with the use of sickles, harvesting can also be carried out with wooden pincers (as in the Province of Asturias, North Spain; Ibáñez et al. 2001) or directly by hand, as we can see in northern Morocco (Fig. 3.1) or among the Bedouin (Simms and Russell 1997). However, some tools are also invisible to ethnographers, who do not mention them either because other tools attract their attention more or because they are used in technical and social contexts they do not observe. A striking example is that of the Yamana in Tierra del Fuego. Most of the ethnographers' accounts mention the tools made from obsidian or glass, especially the projectile points, but hardly cite the tools made from local raw materials and used in domestic contexts. Archaeological excavations of occupations contemporary with those observed by ethnographers in the late nineteenth and early twentieth century show that the real tools differ widely from those described in ethnographic sources (Clemente 1997; Terradas et al. 1999).

Fig. 3.2 Hide working with lithic tools in northern Morocco

3.2.2 Chaînes Opératoires and Technical Processes

Ethnographic observations have contributed a vast literature to understand the technical processes carried out by hunter–gatherer groups and farmers with ways of life comparable with those of prehistoric groups.

The most basic information refers to the techniques used in the procurement and manipulation of resources, for example, about hunting techniques (Frison 1978; Churchill 1993; Hughes 1998; Ellis 1997; Hutchings and Brüchert 1997; Petrequin and Petrequin 1990; Lupo and Schmitt 2003), butchery techniques (Fisher and Strickland 1989; Beyries 1993), hide-working (Gusinde 1931/1982; Clark and Kurashina 1981; Beyries 1999; Rodríguez 1997, 1999; Ibáñez et al. 2002), woodworking (Carneiro 1979; Keeley 1983; Kamminga 1988), work in stone (Roux 1999), crafts in plants (Ibáñez and González Urquijo 2002) and so on.

In addition, ethnography provides significant information about production objectives, such as the characteristics of the products sought, like the shape, size and number. This information is crucial when the technical processes are used to transform perishable products of which no evidence is normally found in the archaeological record (Speck 1937; Silvestre 1994; Holl 2003).

It also informs about the reasons for technical variability. In the well-studied case of hide-working, the variability may be due to the type of animal skins (fish or mammals, of different sizes), the objectives of the production (careful work or not), the production organisation (domestic or specialised work, female or male), which is in turn connected with the economic goal (self-consumption, trade) and social value (Fig. 3.2). Some studies give particular technical details that may be strategic in the performance of a task and later in their detection and identification during use-wear analysis. The use of specific equipment (tools and handles) has been described in connection with particular task conditions. For example, the Gamo people in Ethiopia use scrapers of different sizes to work hide, depending on the type of animal the skin came from, mainly on the size of the animal (cattle vs. sheep/goat; Weedman 2006). However, other nearby groups use scrapers of different sizes depending on the processing stage, large scrapers at first and small ones in the final phases (Brandt 1996).

Another example is the interpretation of the use of scrapers at the Ui1 site, based on an ethnographic reference obtained by studying American and Asiatic groups (Athapaskan, Interior Salish and Koriak; Beyries et al. 2001; Beyries 2008). Here, based on the wear patterns on the edges of the tools, it was possible to determine the procedures followed to process the hides (fixing the tool, type of haft, etc.), as well as the type of hide being worked (fine like that of roe deer or reindeer, or thick like that of elk).

The same note of precaution should be sounded for the technical processes as for the tools. Some technical processes are invisible to ethnographic sources (cf. Clemente 1977) and can lead to mistaken models. Rodríguez (1999) has noted the considerable contradictions between ethnohistorical sources and archaeological evidence in the case of pre-Hispanic populations in the Canary Islands. Written sources describe the high level of technical development in hide-working, with specialisation, complex processes and high-quality products, whereas archaeological research has shown the extension of domestic work with more expedient processing. In this example, the bias clearly lies in the European narrators' interest in a certain type of product: elaborate leather goods that became the object of trade during the period of contact.

From the anthropology of techniques comes another basic contribution: the theoretical developments associated with the concepts of technical process *and chaîne opératoire* (Coudart and Lemonier 1984). These concepts have succeeded in arranging work sequences within a structure of different tasks, and furnish them with technical, economic and social meaning.

A technical process consists of an arranged succession of tasks (the *chaîne opératoire*) which gradually brings the raw material to the form and characteristics of the final product (Pelegrin et al. 1988). Each of these stages or links in the chain of tasks consists of a number of technical acts. These acts are certain movements and individual actions carried out by the worker.

The data provided in the first place by functional analysis, referring to the action of a tool on a substance being worked, consist of these technical acts. In this respect, the actions inferred by functional analysis do not achieve their full meaning if they are not related with those that preceded and followed them, in the context of the *chaînes opératoires* and technical processes they belong to (Ibáñez and González Urquijo 1996). Ethnographic sources, together with experimentation and the deductions based on archaeological evidence, help to construct models of general technical processes, *chaîne opératoire* and technical acts, with their variations, just as we might find them among prehistoric populations.

In many cases, these models must be generic and comparative. This is due to several reasons: the vastness and variability of known technical behaviour, and at the same time, (a) the limited and biased nature of the archaeological record; (b) the existence of many activities carried out without tools or with tools that are not preserved in the archaeological record; (c) the limitations of functional analysis itself, in the precision of the determination of kinematics and above all in the type and state of the worked substances. Consequently, the technical processes are usually reconstructed in their more general aspects, by attempting to locate the main stages in processing such as the procurement, transformation (roughing out, extraction of the blank, shaping and finishing) and repair/maintenance. With a good ethnographic and experimental background, this reconstruction of the technical processes is approached through the information obtained by use-wear observation, like the type and state of the worked substance, the tool kinematics, the association of activities in a single tool, the length of the active zones and the tool shape, the specificity of the implements and the active zones, the intensity of use and the variation and association of activities in an assemblage. To give an example, intense scraping on hard substances, like bone, antler and wood (Clark and Thompson 1954; Campana 1989; McGrath 1970; Hayden 1977; Kamminga 1988) form part of the object shaping stage, while many of the perforation and fine engraving tasks belong to the finishing stage (Ibáñez and González Urquijo 1996).

3.2.3 Production Context

This is the aspect where ethnographic information is able to provide a more important reference background as it can reach the live contexts in which tasks are performed. This perspective shows the relationships of technical activities with environmental conditions or other spheres of economic, social and ideological behaviour. Many instances exist of the use of ethnographic or ethnoarchaeological examples.

Some of these relationships are simple but possess great heuristic power. Beyries (1999, 2008) shows that some characteristics of hide-processing, like the worker's position and how the hide is placed, are correlated with the type of group mobility (nomad or sedentary). The worker-hide position is reflected in tool shape, with the use of convex edges among mobile groups and straight edges among sedentary groups. In fact, this correlation is also observed in the archaeological record, where tools with convex active edges, like end-scrapers, are more common in the Upper Palaeolithic and Mesolithic, in contrast with more frequent straight edges in the Neolithic.

The classic studies by Binford (1977) and Tomka (1993) have provided information about tool management and the cycles of circulation and discard of tools. Based on observations made of Nunamiut eskimos and Australian Alyawara, Binford introduced the concepts of 'curated' and 'expedient' to describe two typical strategies for tool management among hunter–gatherers, or the 'drop' and 'toss' concepts to explain the distribution of manufacturing waste and use, as they differ according to whether the hunter–gatherers' camp is more or less stable and/or specialised.

Brandt's study (1996) of the Konso in Ethiopia is a good reference for the management of lithic waste by sedentary populations. Manufacturing waste and fragments generated by use and repair in areas where children sometimes go are cleaned up and discarded in safe areas outside. However, the waste created while shaping the pieces for hafting, which is carried out around the fire, is left in the same place, as the children are forbidden to go near the fire. The spatial distribution of tasks and the management of waste are different in other groups. Among the Gamo, the place for hide-working, is a specialised area within the compound, which is only visited for this purpose. Repair flakes and used end-scrapers are abandoned in the work-area.

Some ethnographic studies (McGrath 1970), and above all ethnoarchaeological research (Binford 1978; Yellen 1977; Gould 1977; Kelly 1995) have been used to determine residential mobility patterns in hunter–gatherer groups. An important role is played in these models by the association between the types of substances that are processed and the phases in the tasks, and the type of settlements and territorial mobility strategies. This information has succeeded in giving meaning to the data from functional analysis and finding answers to this kind of question in diverse contexts (Plisson 1985; Ibáñez and González Urquijo 1996; Philibert 2002).

In some examples of complex relationships, the type of processing applied depends on or is connected with a wide range of environmental, economic and social variables. One of these is harvesting cereals, as shown by a comparative study of wheat harvesting techniques in regions of the Iberian Peninsula and North Morocco (Ibáñez et al. 2001). In this activity, the use of tools or the type of tool depends on the environmental conditions, the kind of cereal, the objective and scale of production. This in turn is influenced by social conditions (role of cereal production, field size, workers' skill, and so on). Thus, in the north of the Iberian Peninsula, factors like cool wet summers, crops of dressed wheat, lack of interest in storing the straw, and production on a domestic scale allow the use of alternative tools to sickles, such as the wooden pincers that only separate the ears with the grain. In North Morocco, the interest in gathering long straw stems, which are used as roofing material, means that the whole plants are gathered by hand, rather than using a sickle. However, in the south of the Iberian Peninsula, interest on grain and hot dry summers force the use of intensive forms of harvesting, with sickles. The suitable time for harvesting without the grain falling from the ears is reduced to just a few days.

Ethnoanalogical sources inform about major aspects of the social conditions of labour, apprenticeship (Fig. 3.3) or the social division of labour, by sex (Murdock and Provost 1973; Vila and Ruiz 2001; Weedman 2010), by social identity (Brandt et al. 1999; Weedman 2006), by economic condition (Ibáñez et al. 2001) and so on. At a general level, ethnographic literature has been able to reconstruct some well-known trans-cultural rules through the observation of coincidences in the ways of organisation of hundreds of hunter–gatherer groups (Murdock 1967; Testart 1986; Keeley 1988; Hawkes 1993; Marlowe 2005; Kusimba, 2005; Hill et al. 2011).

Other detailed studies have succeeded in determining some examples of the organisation of labour in farming communities and its links with the ways that tools are used. In southern Ethiopia, Brandt (1996) showed that crafts in general and hide-working in particular, among the Konso, Gamo and Wolayta, are low social status work, carried out by marginalised groups. In these extremely complex societies, with castes and rules of avoidance, in some cases the work is carried out only by women (among the Konso), in others by men (the Gamo), and in some cases by both men and women (the Wolayta). In North Morocco, in the Jbala region, hide-working is a male activity (Ibáñez et al. 2002), but we find a plurality of technical

Fig. 3.3 Apprenticeship of reed craftwork in northern Morocco

processes linked to different organisation of crafts within the same society. When the scale of production is domestic, the whole equipment, tools, tasks and final products are simple. However, when specialised crafts workers are involved, more complex processing includes leaving the hides to soak in tanning liquids for a period of time. These craftsmen work part-time and combine this work with other country labour. Although they are not excluded socially as described for the groups in Ethiopia, in general they are poor peasants who live in marginal areas and who resort to craft working to obtain extra farm products, in which they are deficient, often by bartering.

In another ethnoarchaeological study, Roux (1999) sought regularities in the work carried out by modern bead-makers in Khambhat, in order to determine the level of skill of the craftsmen and their productivity. This information was used to study the organisation of labour in the Harappan period in the Indus Valley. Based on the estimates about the beads produced in the Harappan period, the author deduced that there must have been few expert craftsmen and that they would also take part in other kinds of labour, and therefore they would have worked part-time. This intermediate deduction allowed the final conclusion that during this period, a social class of craftsmen still had not developed, and that they worked at the service of elite.

Finally, ethnoarchaeology has also developed interesting associations between the ideological context and social or group identity in connection with tool use (Petrequin and Petrequin 1988; Brandt et al. 1996; Sillitoe and Hardy 2003; Weedman 2010).

3.3 Conclusions

Ethnoanalogical sources (ethnographic, ethnohistorical and ethnoarchaeological studies) have provided a series of structural reference points for functional analysis. Functional interpretations could not be conceived without the contribution of these sources. They determine much of the design of experimental programmes and ultimately frame a large part of technical, economic, social and ideological conclusions that are reached through the functional results.

These sources do not provide pristine data or direct rules of inference. However, they are often able to rule out some of the hypotheses and restrict the range of possible explanations. On the other hand, these data can be used to open new debates, reconsider old results and propose reasoned responses to some of the questions that are raised.

We are aware of the limitations of ethnographic and ethnohistorical sources, full of prejudice and limited and biased descriptions, as well as the problem with ethnoarchaeological information, based on modern groups with a long history of contact with societies on a level of technological development different from prehistoric groups. Another danger in the use of these sources by prehistorians has been called 'positive inference', and consists of searching through the wide ethnographic record to find confirmation for a hypothesis, and leap upon it, making an abstraction of the context of comparison. We have learnt that it is necessary to explore the full range of comparative options offered by the record. This is a strategy that usually enriches the formulation of hypotheses and the interpretation of the results (cf. Owen 1999; Beck Kehoe 1999). The goal is not to find an ethnographic analogy for an archaeological functional inference, but an analogical reference framework in which coincidences and variations are equally important and expressive.

In this context, ethnoanalogical sources are able to improve our understanding of various significant aspects connected with the use of prehistoric tools. We have focussed on the references they provide to understand the tools themselves, to reconstruct the technical processes in which they play a part or to furnish an economic and social background to the tasks documented in the archaeological record. However, these are not the only aspects to which they can contribute. In the introduction we have also mentioned other aspects of behaviour, like tool management, the know-how put into practice, user sex, age and skill, seasonality, production objectives, product management, possession or ownership of the tools, reasons for the division of labour, social conditions of the workers, and the ideological, symbolic and narrative context of technical activity.

Acknowledgements This paper is a contribution forming a part of the HAR2011–29486 and HAR2010–21545-C02–019 projects of the MICINN, Proyectos de Investigación Fundamental no Orientada Program. The authors are grateful to Peter Smith for the English translation.

References

Albasini-Roulin, P. A. (1987). Approche ethno-comparative des emmanchements de l'outillage lithique néolithique de quelques stations littorales du canton de Fribourg (Suisse occ.). In D. Stordeur (Ed.), *La main et l'outil. Manches et emmanchements préhistoriques* (pp. 219–228). Lyon: 15. G.S. Maison de l'Orient (Travaux de la Maison de l'Orient).

Altinbilek, Ç., Coskunsu, G., Dede, Y., Lovino, M. R., Lemorini, C., & Özdogan, A. (2001). Drills from Çayönü: A combination of ethnographic, experimental and use-wear analysis. In I. Caneva, C. Lemorini, D. Zampetti, & P. Biagi (Eds.), *Beyond tools*: *Redefining the PPN lithic assemblages of the Levant* (pp. 137–143). Berlin: Ex-Oriente.

Anderson, P. C. (2007). Le travail Ã l'araire aujourd'hui en Tunisie, le point de vue d'une ethnoarchéologue. In R. Bourrigaud & F. Sigaut (Eds.), *Nous Labourons. Actes du Colloque, Techniques de travail de la terre, hier et aujourd'hui, ici et là-bas* (pp. 247–258). Nantes: Centre d'Histoire du travail.

Ascher, R. (1961). Analogy in archaeological interpretation. *Southwestern Journal of Anthropology, 17,* 317–325.

Barris, S., & Totelin, L. (2000). Un peigne pour des épis: Approche ethnographique des outils de la récolte. In G. Raepsaet & F. Lambeau (Eds.), *La moissonneuse gallo-romaine* (pp. 63–71). Brussels: Université Libre de Bruxelles.

Beyries, S. (1993). Expérimentation archéologique et savoir-faire traditionnel: l'exemple de la découpe du cerf. *Techniques et Culture, 22,* 53–79.

Beyries, S. (1999). Ethnoarchaeology: A method of experimentation. In L. R. Owen & M. Porr (Eds.), *Ethno-analogy and the reconstruction of prehistoric artefact use and production* (pp. 117–130). Tubingen: Mo Vince.

Beyries, S. (2008). Modélisation du travail du cuir en ethnologie: proposition d'un système ouvert Ã l'archéologie. *Anthropozoologica, 43,* 9–42 (with CD-ROM).

Beyries, S., & Petrequin, P. (Eds.). (2001). *Ethno-archaeology and its transfers. British Archaeological Report, International Series 983.* Oxford: Archaeopress.

Beyries, S., Vasil'ev, S. A., David, F., D'iachenko, V. I., Karlin, C., Chesnokov, I. V. (2001). Ui1, a Paleolithic site in Siberia: An ethno-archaeological approach. In S. Beyries & P. Petrequin (Eds.), *Ethno-archaeology and its transfer. British Archaeological Reports International series, 983* (pp. 9–22). Oxford: Hadrian Books.

Binford, L. R. (1977). Forty-seven trips: A case study in the character of archaeological formation processes. In R. V. S. Wright (Ed.), *Stone tools as cultural markers: Change, evolution and complexity* (pp. 24–36). Canberra: Australian Institute of Aboriginal Studies.

Binford, L. R. (1978). *Nunamiut ethnoarchaeology*. New York: Academic Press.

Brandt, S. A. (1996). The ethnoarchaeology of flaked stone tool use in southern Ethiopia. In G. Pwiti & R. Soper (Eds.), *Aspects of African archaeology* (pp. 733–738). Harare: University of Zimbabwe Press.

Brandt, S. A., Weedman, K. J., & Hundie, G. (1996). Gurage hide working, stone tool use and social identity: An ethnoarchaeological perspective. In G. Hudson (Ed.), *Essays on Gurage language and culture* (pp. 35–51). Berlin: Harrassowitz.

Brézillon, M. (1971). *La dénomination des objets de pierre taillée*. Paris: CNRS (IVe supplément Ã Gallia Préhistoire).

Campana, D. (1989). *Natufian and Proto-Neolithic bone tools: The manufacture and use of bone implements in the Zagros and the Levant. BAR, International Series 494.* Oxford: Archaeopress.

Carneiro, R. (1979). Tree felling with the stone axe: An experiment carried out among the Yanomano Indians of Southern Venezuela. In C. Kramer (Ed.), *Ethnoarchaeology: Implications of ethnography for archaeology* (pp. 21–58). New York: Columbia University Press.

Churchill, S. E. (1993). *Weapon technology, prey size selection, and hunting methods in modern hunter-gatherers: Implications for hunting in the Paleolithic and Mesolithic.* In G. L. Peterkin, H. Bricker, P. A. Mellars (Eds.), Hunting and animal exploitation in the later Paleolithic and Mesolithic of Eurasia. American Anthropological Association, Archaeological Paper No. 4, pp. 11–24.

Clark, J. G. D. (1953) The economic approach to prehistory. *Proceedings of the British Academy, 39,* 215–238.

Clark, J. D., & Kurashina, H. (1981). A study of the work of modern tanner in Ethiopia and its relevance for archaeological interpretation. In R. A. Gould & M. B. Schiffer (Eds.), *Modern material culture: The archaeology of us* (pp. 303–321). New York: Academic Press.

Clark, J. D. G., & Thompson, M. W. (1954). The groove and splinter technique of working antler in Upper Palaeolithic and Mesolithic Europe, with special reference to the material from Star Carr. *Proceedings of the Prehistoric Society, 19,* 148–160.

Clemente, I. (1997). *Los instrumentos líticos de Túnel VII: una aproximación etnoarqueológica.* Madrid: Consejo Superior de Investigaciones Científicas.

Coudart, A., & Lemonier, P. (1984). Ethnoarchéologie et ethnologie des techniques. *Techniques et culture, 3,* 157–169.

Ellis, C. J. (1997). Factors influencing the use of stone projectile tips: An ethnographic perspective. In H. Knecht (Ed.), *Projectile technology* (pp. 37–78). New York: Plenum Press.

Fisher, J. W., & Strickland, H. C. (1989). Ethnoarchaeology among Efe pygmies, Zaire: Spatial organization of campsites. *American Journal of Physical Anthropology, 78,* 473–484.

Frison, G. C. (1978). *Prehistoric hunters of the high plains.* New York: Academic Press Inc.

Gould, R. A. (1977). Ethno-archaeology; or, where do models come from? A close look at Australian aboriginal lithic technology. In R. V. S. Wright (Ed.), *Stone tools as cultural markers: Change, evolution and complexity* (pp. 163–168). Canberra: Australian Institute of Aboriginal Studies Prehistory and Material Culture Series No.12.

Gusinde, M. (1931/1982). *Los indios de Tierra de Fuego.* Buenos Aires: CAEA.

Hayden, B. (1977). Stone tool functions in the Western Desert. In R. V. S. Wright (Ed.), *Stone tools as cultural markers. Change, evolution and complexity* (pp. 178–188). Canberra: Australian Institute of Aboriginal Studies Prehistory and Material Culture Series No.12.

Hawkes, K. (1993). Why hunter-gatherers work: An ancient version of the problem of public goods. *Current Anthropology, 34,* 341–361.

Hill, K. R., Walker, R. S., Božičević, M., Eder, J., Headland, T., Hewlett, B., Hurtado, M. A., Marlowe, F., Wiessner, P., Wood, B. et al. (2011). Co-residence patterns in hunter–gatherer societies show unique human social structure. *Science, 331,* 1286–1289.

Holl, A. F. C. (2003). *Ethnoarchaeology of Shuwa-Arab Settlements.* Lanham: Lexington Books.

Hughes, S. (1998). Getting to the point: Evolutionary change in prehistoric weaponry. *Journal of Archaeological Method and Theory, 5,* 345–408.

Hutchings, W. K., & Brüchert, L. W. (1997). Spearthrower performance: Ethnographic and experimental research. *Antiquity, 71,* 890–897.

Ibáñez, J. J., & González Urquijo, J. (1996). *From tool-use to site function: A new methodological strategy applied to Upper Paleolithic sites in the Basque Country. BAR International Series, 658.* Oxford: Tempus Reparatum.

Ibáñez, J. J., & González Urquijo, J. (2002). Cesteros en la Jebala, Rif occidental, Marruecos. *El Pajar, Cuaderno de Etnografía canaria, 13,* 88–93.

Ibáñez, J. J., González Urquijo, J., Peña-Chocarro, L., Zapata, L., & Beugnier, V. (2001). Harvesting without sickles: Neolithic examples from humid mountains areas. In S. Beyries & P. Petrequin (Eds.), *Ethno-archaeology and its transfers. British Archaeological Report, International Series 983* (pp. 23–36). Oxford: Hadrian Books.

Ibáñez, J. J., González Urquijo, J., & Moreno, M. (2002). Le travail de la peau en milieu rural: le cas de la Jebala marocaine. In F. Audoin-Rouzeau, S. Beyries (Eds.), *Le travail du cuir de la Préhistoire Ã nos jours* (pp. 79–97). XXII rencontres internationales d'archéologie et d'histoire d'Antibes, Antibes, APDCA.

Kamminga, J. (1988). Wood artefacts: A checklist of plant species utilised by Australian Aborigines. *Australian Aboriginal Studies, 2,* 26–56.

Keeley, L. H. (1983). Neolithic novelties: The view from ethnography and microwear analysis. In M. C. Cauvin (Ed.), *Traces d'utilisation sur les outils néolithiques du Proche Orient* (pp. 251–256). Lyon: Maison de l'Orient.

Keeley, L. H. (1988). Hunter–gatherer economic complexity and population pressure: A cross-cultural analysis. *Journal of Anthropological Archaeology, 7,* 373–411.

Kelly, R. L. (1995). *The foraging spectrum: Diversity in hunter-gatherer.* Washington: Smithsonian Institution Press.

Kimura, B., Brandt, S. A., Hardy, B. L., & Hauswirth, W. W. (2001). Analysis of DNA from ethnoarchaeological stone scrapers. *Journal of Archaeological Science, 28,* 45–53.

Kusimba, S. (2005). What is a hunter–gatherer? Variation in the archaeological record of eastern and southern Africa. *Journal of Archaeological Research, 13,* 337–366.
Lupo, K. D., & Schmitt, D. N. (2003). Small prey hunting technology and zooarchaeological measures of taxanomic diversity and abundance: Ethnoarchaeological evidence from Central African forest foragers. *Journal of Anthropological Archaeology, 24,* 335–353.
Mansur-Franchomme, M. E. (1987). Outils ethnographiques de Patagonie: emmanchement et traces d'utilisation. In D. Stordeur (Ed.), *La main et l'outil. Manches et emmanchements préhistoriques* (pp. 297–307). Lyon: Maison de l'Orient.
Marlowe, F. W. (2005). Hunter–gatherers and human evolution. *Evolutionary Anthropology, 14,* 54–67.
McGrath, K. (1970). *A model for the use of ethnographic data in the analysis of prehistoric activities.* Master Thesis, University of Pennsylvania, Philadelphia.
Murdock, G. P. (1967). Ethnographic atlas: A summary. *Ethnology, 6,* 109–236.
Murdock, G. P., & Provost, C. (1973). Factors in the division of labor by sex: A cross-cultural analysis. *Ethnology, 12,* 203–225.
Owen, L. R. (1999). Questioning stereo-typical notions of prehistoric tool functions: Ethno-analogy, experimentation and functional analysis. In L. R. Owen & M. Porr Â (Eds.), *Ethno-analogy and the reconstruction of prehistoric artefact use and production* (pp. 17–30). Tübingen: Mo Vince.
Owen, L. R., Porr, M. (Eds.). (1999). *Ethno-analogy and the reconstruction of prehistoric artefact use and production.* Urgeschichtliche Materialhefte, 14. Mo Vince, Tübingen.
Pelegrin, J., Karlin, C., Bodu, P. (1988). Chaînes opératoires: un outil pour le préhistorien. In *Technologie préhistorique.* Notes et Monographies Techniques 25. CNRS, Paris, pp. 55–62.
Perry, L. (2005). Reassessing the traditional interpretation of 'Manioc' artifacts in the Orinoco Valley of Venezuela. *Latin American Antiquity, 16,* 409–426.
Petrequin, A.-M., Petrequin, P. (1988). Ethnoarcheologie de l'habitat en grotte de Nouvelle-Guinee: une transposition de l'espace social et economique. *Bulletin du Centre Genevois d'Anthropologie, 1988*(1), 61–82.
Petrequin, A.-M., Petrequin, P. (1990). Flèches de chasse, flèches de guerre. Le cas des danis d'Irian Jaya (Indonésie). *Bulletin de la Société Préhistorique Française, 87,* 484–511.
Philibert, S. (2002). *Les derniers sauvages. Territoires économiques et systèmes techno-fonctionnels mésolithiques.* BAR International Series 1969. Oxford: Archaeopress.
Plisson, H. (1985). *Étude fonctionnelle des outillages lithiques préhistoriques par l'analyse des micro-usures: recherche méthodologique et archéologique.* Thèse de Doctorat, Paris I.
Rodríguez, A. (1997). La tecnología de la piel y el cuero en la prehistoria de Canarias. Una aproximación etnoarqueológica. *Museo Canario, 52,* 11–31.
Rodríguez, A. (1999). The reconstruction of ancient leather technology or how to mix methodological approaches: An example from the Canary Island prehistry. In L. R. Owen & M. Porr (Eds.) *Ethno-analogy and the reconstruction of prehistoric artefact use and production* (pp. 141–152). Tubingen: Mo Vince.
Rodríguez, A., Jiménez, A. M., Zamora, J. M., & Mangas, J. (2006). El empleo de cantos rodados en la elaboración de la loza tradicional de la isla de Gran Canaria, implicaciones etnoarqueológicas. In I. Briz & A. Vila (Eds.), *Etnoarqueología de la Prehistoria: más allá de la analogía* (pp. 209–226). Treballs d'Etnoarqueologia, 6. Madrid: CSIC.
Rots, V., & Williamson, B. S. (2004). Microwear and residue analyses in perspective: the contribution of ethnoarchaeological evidence. *Journal of Archaeological Science, 31,* 1287–1299.
Roux, V. (1999). Ethnoarchaeology and the generation of referential models: The case of Harappan carnelian beds. In L. R. Owen & M. Porr (Eds.), *Ethno-analogy and the reconstruction of prehistoric artefact use and production* (pp. 153–169). Tübingen: Mo Vince.
Semenov, S. A. (1964). Prehistoric technology. London: Cory Adams & Nackay.
Sigaut, F. (1991). Un couteau ne sert pas Ã couper, mais en coupant: structure, fonctionnement et fonction dans l'analyse des objets. In *25 ans d'études technologiques en préhistoire: bilan et perspectives*, XIèmes. Rencontres internationales d'archéologie et d'histoire d'Antibes. APDCA, Juan-les-Pins, pp. 21–34.

Sillitoe, P., & Hardy, K. (2003). Living lithics, ethnography and archaeology in Highland Papua New Guinea. *Antiquity, 77,* 555–566.
Silvestre, R. E. J. (1994). The ethnoarchaeology of Kalinga basketry: A prelimiary investigation. In *Kalinga ethnoarchaeology: Expanding archaeological method and theory* (pp. 199–207). Washington: Smithsonian Institution Press.
Simms, S. R., & Russell, K. (1997). Bedouin hand harvesting of wheat and barley: Implications for Early Cultivation in Southwestern Asia. *Current Anthropology, 38,* 696–607.
Speck, F. G. (1937). Analysis of Eskimo and Indian skin-dressing methods in Labrador. *Ethnos, 2*(6), 345–353.
Spriggs, M. (1977). Introduction: Where the hell are we? (or a young man's quest). In M. Spriggs (Ed.), *Archaeology and anthropology areas of mutual interest* (pp. 3–17). Oxford: British Archaeological Reports.
Terradas, X. (2005). *Stone tools in ethnoarchaeological contexts. British Archaeological Reports* (S 1370). Oxford: Archaeopress.
Terradas, X., Vila, A., Clemente, I., & Mansur, E. (1999). Ethno-neglect or the contradiction between ethnohistorical sources and the archaeological record: the case of stone tools from the Yamana. In L. R. Owen & M. Porr (Eds.), *Ethno-analogy and the reconstruction of prehistoric artefact use and production* (pp. 103–115). Tubingen: Mo Vince.
Testart, A. (1986). *Essai sur les fondements de la division sexuelle du travail chez les chasseurs-cueilleurs*. Paris: EHESS.
Tomka, S. (1993). Site abandonment behavior among trashumant agro-pastoralists: The effects of delayed curation on assemblage composition. In C. M. Cameron & S. Tomka (Eds.), *Abandonment of settlements and regions: Ethnoarchaeological and archaeological approaches* (pp. 11–24). Cambridge: Cambridge University Press.
Trigger, B. (1989). *A history of archaeological thought*. Cambridge: Cambridge University Press.
Vila, A., & Ruiz, G. (2001). Información etnológica y el análisis de la reproducción social: el caso Yámana. *Revista Española de Antropología Americana, 31,* 275–291.
Walker, J., & Wilk, R. (1988). The manufacture and use-wear characteristics of ethnographic, replicated, and archaeological manioc grater board teeth. In M. Gaxiola & J. E. Clark (Eds.), *La obsidiana en Mesoamérica*. Ciudad México: Instituto Nacional de Antropología e Historia.
Weedman, K. J. (2006). An ethnoarchaeological study of hafting and stone tool diversity among the Gamo of Ethiopia. *Journal of Archaeological Method and Theory, 13,* 188–237.
Weedman, K. J. (2010). Feminine knowledge and skill reconsidered: Women and flaked stone tools. *American Anthropologist, 112,* 228–243.
Wylie, A. (1985). The reaction against analogy. In M. Schiffer (Ed.), *Archaeological method and theory* (Vol. 8, pp. 63–112). London: Academic Press.
Yellen, J. E. (1977). *Archaeological approaches to the present: Models for reconstructing the past*. New York: Academic Press.

Chapter 4
Use-Wear Analysis on Flint Tools. Beyond the Methodological Issues

Juan F. Gibaja and Bernard Gassin

4.1 Use-Wear Analysis and Flint Tools. Questions and Methods

Since the onset of use-wear studies of lithic assemblages, many researchers have focused their analyses on flint tools mainly because:

1. Within archaeological lithic assemblages flint is the most represented raw material, mostly from Middle and Upper Palaeolithic contexts;
2. Flint lithology is the most studied lithic raw material by specialists;
3. Wear alterations in flint elements are most diagnostic since modifications occur in very different traces and within few minutes of work.

Fortunately, during recent years researchers started looking at other raw materials such as obsidian, quartz, quartzite, etc. (Clemente et al. this volume).

Since the origins of the use-wear analysis discipline, methodological questions were always one of the most important issues for researchers, for which huge improvements have been made in technical advances in the field of computer science, microscopy technology and photographic record. Parallel to these technological advances, continuous improvements have been made on the identification of wear trace diversity, such as postdeposition processes, using several experimental blind tests.

Therefore, the use of different microscope types to observe wear traces must be one of the most important methodological issues (Marreiros et al. this volume). During the 1970s and 1980s there were two opposed perspectives regarding the

---

J. F. Gibaja (✉)
Departamento de Arqueología y Antropología, Consejo Superior de Investigaciones Científicas (IMF-CSIC), Institución Milá y Fontanals, C/Egipcíàques, 15, 08001 Barcelona, Spain
e-mail: jfgibaja@imf.csic.es

B. Gassin
TRACES, UMR 5608 du CNRS, Maison de la recherche, 5, allée Antonio-Machado, 31058 Toulouse Cedex 9, France
e-mail: bernard.gassin@ac-nice.fr

different types of microscopes that should be used. One perspective argued for the use of stereoscopic equipment with low magnifications, while the other used the metallographic microscope with high magnifications. Currently, most researchers use both types of equipment together since both approaches complement the available data. Nevertheless, there is a small number of researchers using scanning electron microscopy (SEM) (Martinez 2005) or, more recently, laser confocal microscopy (Ibáñez et al. 2014). Although the degree of details that can be observed on wear traces with SEM microscopes has increased considerably, it has not yet been proven that this technology presents a more accurate diagnostic of the worked material or even a more precise approach to activity evidences. This type of microscope has not been widely used by all specialists, mainly because of its high cost and the time it requires to prepare the pieces to be analysed.

Like in any other archaeological speciality, the results from the use-wear analysis depend greatly from the preservation conditions of the materials. In contexts where archaeological materials are well preserved and have been perfectly recovered, treated and stored, the data obtained will be excellent. However, before starting the analysis we should start with an assessment of the material's condition and predict the possible outcome in terms of preserved data.

The nonrandom distribution of wear traces (chipping, rounding, polish and striation) on a tool's surface allows us to determine the used edge areas. The distribution patterns of wear traces lead us to identify the movement made during the activity: parallel or perpendicular to the edge or on the central axis of a pointed tool (a projectile or a tool used to pierce through rotary movement). For this purpose, the use-wear analyst observes the orientation of the striations, the chipping distribution (unifacial, bifacial or alternating), the polish and edge rounding asymmetry. On linking the wear traces observed on the archaeological tools with those obtained from experimentation regarding the same activity, it is possible to identify, with more or less accuracy, the worked material. We observe the morphology, size and number of edge damage scars, the extension and distribution of the micropolish, its microtopography, morphology and frame, the striations' morphology, number and distribution (e.g. Plisson 1985; Gonzalez and Ibanez 1994; Van Gijn 1989; Gassin 1996). In the next section, we use two archaeological case studies to illustrate to the reader what we have explained.

4.2 Functioning and Function: Lithic Tools and the *Chaîne Opératoire* Concept

Use-wear observations interpreted on the basis of experimental references (see above) allows us to determine the "functioning" of the tools: what is the active area during work, in what position was the tool during use, which movement was used and what the worked material was. Thus, we will reserve the term function to refer to more developed data, supported by archaeological record and technological data (Sigaut 1991). It is not only to understand how the tool was used but also to know at the same time more precisely to what stage it belongs within the *chaîne opératoire* sequences.

4.2.1 Abrasive Wear Traces: From Hypothesis to the Proposed Functionality

During the past decades, researchers have characterized wear traces from nonwoody plants, mainly from work done on certain plants such as cereals (wheat and barley), fern, rush or reeds. Such characterization could not ignore other factors that influence the wear traces generated by contact with nonwoody plants, such as: (1) the place where plants are cut, (2) the use of other materials, (3) whether they were picked fresh or not, (4) whether harvested plants had been planted on land previously prepared for cultivation etc. Nevertheless, as a general definition, cutting nonwoody plants, especially cereals, usually causes edge bifacial chipping associated with slight edge rounding, and a much extended micropolish with flat morphology and compact frame which develops up to the central arises on the dorsal face of the blades or flakes. Within the polish there are numerous striations of different shape and size, mainly if the cut is made from plants near the ground (Gibaja 2003).

When we analysed the flint tools of various Neolithic sites from northwestern Spain and southeastern France, however, we note that other than the pieces with clear wear traces of cereals, there are pieces with edges showing traces related to cutting plants associated with other traces made by the contact with some abrasive material. This duality is reflected by an intensive abrasion, abundant striations, plant polish modified by some abrasive material and edge rounding together with chipping.

Our experimental data base did not allow us to determine the origin of these wear traces. Until then this type of traces had been associated by other researchers with cutting dry skin, with or without abrasive materials, with craft activities in which they touch the clay used in pottery work, with the extraction of sand blocks or with the cereal threshing.

Among this set of tasks, the cereal threshing caused the most similar traces, but they were infinitely more developed. For this reason we decided that we should indeed think of an activity related to processing cereals, which simultaneously cuts edge stems and contacts with a mineral such as the ground.

We conducted two types of experiments: (1) cutting cereals near the ground so that there was a continuous contact between the flint tool and the ground and (2) cutting the stems above the ground to separate the ear and/or the root, in order to get stems with certain measures. These experimentations gave satisfactory results. The presence of traces associated with abrasive contact was identified on the tool ends that had come into contact with the ground surface when used to cut the stems near the ground. When we cut the stems on the ground to separate parts, these traces were present all over the entire edge. In summary, our experiment showed that these types of tools with such wear traces were used routinely to process cereals after the cutting process.

4.2.2 Scraping Flint Tools, from Functioning to Function

Flakes and blades used for scraping soft mineral substances have been identified in numerous *Chasséen* (Middle Neolithic) archaeological sites in the region of Provence, France (Grotte de l'Eglise supérieure, Baume Fontbrégoua, Grotte G and Villa Giribaldi).

Experimentation with tools used to scrape the walls of ceramic vessels has allowed us to interpret the traces generated by this activity and distinguish between two ways of scraping (in positive and negative modes) (Fig. 4.1: 1–2). Other factors that influence wear traces characteristics are the moisture of the clay and the fineness of the temper.

Experimental data allowed us to determine that the vessel walls were scraped in a positive way when the clay was drying up (the consistency was leatherlike). On the basis of a comparison with the production of modern potters or the reproduction of experimental ceramic vessels, similar to those made during the Neolithic period, we propose that these tools were used for the wall thinning and/or the bevelling of the lips, after shaping, when the clay was still drying (when clay was moist enough to produce regular chips when scraping, but was sufficiently dry/rigid to prevent twisting).

The functional analysis of numerous burins from *Chasséen* archaeological sites in the south of France shows that most of them are used with the lateral edges to scrape silica-rich plants like reeds (Fig. 4.1: 3–4). The face in front of the movement (rake face) is always the burin-negative facet; it is concave and the working angle with the material is lower than 90° (negative rake angle); the opposite face (flank face) is the ventral face of the blade; it is plane or convex and the clearance angle is very low. The rake face bears a very bright and very invasive polish with a compact linkage of polished area and a snow-melting microtopography without any striation or linear indicator. The polish on the flank face is not invasive; it is very smooth and bright with striations and linear indicators almost perpendicular to the edge but always slightly oblique.

These burins are used to scrape silica-rich vegetal branches or stems for the removal of thin chips, for instance during a finishing work, like final shaping of arrow shafts.

4.3 Lithic Production Systems

Lithic functional studies and technological analysis play an important role together to understand lithic production systems.

Experimental piece (B. Gassin). Scraping clay pottery with a positive cutting (or rake) angle. The polish is rather symmetric on both faces; *3*: Auriac P. IV, (Carcassonne, Aude, France). Middle Neolithic. Burin with a dissymmetric plant polish, interpreted as the result of scraping siliceous plants with a negative cutting (or rake) angle; *4*: Experimental piece (B. Gassin). Scraping green reeds (*Arundo donax L.*) with a negative cutting (or rake) angle. The polish on the rake face (on the *left*) is different (snow-melting appearance and invasive polish) from the one on the flank face (on the *right*)

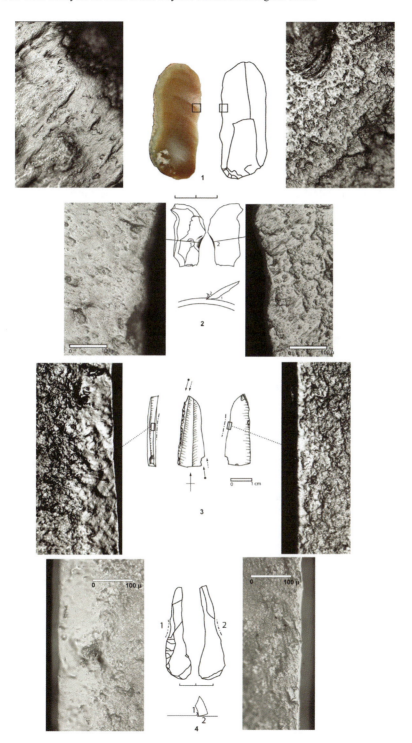

Fig. 4.1 *1*: Grotte G, (Baudinard, Var, France). Middle Neolithic. Blade with an invasive polish on both faces, interpreted as the result of scraping pottery still wet during the drying process; *2*:

4.3.1 Understanding a Production: Products and Waste

The use or nonuse of certain lithic tools reflects the knappers' intentions, allowing to distinguish between first-intention products and waste products.

A technological and functional analysis of lithic industries from the Neolithic age in Provence (Courthézon-Le Baratin and Nice-Giribaldi) shows that, either in parallel or within the laminar *chaînes opératoires*, there are stages of knapping of little flakes from direct percussion.

In the archaeological site of Baratin, thick flakes were extracted and retouched using hard hammers during the configuration and final phase of the blade cores exploitation. In Nice-Giribaldi, flakes were imported and modified using bifacial retouch with soft stone hammers.

The retouched flakes are generally described as shaped tools (denticulated tools resulting from Clactonian notches, thick scrapers, bifacial pieces from percussion), but they must be seen as simple technical processes that are implemented so as to knap little flakes designed to be used as tools within the context of a domestic production (Fig. 4.2: 1, 2, 5, 6, 8). The tools obtained through such processes play a specific part in the technical system: they are used for short durations and in a restricted number of functions (scraping wood, grooving bone at Le Baratin; scraping and grooving bone, cutting soft materials at Giribaldi), which contrasts with the more intensive and varied uses of blades. At Le Baratin, the "retouched" by-products (denticulated and thick scrapers) are never used with the retouched parts (Fig. 4.2: 3, 4, 7), but, at Giribaldi, some bifacial pieces are used to scrape, groove or bore bone, or to cut soft materials.

In other archaeological sites the use-wear analysis shows that the flakes from bifacial retouch were not first-intention products. During the Late Neolithic from Motte aux Magnins, French Jura, V. Beugnier's study shows that bifacial retouch flakes were not used and can be considered as waste products (Beugnier 1997). Thus, flakes extracted during the configuration of handaxes in the Mousterian of Acheulean tradition, studied by Claud (2008) were used in an occasional and opportunistic way, while the final handaxes, due to their edge morphological characteristics and easier edge resharpening, were used for butchering and wood working.

In the final Middle Palaeolithic lithic assemblages from El Kown, Syria, bladelets extracted from what was becoming the proximal part of Levallois blades or flakes, were initially interpreted as preparation elements for the extraction of Levallois flakes and blades; however use-wear analysis (Boeda and Bonilauri 2006) showed that they were first-intention products, hafted and used for butchering.

4.3.2 Design of the Tools

Use-wear studies allow us to understand the functional dimension of the tool's design, by identifying the active areas, their morphology and way of functioning. For example, the burins from Southern *Chasséen* culture were used to scrape

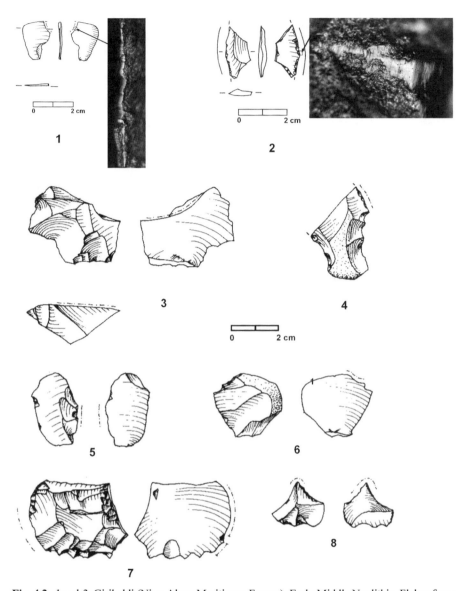

Fig. 4.2 *1* and *2*: Giribaldi (Nice, Alpes-Maritimes, France), Early Middle Neolithic. Flakes from bifacial debitage. *1*: scraping bone; *2*: sawing or incising bone; *3–8*: Le Baratin (Courthezon, Vaucluse, France), Early Neolithic. *3, 4, 7*: notched or denticulated flakes, retouched by direct percussion with hard hammer. Used zones are not on retouched sides. *5, 6, 8*: used little flakes ("retouch" flakes) for scraping wood (*5* and *6*) and piercing soft stone or pottery (*8*)

(Fig. 4.1: 3), using the edge between burin facet and ventral face, stiff vegetal material with high silica content (Gassin 1996). Instead, burins from the Late Upper Palaeolithic from Northern Iberian Peninsula were used to work bone and antler:

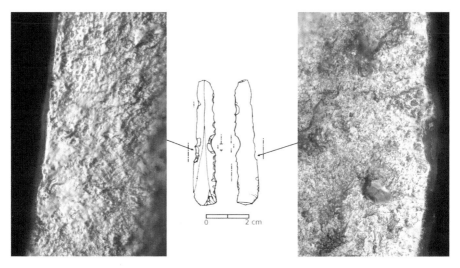

Fig. 4.3 La Grange (Surgères, Charente-Maritime, France). Late Mesolithic. Scraping with a negative rake a vegetal material. The rake face is the retouched one (on the *left*). 200x

grooving using the burin tip, scraping with the burin facet, scraping and cutting with the non-retouched lateral edges. Instead, from the same chronological and geographic area, the carinated burins were not tools, but were used as cores for bladelets extraction, and these products were modified as backed projectiles elements (Ibañez and Gonzalez 2006a). In the Late Mesolithic industries from western Europe, VII–VI millennium cal BC, notches on blades were produced to scrape with a negative rake angle different materials (e.g., wood, vegetal material, bone) (Fig. 4.3).

4.3.3 Studying Lithic Assemblages and Raw Material Management

Lithic assemblages from the Neolithic archaeological sites often present debitage products extracted from different reduction sequences and raw materials. Local raw materials are sometimes represented with debitage products from all the *chaîne opératoire* sequences; exogenous raw materials are frequently present as "ready-to-use" blades or preconfigurated nucleus. Thus, there is evidence for various production cycles of blanks: imported blades show evident traces of long-time use, were frequently transported between sites, and edges were modified and recycled; at the same time, flakes and blades extracted within the campsite were used in an expedient way. Such contrast in lithic managements is well documented during the Middle Neolithic in Grotte de l'Église supérieure, France, or Franchthi, Greece (Perlès and Vaughan 1983), and such data are responsible for the onset of the "raw material management" concept.

4.4 Exchanges and Interactions

We present two case studies that clearly show how use-wear analysis is an important discipline for the debate and hypotheses related with raw materials and ideas exchange and spread, or population movements.

4.4.1 Spreading and Exchange

An integrated approach, through lithic technology and use-wear analysis, is a way to understand long-distance diffusion networks of lithic products. One can investigate the diffusion of these products, from raw material sources up to remote consuming sites, by integrating their position in the *chaînes opératoires* of the productions, the level of know-how implemented by the producers, and the circumstances of their use and management.

During the Middle Neolithic, the stone tool production in flint from the western Provence was massively diffused in several cultural spheres: the Southern *Chassey* culture in the south of France, the *Montbolo* and *Sepulcros de Fosa* cultures in northeast of Iberia. Taking into account the proportion and the absolute quantity of these imported products, we can distinguish several impact zones:

- A production area, in the immediate vicinity of the extraction sites of raw material, with places of local production, where the *bédoulien* flint represents the totality or at least a very high percentage of the lithic tools.
- A vast zone of massive diffusion, where numerous receiving or consumer sites comprise a majority of imported *bédoulien* flint, up to 300 km to the west or the east.
- A remote zone, in the northeast of Iberia, at a distance of more than 400 km, where the production of "*melado*" flint (most of them bédoulien flint) has an unequal distribution: while abundant in funeral contexts (Bòbila Madurell, Sant Quirze del Vallès, Barcelona), they rarely occur on settlement sites (Ca n'Isach, Palau-Savardera, Girona). Moreover, the products in "*melado*" flint, far from decreasing in quantity from the Pyrenees in the north towards the south, are concentrated in the Vallès region. It is possible to distinguish differences in the management methods used (intensity of use, resharpening and recycling, ranges of uses of the productions) according to the technological categories of the diffused products and according to the region.

At la Combe (Caromb, Vaucluse, France), situated at the head of the diffusion networks only a few kilometers from the sources of raw material, where cores were shaped out and the *débitage* of blades took place, the majority of the used blades were used by the non-retouched edges, and there was no maintenance or recycling of the blades by retouch.

The management of blades in unheated *bédoulien* flint within the area of massive diffusion can be described through the example of sites from Provence and

Languedoc. At the Grotte de l'Eglise, in Provence, the majority of imported blades were used in several different zones, both untreated edges and retouched edges, whereas the bladelets obtained by pressure on imported heated flint and the flakes from local or from imported flint, mainly knapped on the spot, are in their vast majority used without retouch (Fig. 4.4). It appears that the retouch was frequently a way of resharpening or of recycling blanks first used untreated. The imported blade products are primarily characterized by their extreme functional multipurpose.

Some patterns of local circulation of imported blanks have been highlighted in Languedoc and Roussillon sites. The functional spectrum of the site of Auriac near Carcassonne supports the hypothesis of a bladelets (knapped by pressure after heat treatment) redistribution site: the bladelets have a low intensity of use, and there is no indication of agriculture or craft activities (Torchy and Gassin 2011).

At the cave of Montou, in a *Montboló* context, it has been shown, by the presence of cores in a terminal phase of production and by a few small flakes that the bladelets in heated flint were produced on the spot. These bladelets (approximately 15% of the lithic industry) probably concern the end of the *débitage*, the cores having already been the object of earlier debitage in other places. The concept of intermittent debitage has been proposed (Léa 2005). There would be a circulation of cores within a local territory, with phases of debitage when necessary, according to the needs linked to the tasks to which the occupants of the site devote themselves. In this specific case, the bladelets were used to cut plants and soft animal material. Likewise, the blades in *bédoulien* flint, resharpened, transformed and recycled to the extreme, are at the end of the cycle of use and show a long and complex chronology of uses. Only the last uses of these blades would be related to the occupation of the site, and thus with its function. They were used before retouching to collect plants, and after retouching to scrap and split plant stems and for the production of pottery. The blades in unheated *bédoulien* flint and the cores in heated *bédoulien* flint would belong to some mobile equipment, which the users took with them during their cycles of exploitation of the territory (Fig. 4.5).

In northeast Iberia, in the zone of the furthest diffusion, and outside the cultural context associated with the production of these blades, one notes a marked investment in funeral rituals. The presence in some burials of Bòbila Madurell of unused blades that present connections between them, suggest that in these cases the aims of the lithic production was the obtaining of products to accompany the buried corpse (Gibaja 2003).

Differences in the position of the sites in the diffusion network can be demonstrated: one can oppose the cemetery of Bòbila Madurell, where there are cores and most blades are used non-retouched, and where the narrowest blades arc less used than the large blades, to the cemetery of Camí de Can Grau (Granollers, Barcelona), where there are not cores and the majority of blades were used already retouched and where there is a high use of all the blades, including the narrowest (Gibaja 2003). Bòbila Madurell could be a redistributing site, controlling the diffusion, and Camí de Can Grau could be a consuming site.

During the Final Neolithic, use-wear studies on chert tools from Grand Pressigny, France (knifes and blades) distributed in a vast territory, show the presence

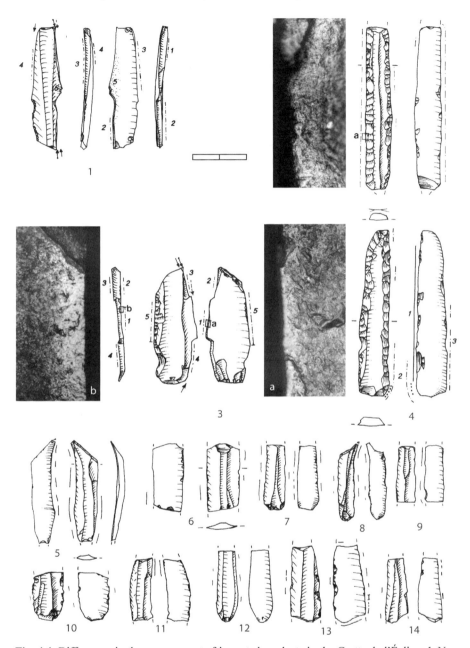

Fig. 4.4 Differences in the management of imported products in the Grotte de l'Église. *1*: Non heated *bédoulien* flint. Used to cut vegetal (used zone *5*), then retouched in burin, and used to scrape vegetal (used zones *1–4*); *2*: Non heated *bédoulien* flint. Scraping hide with both sides; *3*: First used to scrape hide (used zone *5*), and then used and rejuvenated as a burin to scrape vegetal; *4*: Nonheated *bédoulien* flint. Cutting vegetal (used zone *1*), then retouched and scraping hide (used zone *2*). Scraping hide with the other side (used zone *3*); *5–14*: Heated *bédoulien* flint. Bladelets used in butchering. (Gassin 1996)

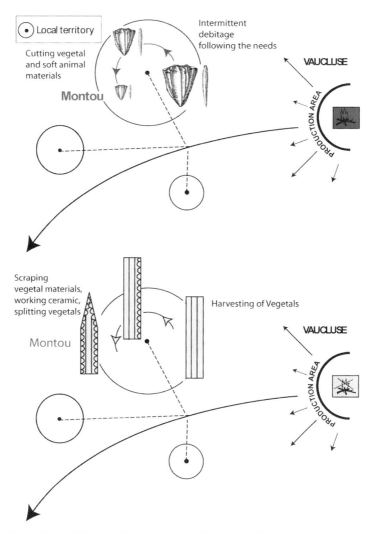

Fig. 4.5 Intermittent debitage of heated cores and curation of imported nonheated Bédoulien blades in Montou cave. (Lea 2005; Gassin et al. 2011)

of different status according to the distance from production areas. Such knifes and blades have high durability, are used as harvesting tools and later modified and recycled for other activities (e.g. scrapers for working hide, lighters) (Beugnier and Plisson 2004). In the Netherlands, the knifes found in burials show wear traces suggesting that they were frequently removed from and put back in a leather sheath: they were maybe sheathed and unsheathed to be shown during ceremonies (Van Gijn 2010).

These questions, related with social organization, are also present in archaeological PPNA and PPNB contexts in the Near East (Astruc et al. 2003; Ibáñez and González 2006b)

4.4.2 Agricultural Techniques and the Neolithization in the Occidental Mediterranean

The morphology of lithic tools, the way of using them and the technological processes used to produce such tools, are associated with technical traditions that represent one of the most diagnostic identity elements within human populations. The study of geographic and chronological distribution of these technological traditions allow us to infer cultural changes, contacts and diffusion. One of the most important and diagnostic composite tools for the first Neolithic farmers is the sickle. Such importance is illustrated when in the absence of direct evidence for agriculture, such as carpological data, the presence of sickle elements is used as an indirect evidence for agriculture in some archaeological sites.

Recently, a group of researchers started a research project that focuses on the knowledge of the first Neolithic sickles in the Occidental Mediterranean territory, in order to identify differences, such as shape and technological production system among sickles, between different geographic areas (Ibáñez et al. 2008; Gassin et al. 2010; Gibaja et al. 2010).

At the moment all data seem to indicate the presence of different types of sickles regarding to the presence or absence of lithic elements, nature of these lithic components and hafting design. In summary:

- In southern Iberian Peninsula, Andalucía and Valencia, and Portuguese Estremadura Neolithic sickles were composed by small blades insert in a diagonal position in the hafting and create a denticulate line.
- In the northwestern Iberian and southeastern France, larger blades and flakes were used in a parallel position to the haft.
- In central Iberian Peninsula, and also present in the archaeological site of La Draga (Girona) and southeastern France, data show the presence of sickles composed by a medium-size blade insert in diagonal position.
- In northern Iberia and southeastern France the analysed data show the presence of abrasive wear traces, which means that these tools were used in sickles to cut cereals near the ground (cf. supra).
- In the Cantabrian region, although other evidences might show the presence of agricultural activities, there is no evidence of sickle lithic tools. These data led us to believe that the used techniques do not leave any evidence in the archaeological record (i.e. cereals were gathered by hand or by using a wood tool called "mesorias").

Such technotypological differences among sickles between different geographic areas are not associated with differences regarding the cereal species; however, at this moment, the carpological data are still uneven (Fig. 4.6). This has led us to argue that perhaps such geographic distribution of sickle typology in the Iberian Peninsula and France are associated with the introduction of Neolithic agriculture through two separate ways: a northern one through the French coast and a southern one from northern Africa. Currently, in order to answer to these questions we start working on Neolithic contexts in Italy and northern Morocco.

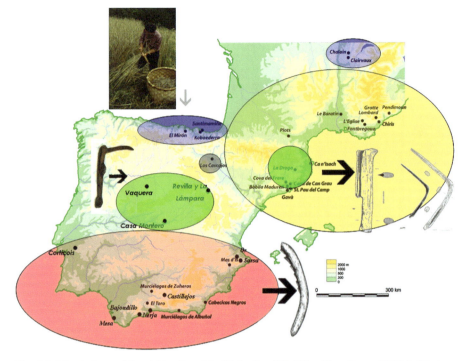

Fig. 4.6 Morphology of the sickles from Neolithic sites (VI–Vth millennium cal BC) in Western Mediterranean

4.5 Approaching Economic and Social Organisation Using Use-Wear Analysis

One of the most important aims in use-wear analysis is to know which activities were made on the campsite, and to write about some aspects of social organization. In this part we present some interesting case studies.

4.5.1 Activities Made Within Archaeological Site

In the Upper Palaeolithic, the Dordogne French region shows high human occupation during the Solutrean technocomplex. From all the published literature for the Solutrean in this region, we focus on the research carried out by J.M. Geneste and H. Plisson on the relationship between morphotechnology and functional studies on Solutrean lithic projectiles from four archaeological sites: Combe Saunière, Placard, Fourneau du Diable and Pech de la Boissière (Plisson and Geneste 1989; Geneste and Plisson 1993).

One of the interesting use-wear results is related with the fragmentation of the projectile points and the representation of these fragments in the different sites.

The experimental data compared with archaeological observations on points from these assemblages showed that these tools were used as projectiles (although no definite criteria were found to distinguish between bow and arrow or propellant *atlatl*), and that the degree and the characteristics of the fracturing were linked with factors like the skeletal part of the prey with which the point was in contact, raw material used to produce the points, the weight and length of the points and how these weapons were hafted.

In these sites, the proximal parts of the points were more numerous than the distal fragments. Their interpretation was that the shafts were saved, together with the proximal part of the broken points, which were damaged when the contact between the projectile and the animal bone or any other hard material occurred. The broken tool was extracted from and replaced by a new projectile in the campsite. The hunted animals were transported and butchered in the campsite. Some distal fragments of the projectile points were extracted from the animals and discarded in or near the settlement. Thus, the site was not only used for hunting activities, but at the same time was a place for processing and consumption of the prey after hunting, and where the projectiles were made and repaired. Other studies about palaeolithic sites function involve the whole lithic industry (Ibañez and Gonzalez 1996).

Another example is the use of spatial analysis in different Neolithic sites. The main goal linking spatial analysis and use-wear studies is to identify and locate tools and activities within the site. The tools distribution within the site allows us to identify possible areas associated with distinct activities.

In the site of Chalain (France) this approach shows the existence of working areas within the site related with working bone (Beugnier 1997). Opposed to that in the site of Khirokitia (Cyrus) or Motte-aux-Margins (France), the spatial distribution shows a homogeneous pattern, and there is no clear evidences for different working areas (Beugnier 1997; Astruc 2002).

From a broader perspective, the use-wear analysis contributes to define sites with different functionality within a geographic area: hunting activities, places associated with farming activities, workshops, burials and other handcraft works.

4.5.2 *The Living and the Dead. Tools for Production, Goods for Reproduction*

It is evident that one of the most debated topics in archaeological discussion is associated with the social and symbolic world during prehistory. The comparative study of domestic and burial contexts is one of the most important ways to understand social organization (Fig. 4.7). An example is the use-wear studies done on tools from the most important northeast Iberian Neolithic cemeteries (Bòbila Madurell, Camí de Can Grau or Sant Pau del Camp). These burial practices are so important during this period that this culture was called "*Cultura de los Sepulcros de Fosa*" by Bosch Gimpera at the beginning of the twentieth century. These structures are

Fig. 4.7 Individual graves in the cemetery of de Can Gambús 1 (Sabadell, Barcelona, Spain). Photographs from J. Roig y J.M. Coll (Arrago S.L.)

graves mainly made for one individual, male, female or juvenile, which are associated with different objects deposited as accompaniment: lithic and bone tools, beads, ceramic vessels, faunal remains etc. (Gibaja 2003).

Thus, use-wear analysis focuses on the associations of objects and on the function of lithic tools regarding age and gender of the individuals. The use of statistical analysis allow us to argue that some individuals had an important asset composed by numerous objects of high quality (some of the lithic raw materials from those tools are from other geographic areas such as southeastern France, Alps or Sardinia). Nevertheless, there is a regular distribution of such tools related to the individual's gender and age. Among the most characteristic tools there are the axes, cores and projectiles (point and geometric arrowheads) associated with adult or old male individuals.

Regarding the functionality of the lithic tools, we observed that males were associated with tools used for butchering and projectile arrowheads, and females with tools used for hide working. Children usually were associated with beads, although some adults (male or female) sometimes got beads too. Blades and a few flakes were not associated with any gender or age category. Finally, one of the most important tasks for the community subsistence, farming, is associated with tools deposited in graves with all individuals.

Such differences in burial accompaniment may be explained by social differences between families and individuals: among the community some people had access to different goods; differences in the deposits according to the gender could reflect differences in activities devoted to males and females. Males and females had different quotidian tasks.

A lot of objects or tools were specifically produced in order to be used as funerary deposits, or left as gifts in the individual graves without showing signs of wear, because of brief use or resharpening, in a perfect working order. A good example is the prismatic cores which were exploited to extract big blades used as gifts in the individual graves, as well as axes showing perfect preservation, geometric and pointed arrowheads, and bone awls. So these tools pass from a use-value in the production sphere to status of goods for social reproduction in a symbolic sphere.

Acknowledgements Most of the topics presented here occurred from projects financed by the Ministerio de Economía y Competitividad (HAR2011–23149) and the European Research Council (ERC) funded through an Advanced Grant (ERC-AdG-230561).

References

Astruc, L. (2002). *L'outillage lithique taillé de Khirokitia. Analyse fonctionnelle et spatiale. Monographies du CRA 25.* Paris: Editions du CNRS.
Astruc. L., Abbes, F., Ibáñez, J. J., & González, J. E. (2003). "Dépôts", "réserves" et "caches" de matériel lithique taillé au Néolithique précéramique au Proche-Orient: Quelle gestion de l'outillage? Paléorient, 29(1), 59–78.
Beugnier, V. (1997). L'usage du silex dans l'acquisition et le traitement des matières animales dans le néolithique de Chalain et Clairvaux: La Motte-aux -Magnins et Chalain 3 (Jura, France) 3700-2980 av. J.-C. Paris: Thèse de doctorat, Université de Paris X.
Beugnier, V., & Plisson, H. (2004). Les poignards en silex du Grand-Pressigny: fonction de signe et fonctions d'usage. In C. Constantin, & P. Bodu (Eds.), *Approches fonctionnelles en Préhistoire*, Actes du XXVe congrès préhistorique de France, Nanterre, 24–26 novembre 2000 (pp. 139–154). Paris: Société préhistorique française.
Boëda, E., & Bonilauri, S. 2006. The intermediate Paleolithic: the first bladelet production 40,000 years ago. *Anthropologie, XLIV*(1):75–92.
Claud, E. (2008). Le statut fonctionnel des bifaces au Paléolithique moyen récent dans le Sud-Ouest de la France. Étude tracéologique intégrée des outillages des sites de La Graulet, La Conne de Bergerac, Combe Brune 2, Fonseigner et Chez-Pinaud/ Jonzac. Thèse de Doctorat, Université Bordeaux 1, 546 pp.
Gassin, B. (1996). *Evolution socio-économique dans le Chasséen de la grotte de l'Eglise supérieure (Var): Apport de l'analyse fonctionelle des industries lithiques. Monographie du CRA 17.* Paris: Editions CNRS.
Gassin, B., Bicho, N., Bouby, L., Buxo, R., Carvalho, A. F., Clemente, I., Gibaja, J. F., González, J., Ibáñez, J. J., Linton, J., Marinval, P. H., Márquez, B., Peña-Chocarro, L., Pérez, G., Philibert, S., Rodríguez, A., & Zapata, L. (2010). Variabilité des techniques de récolte et traitement des céréales dans l'occident méditerranéen au Néolithique ancien et moyen: facteurs environnementaux, économiques et sociaux. In A. Beeching, E. Thirault, & J. Vital (Eds.), *Économie et société à la fin de la Préhistoire. Actualité de la recherche.* Documents d'Archéologie en Rhône-Alpes et en Auvergne N° 34 (pp. 19–37). Lyon: Publications de la Maison de l'Orient et de la Méditerranée.
Gassin, B., Léa, V., Astruc, L., & Linton, J. (2011). Lithic management in the Chassey culture Neolithic. In L. Longo (Ed.), Integrated methodological approaches to the study of lithic technology. Proceedings of the International Conference-Florence-13–15 décembre 2007. Human Evolution, Special Issue, 143–160
Geneste, J. M., & Plisson, H. (1993). Hunting technologies and human behavior: Lithic analysis of Solutrean shouldered points. In H. Knecht, A. Pike-Tay, & R. White (Eds.), *Before Lascaux. The complex record of the early upper Paleolithic* (pp. 117–135). Boca Raton: CRC Press.

Gibaja, J. F. (2003). *Comunidades Neolíticas del Noreste de la Península Ibérica. Una aproximación socio-económica a partir del estudio de la función de los útiles lítcos.* British Archaeological Reports (International series) (S. 1140). Oxford: Hadrian Books Ltd.

Gibaja, J. F., Ibáñez, J. J., Rodríguez, A., González, J. E., Clemente, I., García, V., & Perales, U. (2010). Estado de la cuestión sobre los estudios traceológicos realizados en contextos mesolíticos y neolíticos del sur peninsular y noroeste de África. In J. F. Gibaja, & A. F. Carvalho (Eds.), *The last hunter-gatherers and the first farming communities in the South of the Iberian peninsula and North of Morocco.* Promontoria, 15, 181–189.

González, J. E., & Ibáñez, J. J. (1994). Metodología de análisis funcional de instrumentos tallados en sílex. Cuadernos de Arqueología 14. Universidad de Deusto. Bilbao.

Ibáñez, J. J., & González, J. E. (1996). *From tool use to site function: Use-wear analysis in some final upper Palaeolithic sites in the Basque country.* British Archaeological Reports (International series), 658. Oxford: Hadrian Books Ltd.

Ibáñez, J. J., & González, J. E. (2006a). La complexité fonctionnelle des burins: Exemples de la fin du Paléolithique supérieur cantabrique et du Néolithique précéramique de Syrie. In M. Araujo, J.-P. Bracco, & F. Le Brun-Ricalens (Eds.): *Burins préhistoriques: Formes, fonctionnements, fonctions.* ArchéoLogiques, 2, 297–318.

Ibáñez, J. J., & González, J. E. (2006b). Evolution technique et société dans le Néolithique du moyen Euphrate. In L. Astruc, F. Bon, V. Léa, P. Y. Milcent, & S. Philibert (Eds.), Normes techniques et pratiques sociales: de la simplicité des outillages pré- et protohistoriques, actes des rencontres 20–22 octobre 2005/ sous la dir. de. APDCA, Antibes, 359–374.

Ibañez, J. J., González, J. E., Gibaja, J. F., Rodríguez, A., Márquez, B., Gassin, B., & Clemente, I. (2008). *Harvesting in the Neolithic: characteristics and spread of early agriculture in the Iberian peninsula. Prehistoric Technology. 40 Years Later: Functional Analysis and the Russian Legacy. British Archaeological Reports (International series).* Oxford (Reino Unido), Hadrian Books Ltd., 183–195.

Ibáñez, J. J., González, J. E., & Gibaja, J. (2014). Discriminating wild vs domestic cereal harvesting micropolish through laser confocal microscopy. *Journal of Archaeological Science*, 48, 96–103.

Lea, V. (2005). Raw, pre-heated or ready to use: Discovering specialist supply systems for flint Industries in Mid-Neolithic (Chassey culture) communities in Southern France. *Antiquity, 79/303,* 51–65.

Martinez, K. (2005). Análisis funcional de industrias líticas del Pleistoceno Superior. El Paleolítico Medio del Abric Romaní (Capellades,Barcelona) y el Paleolítico Superior de Üçagizli (Hatay, Turquía) y el Molí del Salt (Vimbodí, Tarragona). Cambios en los patrones funcionales entre el Paleolítico Medio y el Superior. Tarragona: Tesis Doctoral, Universitat Rovira i Virgili.

Perlès, C., & Vaughan, P. (1983). Pièces lustrées, travail des plantes et moissons à Franchthi, Grèce (Xe-IVe mil . BC). In M.-C. Cauvin (Ed.), *Traces d'utilisation sur les outils néolithiques du Proche-Orient* (pp. 209–224). Lyon: GIS-Maison de l'Orient. (Travaux de la Maison de l'Orient, 5).

Plisson, H. (1985). Etude fonctionnelle d'outillages lithiques préhistoriques par l'analyse des micro-usures: Recherche méthodologique et archéologique. Paris: Thèse de doctorat, Université de Paris I, Panthéon Sorbonne.

Plisson, H., & Geneste, J. M. (1989). Analyse technologique des pointes à cran solutréennes du Placard (Charente), du Fourneau du Diable, du Pech de la Boissière et de Combe Saunière (Dordogne). *Paleo, 1,* 65–106.

Sigaut, F. (1991). Un couteau ne sert pas à couper, mais en coupant. Structure, fonctionnement et fonction dans l'analyse des objets. 25 ans d'études technologiques en Préhistoire : bilan et perspectives. XIe Rencontres Internationales d'Archéologie et d'Histoire d'Antibes. Juan-les-Pins: APDCA, 21–34.

Torchy, L., & Gassin, B. (2011). Le silex bédoulien sur les sites chasséens du Languedoc: étude fonctionnelle, statut des sites et réseaux de diffusion. *Gallia Préhistoire, 53,* 59–84.

Van Gijn, A. (1989). The wear and tear of flint. Principles of functional analysis applied to Dutch Neolithic assemblages. Analecta Praehistorica Leidensia 22.

Van Gijn, A. (2010). *Flint in focus. Lithic biographies in the Neolithic and Bronze age.* Leiden: Sidestone Press, 289 pp.

Chapter 5
Use-wear Analysis of Nonflint Lithic Raw Materials: The Cases of Quartz/Quartzite and Obsidian

I. Clemente Conte, T. Lazuén Fernández, L. Astruc and A. C. Rodríguez Rodríguez

5.1 Introduction

Ever since the beginnings of traceology as a scientific method of analysis, the raw material was seen to be one of the most influential variables in the formation and development of use-wear marks (Semenov 1957). This is not only the consequence of differences in the mineralogical composition of each rock, as other characteristics such as granulometry, cementation and position of the different minerals, mineral structure, type of fracture and hardness are also influential (Hayden 1979; Clemente Conte 1997; Rodríguez Rodríguez 1997; Astruc et al. 2001). Thus, the degree of homogeneity and heterogeneity of the different rocks used as raw material for the manufacture of different implements also influences the specific characteristics of the use-wear marks.

The marks that form on the edges and surfaces of tools, whatever the raw material is, are generally always the same: macro- and microscars, rounding/blunting of the edges, striations and micropolish. In all cases, the equipment used to observe the stone tools is the same: a binocular magnifying glass (up to 90X) to observe the number of edges used and the nature of the traces (if they are found

---

I. Clemente Conte (✉)
Dpto. de Arqueología y Antropología, IMF-CSIC, Barcelona, Spain
e-mail: ignacio@imf.csic.es

T. Lazuén Fernández
PACEA, UMR 5199, CNRS-Université Bordeaux, Bât B18,
Allee Geoffroy St Hilaire, 33615 Pessac Cedex, France
e-mail: t.lazuen@pacea.u-bordeaux1.fr

L. Astruc
CNRS/ArScan, Du village à l'Etat au Proche-et Moyen-Orient, Nanterre, France
e-mail: laurence.astruc@gmail.com

A. C. Rodríguez Rodríguez
Dpto. Ciencias Históricas, Universidad de Las Palmas de Gran Canaria,
Las Palmas de Gran Canaria, Spain
e-mail: arodriguez@dch.ulpgc.es

on one or both faces, the characteristics of the scarring etc.) and a metallographic microscope (between 100 and 500X) to analyse the specific features of the micropolish generated by working each kind of raw material. In certain cases we may use other types of microscopes, e.g. scanning electron microscopes (SEM) to analyse surface compositions or for residue analysis, or confocal microscopes to analyse surface roughness, areas of polish and so on. However, the form and appearance of the traces may vary, depending on the raw material used for the implements. Therefore, polish which is glossy on flint may be matt on other raw materials such as obsidian. There are traces like those known as corrosion for quartz crystals in quartzite (Clemente Conte 1997; Clemente Conte and Gibaja Bao 2009; Gibaja et al. 2009; Leipus 2006; Leipus and Mansur 2007) or the similar "corrosion" that is even more evident in obsidian, while it is practically nonexistent in flint.

This means that the use-wear marks on each rock, and other raw materials from animals (bone, antler, shells, etc), may exhibit specific traits and these should be interpreted and determined through the use of different magnifications, the application of certain filters and optical prisms, and so on (See H. Plisson's paper in this volume, and Plisson and Lompré 2008; Gyria and Plisson 2009).

In this chapter we are going to describe the specificities of the use-wear marks that can be seen both in heterogeneous rocks like quartzite, and in homogeneous rocks such as obsidian.

5.2 Tools Made from Quartz (T.L.F.)

Quartz is a ubiquitous mineral. Its formation is generally associated with hydrothermal phenomena, and it outcrops in veins. It is found in two varieties, as hyaline or automorph quartz (rock crystal) and a milky or xenomorph quartz. It may be of different colours depending on the impurities it contains. Unlike other rocks with a similar composition (flint, jasper, chalcedony), quartz is macrocrystalline, rather than cryptocrystalline (Huet 2006; Ballin 2008; Driscoll and Menuge 2011). Also, unlike rocks such as quartzite, in quartz the crystals are joined together without any type of cement, although it may contain impurities and fluids trapped between the crystals (Kamminga 1982). It hardly ever displays exfoliation, and therefore the fractures are conchoidal, although the boundaries between crystals and the planes of weaknesses generated during the formation or tectonic pressure suffered by the veins may disguise them.

Although quartz crystals are extremely hard and resistant—more than flint or any other rock used in prehistory for chipped implements (cf. Huet 2006)—their aptitude for knapping and use depends precisely on the joints between the crystals. There is a great variability, but some good-quality quartz blocks provide as sharp and efficient edges as the best rocks. Counterintuitively, several studies have pointed out the great potential of quartz tools for cutting tasks (Bracco and Morel 1998; Huet 2006; Knight 1991).

5.2.1 Experimental Programmes

Quartz has sometimes been thought of as inappropriate for functional analysis due to its irregular fracturing pattern, its surface texture, its high reflectivity and hardness (Sussman 1985). Probably for this reason, few functional studies and experimental programmes have been reported in scientific literature.

In the experimental field, the most significant contributions have been made by Sussman (1985, 1988) and Knutsson (1986, 1988a, b), who used SEM and optical microscopes for their observations.

Knutsson's work provided a model for quartz deformation based on mechanical and abrasive phenomena, and the solution and precipitation of silica. In this author's opinion, wear in quartz is more complex than in flint and therefore more informative (Huang and Knutsson 1995).

In this model, polish is produced by the contact with substances rich in silica and by the abrasion and precipitation of this mineral. Sussman (1985, 1988) links the appearance of polish with working wood, antler and bone, and it is restricted to the high zones of the microtopography. However, the best-developed polish would be caused by working with plants, with notable variations depending on the resistance of the stalks and the humidity level. Some phenomena produced on the surface of the polish or the crystals, like pits, appear due to contact with substances rich in calcium (bone, horn and shells) and are the consequence of the selective solution of crystalline silica in the most vulnerable parts of the structure, such as fractures and intercrystalline boundaries (Knutsson 1988a).

Sussman (1985) also notes the appearance of more marked rounding (identifiable with both optical microscopes and SEM) with certain kinds of tasks, especially scraping dry hide with additives.

Fracturing is the basic and most common evidence of use due to material fatigue, because of the lesser tensile and compression resistance of quartz (cf. Tallavaara et al. 2010). Striations are associated with microfractures because these free small quartz particles chafe the crystalline layer. Sussman (1988) links the presence of comet-shaped striations with working bone and antler. Knutsson (1988a) finds that the presence of fractures and striations hidden beneath a layer of amorphous silica coming from depressed areas is a characteristic of wood working.

In this model, the adhered residue of the worked substances would be deposited in areas of least friction and would tend to build up volume on the surface. Their persistence in time and even after cleaning the lithic artefacts would be explained by the adhesive covering created by the solution of quartz particles during the use (Knutsson 1986; Fullagar 1986).

5.2.2 Possibilities and Limits of Functional Analysis in Quartz

The possibility of functional analysis in quartz has raised some doubts (Sussman 1985) because of the lesser development and different characteristics of such diagnostic marks as polishing, in comparison with those found on flint. However, quartz shares marks of similar characteristics (flaking, striations and rounding), as well as additional kinds of alterations, such as the figures of corrosion. In addition, it seems to conserve the marks comparatively better than quartzite, and above all, than flint; at least in old cave deposits (Lazuén et al. 2011). Flint seems to be more vulnerable to chemical alterations that cause surface solution (cf. Huang and Knutsson 1995), which is especially significant in assemblages of older chronologies. It has been suggested that use-wear marks in quartz might benefit from a slight chemical solution, which heightens the traces, as some of them might be hidden by layers of redeposited silica. This is what K. Knutsson has chosen to call the "quartz paradox" (Knutsson 1988a, b). In fact, a specific study by Derndarsky and Ocklind (2001) explored the possibility of detecting striations and fracture cones in subsurface layers of the objects with fluorescent tincture and the use of confocal microscopy. They achieved certain success in the application to the identification of marks on objects from deposits with postdepositional alterations.

Few specific studies have been made about the alterations produced on the quartz surface, apart from some references to eolic alteration (Knutsson and Lindé 1990), and some of the chemical attacks mentioned above (Knutsson 1988a, b). However, in some of the archaeological series the existence of an alteration known as "soil sheen" has been observed (Levi-Sala 1996), which would be the result of chemical and mechanical action within the sediment itself, favoured by soil acidity (Lemorini 2000; Plisson and Mauger 1988). In quartz, this phenomenon is seen basically in the appearance of striations in disordered directions, with very variable lengths and widths, and other types of corrosion on the crystal surfaces (Lazuén et al. 2011).

5.2.3 *Applications in Archaeological Assemblages*

Few functional studies have been made on quartz assemblages. In 1975 Broadbent and Knutsson carried out a first study of remains from Neolithic sites in northern Europe, with a binocular magnifying-glass. From the early 1980s onwards, R. Bradley extended the observations with metallographic microscopes to identify the types of wear described by L.H. Keeley for flint. She achieved the first results in the study of the Scottish Neolithic site of Tougs, where the author succeeded in concluding that un-retouched implements were used above all in scraping tasks (Bradley 1986).

Part of the functional studies on quartz has focused on sites in northern Europe, where it is the most abundant raw material. At the Neolithic site of Bjurselet (Sweden) a total of 26 quartz objects with clear use-wear marks were employed mostly for cutting but also to make grooves, to perforate and scrape (Knutsson et al. 1988). Derndarsky and Ocklind (2001) published the study of two samples of quartz endscrapers from the Swedish Neolithic sites of Görviksudden and Gärdselbäcken, with limited results partly due to the postdepositional alterations suffered by these assemblages.

Another part of the studies has been applied to European, African and Asian Palaeolithic sites. Some of the first applications were undertaken at Lower Palaeolithic sites like Olduvai (Sussman 1987) and L'Aragó (Pant 1989). In 1995, Huang and Knutsson published a study of three small collections from early to late Middle Palaeolithic sites in China. The assemblages had suffered a high level of alteration, and only four objects conserved determinable use-wear marks. At the French site of Payre, a functional study undertaken with SEM included some quartz tools. The results showed that these tools would have been used to saw, scrape and work with meat, although use-wear marks were only seen on three artefacts (Moncel et al. 2008).

H. Plisson's functional analysis has also succeeded in determining whether carinated objects from the Gravettian level at Lapa do Anecrial were used as cores or endscrapers (Almeida et al. 2007). The absence of use-wear marks proved that these objects were used to obtain bladelets.

Perhaps one of the clearest proofs of the efficacy of quartz as a lithic implement in Prehistory is its association with the manufacture of hunting weaponry. This is the case of the quartz and rock crystal segments from the Howiesons Poort layer in Sibudu Cave (South Africa). Evidence of hafting and use with animal substances was identified through the study of microresidue (Delagnes et al. 2006) and impact fractures (Lombard 2011). In Europe, the use of quartz hunting points has been documented at the site of Cova Eirós, an early Middle Palaeolithic site. In this level, where quartz is the dominant raw material, it has also been possible to document primary butchery tasks, the preparation of wooden objects and scraping dry hide (Lazuén et al. 2011).

Another field where studies of quartz tools are especially relevant is that of later prehistory in Oceania, where the research has been based mostly on the analysis of residues conserved on the edges (Fullagar 1986). A recent study of a collection of tools from three Lapita sites (after 3000 bp) in Vanuatu Archipelago has shown that quartz flakes were used to engrave wood, pierce shells and scrape hides (Kononenko et al. 2010).

5.3 Function of Quartzite Implements (I.C.C.)

5.3.1 Methodological Aspects for the Microscopic Analysis of Heterogeneous Rocks

As flint is the raw material most commonly used by prehistoric societies to manufacture part of their tool kit, it has always been allotted more study time, at least in the countries where functional analysis was first applied and developed. Although some researchers maintained an interest in determining the function of implements made from other rocks, like quartz, obsidian, basalt or quartzite (Semenov 1957; Greiser and Sheets 1979; Beyries 1982; Plisson 1985, 1986; Knutsson 1988;

Sussman 1988 etc.). They have only been given close attention in recent decades, particularly in those geographical regions where these raw materials are more abundant or where flint is practically inexistent (e.g. Clemente Conte 1997; Rodríguez Rodríguez 1997; Mansur 1999; Gibaja et al. 2002; Leipus 2006; Leipus and Mansur 2007).

In our case, in earlier studies we have noted the various problems that arise when heterogeneous rocks are analysed under the microscope. We agree with the descriptive definition that Leipus and Mansur (2007, p. 183) give of these rocks: "In this context, we use the term 'heterogeneous raw materials' for those formed by a generally micro or cryptocrystalline matrix of variable composition and crystals included within that matrix. ...en the case of heterogeneous materials, matrix and crystals react differently and in consequence microscopic use-wear analysis should focus on different criteria from those used to analyse 'homogeneous' raw materials. This approach involves a mixed analysis in which the alterations produced on the matrix and on the fracture surfaces of the quartz crystals are analysed in a complementary way". Thus we have described the use-wear marks observed on both the matrix and the crystals of our experimental specimens made from raw materials such as quartzite and rhyolite (Clemente Conte 1995/2008, 1997; Clemente Conte and Gibaja Bao in press; Gibaja et al. 2002). That is why in this work we want to emphasize two methodological aspects enabling the determination of the kinematics carried out with the implements and the approximate hardness or abrasiveness of the worked materials.

But before discussing these topics, we would also like to make a brief comment about another methodological aspect. We are referring to the necessity of approaching the analysis of these rock types from another viewpoint, as we believe they should be examined and recorded with a greater magnification than used for rocks with a more homogeneous surface, such as flint, obsidian and hyaline quartz, for example.

The result of the mineralogical composition of heterogeneous rocks is the distinctly irregular topography of their surfaces. This means that, in general, only the highest points in the microtopography are in direct contact with the material being worked. Therefore, the micro use-wear traces are formed in much smaller areas than in homogeneous rocks. In addition, the traces do not form or develop in the same way in the matrix as in crystals, and consequently, in order to observe specific features of the wear traces we need to use greater magnifications (Clemente Conte 1997; Gibaja et al. 2002; Mansur 1999; Mansur and Lasa 2005; Leipus 2006; Leipus and Mansur 2007). Whereas for flint it is normal to use 10X and 20X lenses, which with 10X eyepieces result in magnifications of 100 and 200 times, we propose that these should at least be doubled for the analysis of heterogeneous rocks. If an optical duplicator is fitted between the microscope lenses and the eyepieces, we shall also be able to obtain images with a double magnification.

In general, micropolish is more highly developed on the surface of the quartz crystals than on the matrix. But this is not the only modification they undergo, as they may also be fractured, cracked, splintered, striated, rounded, smoothed, pecked

Fig. 5.1 a Dry hide scraping use-wear traces on a quartz sidescraper from Cova Eirós, metallographic microscope 200X. **b** The same area at 500X. **c** Wood scraping use-wear traces on a quartz sidescraper from Cova Eirós, 200 X magnification. **d** Percussion traces on the distal end of a quartz denticulate from Cova Eirós. Stereomicroscope 11X

or corroded (Clemente Conte 1995/2008; Gibaja et al. 2002). All these alterations may or may not occur at the same time on the same edge. Thus, in a small area of the edge we may find several crystals together and each one may have a different appearance. For instance, one crystal may present a diagnostic polish; another may have microcracks in one of its sides; yet another may be "corroded"; and a fourth could have clear technological marks (e.g. waves, hackles etc.), with sharp edges which give it a very fresh appearance, as it had just been knapped.

Whereas in homogeneous raw materials the micropolish develops and is distributed over wider surfaces, in the case of implements made from heterogeneous raw materials it is located in small surface areas, first over the surface of a few crystals, and then if the working time is longer, also over the matrix (except when extremely abrasive materials are worked, such as leather or minerals and rocks, as then the crystals tend to be removed and the microwears develop on the rock matrix). For this reason, we propose observing the quartz crystals one by one, as if each of them was a whole edge. The analysis of the different modifications they have undergone, as well as the location and distribution of some marks on their surfaces, can indicate attributes in relation with the kinematics used and with the hardness and abrasiveness of the worked material (Fig. 5.1).

5.3.2 Kinematics Indicator Marks

Most microwear specialists believe that striations and/or linear marks are the features par excellence that most reliably reflect the implement kinematics (e.g. Semenov 1957; Keeley 1980; Mansur 1982; Plisson 1985; González Urquijo and Ibáñez Estévez 1994). In the rock types that we are dealing with, these striations as such only appear on the surfaces where micropolish has developed, or in some crystals, and are not as common or frequent as in homogeneous materials. The scratches, just as in the case of other raw materials, are positioned parallel to the edge in longitudinal cutting actions and oblique or perpendicular to the edge in transversal actions, as can be seen in Figs. 5.3a, f and 5.4c.

In addition to the striations, other traces provide information about the kinematics made with the implement. Thus, for instance, the situation of the microscarring with respect to the sides of the crystals also varies according to the kinematics produced with the tool. In transversal and unidirectional actions they are mainly on the edges of the crystals nearest to the active edge and are oriented parallel to it. In contrast, with longitudinal actions they are located on the edge of the crystals that are oriented perpendicularly to the edge, on one of them when the action is unidirectional and on two of them when it is bidirectional (Fig. 5.2b, c)—in the case of longitudinal actions, especially with materials of medium-high hardness, some scarring may occur on the side nearest and parallel to the edge, just as in transversal actions. This is due more to the direct pressure of the worked material on the side of the crystal than to the kinematics of the tool. On occasions, some crystals are completely fractured as a consequence of the use of the tool and, and if they do not suffer any other alterations, present a fresh surface with clear technological features—waves, hackles etc.—as is the case of the example in Fig. 5.2e. These technological features may also indicate where the force was produced in connection with the kinematics and which caused the fracture of the crystal.

Sometimes, both the sides and edges of the crystals are rounded and take a certain orientation according to the implement kinematics. This is positioned in the same way as the micro-scarring that we have described above. For example, in Fig. 5.2a, c, it can be seen that both crystals indicate a longitudinal cutting action. This effect is even more pronounced when the micro-polish is well-defined (Fig. 5.3). In addition, certain features appear on the surface of some micropolishing that can indicate the movement that the tool has made. For example, in the case of the bone micropolish (Fig. 5.3a, b, c) a series of "microcracks" can be seen oriented in the opposite direction to the kinematics that were made. In this case, they are oriented parallel to the edge in the case of transversal actions and perpendicular to the edge in the case of longitudinal actions. Also in the case of bone, "grooves" and/or elongated depressions may occur with an orientation coinciding with the movement made (Fig. 5.3b).

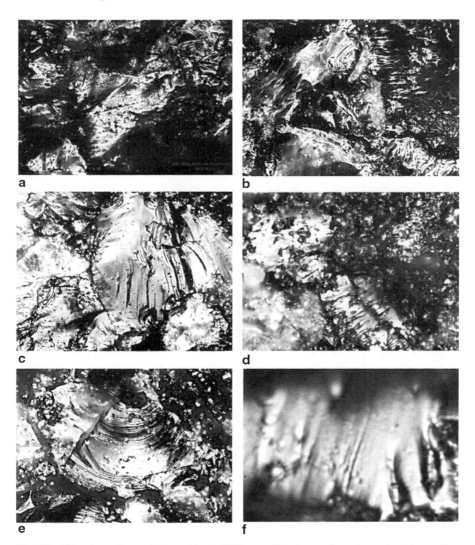

Fig. 5.2 Alterations observed in crystals at 400X magnification. **a** Corrosion, oriented rounding of edges and striations resulting from sawing fresh pine-wood, 30'. **b** Smoothed crystal splintered on one side indicating a longitudinal action, same experimental implement as the previous photograph. **c** Smoothing and rounding of a crystal with cracks on one side, indicating a longitudinal and bidirectional action sawing fresh box-wood for 30'. **d** Corrosion, rounding and striations resulting from cutting fresh bone, 10'. **e** "Fresh fracture" of a crystal which had previously been smoothed by scraping fresh box-wood, 30'. **f** Striations on a micro-polish surface resulting from scraping fresh pine-wood, 30'

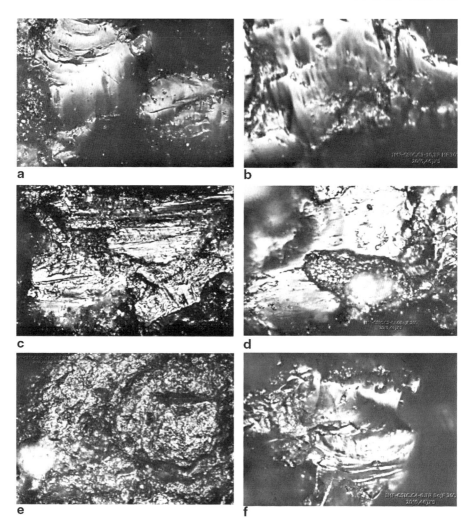

Fig. 5.3 Surfaces, crystals and matrix with micropolish, all at 400X magnification. **a** and **b** Micropolish resulting from scraping fresh bone, 30'. **c** Micropolish with striations resulting from sawing fresh bone, 10'. **d** Micropolish resulting from cutting fresh box wood, 30'. **e** Micropolish of matrix resulting from scraping dry hide, 30'. **f** Micropolish resulting from scraping fresh box wood, 30'

5.3.3 Use-wear Indicating the Hardness/Abrasiveness of the Worked Material

Normally, in microwear analysis of homogeneous raw materials, the scarring produced on the edges of the implements has been considered a good indicator of the hardness of the worked material and is sometimes the main object of the analysis to

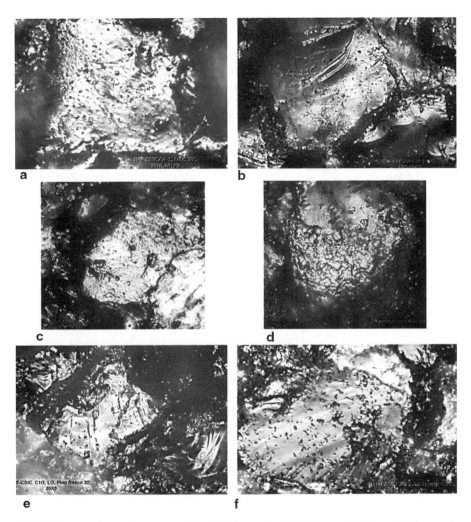

Fig. 5.4 Aspect of corrosion on crystals, all photographs at 400X magnification. **a** Cutting meat, 30'. **b** Scraping fresh skin, 30'. **c** Cutting fresh skin, 15'. **d** Scraping dry hide, 30'. **e** Cutting fresh pine-wood, 30'. **f** Scraping fresh bone, 30'

determine the use (Tringham et al. 1974; Odell 1983 etc.). In the case of quartzite and heterogeneous rocks, the scarring of the edge is not as clear as in the other rocks, as it is less frequent and smaller in size. This depends, however, on the degree of cohesion of the grains and the type of fracture they display. Nevertheless, the scarring is more noticeable on edges that have worked hard materials than on those that have worked softer ones, in the same way as the action is reflected in their distribution, as occurs with other raw materials. In any case, as we have noted in previous publications (Clemente Conte 1995/2008, 1997; Clemente Conte and Gibaja Bao in press; Gibaja et al. 2002), we agree with M. Leipus and M.E. Mansur in this respect when they state that: "*In general, the degree of cohesion among grains in the materials and their tenacity means that the edges tend to become rounded through the loss of grains rather than through fracture*" (Leipus and Mansur 2007, p. 186).

Regarding other types of alterations affecting the surfaces of the quartz crystals through their use, we would like to clarify certain aspects related with what we call "corrosion" (Fig. 5.4).

We have given this name to the aspect of crystals as a result of the loss, disappearance or solution of part of their original surface. This corrosion may take several forms:

- Isolated. They are "hollows" of various sizes and shapes that are generally positioned towards the inner part of the crystals. When they are small- or medium-sized, we describe them as "pecked"; and when they are large, as is more common if hard materials are worked, we call them "large extractions".
- Continuous. This occurs on the periphery and edges of the crystals as the consequence of continuous pecking, wholly or almost wholly destroying the original surface. It usually occurs when very abrasive materials are worked and is also a good indicator of the kinematics produced with the implement. This effect is called "continuous breakage".

The photographs in Fig. 5.2 show several aspects displayed by crystals altered by "corrosion" after working various kinds of material. Thus, when they have worked soft materials of animal origin (meat, fresh skin), the corrosion appears as abundant small-sized pecking, with spherical shapes and clear bases (as if silted up), which give the crystal a generally rough appearance (Fig. 5.4a, b, c). In contrast, in implements that have worked harder and more rigid materials, such as wood and bone, the pecking is larger, generally irregular in shape and with a dark base (Figs. 5.2d and 5.4e, f); and in some cases, if the bone and wood is hard or dry, they increase in size to become "large extractions" (Fig. 5.4f).

If very abrasive materials, like dry hide, are worked, the crystals are affected by the phenomenon we have called "continuous breakage". This mainly affects the periphery of the crystals and consists of the disappearance of the crystal through corrosion, uncovering the matrix where the micropolish develops. Normally, this modification is located on the sides of the crystals nearest the edge and is located on one of the sides, as we have seen above for striations and rounding, depending on the kinematics of the implement (Fig. 5.4d).

It is common to find corrosion on the crystals of archaeological materials that have undergone some type of postdepositional alteration. Heterogeneous raw materials are usually more resistant to these types of alterations than homogeneous kinds, and this fact can be verified in the artefacts from a same site. Corrosion is practically the only alteration that is detected, but whereas in the experimental materials it is practically limited to the area of the active edge, when it is a postdepositional alteration it is seen in other parts of the surface. The appearance of this "corrosion" may vary depending on the kind of sediment in which it occurs. In the same way, poor storage, transport and treatment of the lithic artefacts by the research team may also produce these alterations (Figs. 5.5 and 5.6).

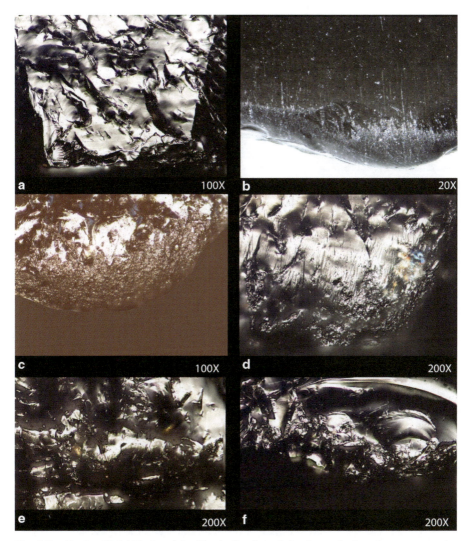

Fig. 5.5 a Cutting fresh hide (goat) for 20 min. Patches of abrasion and a few short narrow striations. **b** Scraping dry hide (deer) for 10 min. Very rounded edge and long striations. **c** Scraping ochered-cured wet hide (goat) for 40 min. Very rounded edge, severe abrasion, slight polish and some narrow striations. **d** Scraping resin (dragon tree blood) -cured dry hide (goat) for 40 min. Rounded edge with severe abrasion, polish and both shallow and rough-bottomed striation. **e** Scraping soaked bone for 45 min. Patches of grainy polish and short striae. **f** Sawing fresh bone for 5 min. Abrasion, little patches of grainy polish and some striations

5.4 Obsidian Tools (L.A. and A.R.R.)

Obsidian is a silica-rich volcanic glass (use-wear analysis on tools made of volcanic raw materials such as basalt, phonolith or rhyolith are not mentioned in this paper—Keeley 1981, Rodríguez Rodríguez 1993b, 2009, Clemente Conte 1997,

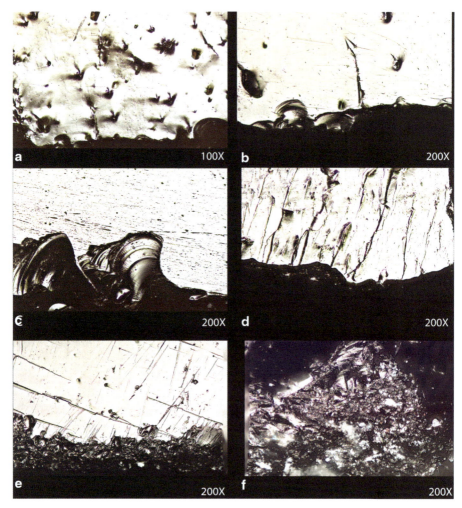

Fig. 5.6 a Cutting barley for 150 min. Rounded edge, polish and striae. **b** The same tool. A detail of the edge and scales with polish and striae (shallow, rough-bottomed and intermittent). **c** Sawing fresh softwood for 30 min. Polish and very dense intermittent striation. **d** Whittling dry hardwood for 60 min. Polish very restricted to the edge, attrition and short striations. **e** Scraping soft limestone for 20 min. Heavy and regular abrasion, rough-bottomed and deep striations. **f** Boring shell (*columbella rustica*) for 5 min. Intense attrition and some linear components

Toselli et al. 2002—neither is research on the manufacture of obsidian prestige objects—Astruc et al. 2011). Because of its glassy texture, it is thus one of the most homogeneous rocks with a very low mineral content, less than 5% in volume (Poupeau et al. 2007). Intra- and intersource variations are well known and concern colours, banding, amount of spherulites, mineral contents, geochemical compositions, magnetic properties and Raman structures (Feinberg et al. 2009; Bellot-Gurlet et al. 2010). Variations in raw material physical and chemical properties determine the surface topography of the knapped tools, the mechanical behaviour of the artefacts under specific constraints due to use or postdepositional damages (i.e. etching, brittleness, abrasion, striation, development of "polishes"). Consequently, as in the case of flints, the variability of obsidian as a raw material has to be taken into account when use-wear analysis is concerned. Wear attributes will develop in a different way on different kind of obsidians.

5.4.1 Experimental Programmes

The first analyses of obsidian artefacts on the basis of consistent experimental research were conducted by Semenov (1972) and his students from the Experimental-Traceological Laboratory at St. Petersburg (Arazova 1986). The reference book for obsidian use-wear analysis has been published by L. Hurcombe: "Use Wear Analysis and Obsidian: Theory, Experiments and Results". The author presents an experimental programme of 169 tools (Hurcombe 1992, pp. 132–133) that have been used for different motions on diverse worked materials (wood and soft plant treatment, butchery, meat and fish processing, and animal material such as skin, hair, bone and antler. Damages due to manufacture of tools (hard and soft hammer technique, pressure flaking) and chemical and physical damages are also investigated. Setzer (2004) focused on a low-power approach and presents an experimental corpus of 80 tools used following different motions on various worked material. The author brings a quantification of the edge attrition of these tools, which are made of Sardinian obsidians of different origins. More recently, N. Kononenko provides a comprehensive analysis of experimental and archaeological study of use-wear and residues on obsidian artefacts from Papua New Guinea (2011). The experimental corpus includes 292 tools used on palms, soft and hard woods, nonwoody plants, fish, chicken and human skin, shell and clay. The experiments are highly documented with 225 colour plates.

The relation between obsidian tools and the activities in which they are employed has been further explored with two experimental programmes. The first focused mainly on hide processing on the basis of the ethnographic knowledge of A. Rodríguez Rodríguez, and, on bone and antler treatment with the help of two bone tool analysts, R. Christidou and A. Legrand. The second dealt with the question of the efficiency of sickles (manufactured with flint or obsidian inserts) during harvesting (experiments took place in 2009 Kızılkaya, Cappadocia (Astruc et al. 2012)).

5.4.2 Possibilities and Limits of Use-wear Analysis on Obsidian Artefacts

Volcanic glasses are sensitive to postdepositional damage depending notably on the soil composition, water content and thermal variations. Major scarring, edge and surface rounding and smoothing, scratches and abrasion features and gain in opacity can be observed. Microscopic fracture and microscopic dissolution of the surface of the obsidian are the most specific behaviour of the raw material when postdepositional damages are concerned. These latter two phenomena can be associated on the same tools causing in some cases very severe fractures of the edge. It is not rare that alterations underline the presence of striation (see experimental tools in Hurcombe 1992, Pl. 109–110 and archaeological ones in Astruc 2011).

The four main wear attributes are scarring, striation, smoothing/abrasion and polish. As obsidian is a highly brittle material, scarring is developed in most cases on used implements after a short time of use. Nevertheless, in very well-preserved contexts, some archaeological tools used to cut or shave soft animal tissues did not exhibit macroscopic scarring. Types of scars are identical to other raw materials as they were formerly described in the Ho Ho Classification (Hayden 1979). Striation also develops quite rapidly. Thus, after short time of use even on soft material, the tool motion can in general be observed. Linear components and striae show a larger variability of morphologies than on flint tools. The formation of striations has been studied by Mansur (1982) on flint tools and for obsidian artefacts by Corruccini (1985) and Hay (1977) and discussed by Hurcombe (1992, pp. 57–58) who distinguishes: sleeks (ribbon-like smooth-bottomed trough, Mansur 1982), roughed bottom striations (rough bottom trough, Mansur 1982), intermittent striations, fernlike striations, crescent crack rows and flaked linear fractures.

Abrasion features on the surfaces (i.e. exfoliation, comets) and smoothing of the edge are easily developed too, following models which are relatively similar to what is observed on flint: during contacts with grit, soil (while harvesting for instance, work of mineral material such as soil, clay, soft or hard rocks, treatment of hide, notably. As scarring is relatively important whatever the type of contact is, smoothing occurring after a stabilization of the edge is probably less common than for flint tools.

Experiments have demonstrated that polishes are developed on obsidian tools. They are in general less visible as the surface of the obsidian is highly reflective. Experience in use-wear analysis of flint tools is therefore recommended to locate the areas showing the polish, in general perceptible by slight changes in surface microtopography, striation or abrasion feature. Parameters used when other kinds of raw materials are concerned such as the "trame", the limit or the extension of the polish, are in general difficult to observe. Nevertheless, the identification of polishes is possible. Its identification is usually easier looking at abraded places or analysing the microtopography changes at the very edge or in relation to scarring. Highly identifiable is the polish produced while cutting siliceous plants such as cereals or reeds. When well developed, the general morphology of the wear is in these cases really similar to that seen on flint tools.

The definition of the polish is again in question. Hurcombe proposed following Anderson (1980) and Fullagar (1991) that polish could be explained by the colloidal silica theory (exchange between the colloidal surface of the obsidian and the silica bodies of the plants). Ongoing research in tribology (science of wear) and nanorheology is being conducted to attain a better understanding of the wear processes on obsidian. This domain of research is based on numerous questions and to solve them is a difficult task. The current studies demonstrate that striation will depend notably on the worked material, the speed and load during the contact, and reveals the ductile and brittle behaviour of the glass. Further questions asked are the following: does striation affects the obsidian or a transformed layer (additive or not?) formed at the surface of the tool? Can polishes be described as transfer layers? If it is the case, what is the behaviour and degree of adherence of these layers?

5.4.3 Use-wear Analysis on Obsidian Tools in Different Archaeological Contexts

Various research projects have been conducted on obsidian tools in different geographical and cultural contexts. They are still insufficiently developed. Compiling the literature, it is obvious that the work done on each obsidian procurement area and diffusion zone is scarce. Analyses on Neolithic sites conducted in western Mediterranean contexts are the most common (Hurcombe 1992; Iovino 1996; Tykot et al. 2006; Setzer 2004) together with Eastern Mediterranean (Vaughan 1981; Vaughan and Perlès 1983), Near-East (Ibáñez et al. 2007, 2008), Anatolia (Altınbilek and Iovino 2001; Anderson np; Anderson 1994; Anderson and Formenti 1996; Astruc et al. 2008; Ataman 1988; Caneva et al. 1996) and Cyprus (Astruc 2011). In the Caucasus, several Palaeolithic, Neolithic and Chalcolithic assemblages have been analysed (Arazova 1986; Badalyan et al. 2010; Kazaryan 1993). In Africa, the research is relatively scarce and focused on recent archaeological periods, such as the Later Stone Age on the coast of Eritrea or the Prehispanic period in the Canary Islands (Beyin 2010; Rodríguez Rodríguez 1993a, 1998, 1999). A long-term tradition of studies exists in America, starting with the analysis of artefacts from the Meso-American civilizations (Lewenstein 1981, 1991; Aldenderfer and Kimball 1989; Aoyama 1993, 1995) but the whole continent is now involved (Mansur-Franchomme 1987, 1988; Kay 1996). Following the work of R. Torrence who had a tremendous impact on obsidian researches, the recent PhD of N. Kononenko on Papua New Guinea (2011) added to this patchy literature one of its best methodological and archaeological applications.

To conclude, it can be said that the observation of wear attributes (scarring, striation, smoothing, polish) on obsidian tools, like for artefacts made of other raw materials, can lead to diagnostics on the function of the implements. The observations have to be combined in three dimensions, taking into account the raw material variability. As polishes are less perceptible on obsidian surfaces it is likely that the detail in diagnostic would be less important when obsidian tools are concerned. Experiments are in any case highly needed to reinforce our methodology, using raw material identical to the archaeological material, and, relying on well-defined and adapted protocols.

Acknowledgements The work on obsidian tools has been partly funded by the project of the Agence Nationale de la Recherche ANR-08-BLANC-0318-CD9, *ObsidienneUs* (dir. L. Astruc).

References

Aldenderfer, M. S., & Kimball, L. R. (1989). Microwear analysis in the Maya Lowlands: The use of functional data in a complex-society setting. *Journal of Field Archaeology, 16*(1), 47–60.

Almeida, F., Brugal, J.-P., Zilhão, J., & Plisson, H. (2007). An upper Paleolithic Pompeii: Technology, subsistence and paleoethnography at Lapa do Anecrial. In N. F. Bicho (Ed.), *From the Mediterranean basin to the Portuguese Atlantic shore: Papers in honor of Anthony Marks* (pp. 119–140). Faro: Actas do IV Congresso de Arqueologia Peninsular. Promontoria Monográfica 07.

Altınbilek, Ç., & Iovino M. R. (2001). From shape to function: Notes on some end-scrapers from Çayönü. In I. Caneva, C. Lemorini, D. Zampetti, & P. Biagi (Eds.), *Beyond tools. Redefining the PPN lithic assemblages of the Levant* (pp. 161–164). Berlin: Ex Oriente. (Proceedings of the third workshop on PPN chipped lithic industries, 1–4 November 1998, Venice).

Anderson, P. (np). *Functional interpretation of obsidian tools in Aşikli (Pre-pottery Neolithic, Central Anatolia): Microscopic and experimental data*. Poster presented at the XIth Arkeometri Sonuçlari Toplantisi, Ankara, May 1995.

Anderson, P. C. (1980). A testimony of prehistoric tasks: Diagnostic residues on stone tool working edges. *World Archaeology, 12*, 181–194.

Anderson, P. C. (1994). Reflections on the significance of two typological classes in the light of experimentation and microwear analysis: Flint sickles and obsidian "Çayönü tools". In H. G. Gebel & S. K. et Koslowski (Eds.), *Neolithic chipped stone industries of the fertile crescent* (pp. 61–82). Berlin: Ex Oriente. (Proceedings of the first workshop on PPN chipped lithic industries).

Anderson, P., & Formenti, F. (1996). Exploring the use of abraded obsidian "Cayönu tools" using experimentation, optical and SEM microscopy, and EDA analysis. In S. Demirci, A. M. Özer, & G. D. et Summers (Eds.), *Archaeometry 94* (pp. 553–566) Ankara: Tübitak. (Proceedings of the 29th symposium on archaeometry, Ankara, 9–14 May).

Aoyama, K. (1993). Experimental microwear analysis on Maya obsidian tools: Case study of the La Entrada Region, Honduras. In P. C. Anderson, S. Beyries, M. Otte, et al. (Eds.), *Traces et fonction, les gestes retrouvés* (Vol. 2, pp. 423–432). Liège: Université de Liège. (ERAUL; 50. actes du colloque international de Liège, 8–10 décembre 1990).

Aoyama, K. (1995). Microwear analysis in the Southeast Maya Lowlands: Two case studies at Copán, Honduras. *Latin American Antiquity, 6*, 129–144.

Arazova, R. (1986). *Stone agricultural tools of early farmer societies of Azerbaijan*. ELM, Baku.

Astruc, L. (2011). Du Gollü dağ à Shillourokambos: de l'utilisation d'obsidiennes anatoliennes en contexte insulaire. In J. Guilaine, F. Briois, & J. D. Vigne (Eds.), *Shillourokambos, un établissement néolithique pré-céramique à Chypre. Les fouilles du secteur 1*. (pp. 727–744). Athens: Editions Errance, Ecole française d'Athènes.

Astruc, L., Jautée, E., Vargiolu R., & et Zahouani H. (2001). La texture des matières siliceuses et son influence sur le nature et le développement des traces d'usure: apports des méthodes expérimentales. L'exemple des cherts de la formation de Lefkara (Chypre). In L. Bourguignon, I. Ortega, & M.-Ch. Frère-Sautot (Eds.), *Préhistoire et approche expérimentale* (pp. 205–224). Montagnac: Editions Monique Mergoil.

Astruc, L., Kayacan, N., & Özbaşaran, M. (2008). Technical activities held at Musular: First approach through use-wear analysis. *Arkeometry sonuçları toplantısı, 23*, 165–172.

Astruc, L., Vargiolu, R., Ben Tkaya, M., Balkan-Atlı, N., Özbaşaran, M., & Zahouani, H. (2011). Multi-scale tribological analysis of the technique of manufacture of an obsidian bracelet from Aşıklı Höyük (Aceramic Neolithic, Central Anatolia). *Journal of Archaeological Science, 38*(12), 3415–3424.

Astruc, L., Ben Tkaya M., Torchy, L., et al. (2012). *De l'efficacité des faucilles proche-orientales: Approche expérimentale*. BSPF, 2012/4, 671–687.

Ataman, K. (1988). *The chipped stone assemblages from Can Hassan III: A study in typology, technology and function.* PhD Thesis, Institute of Archaeology, University College, London, December 1988.
Badalyan, R. S., Harutyunyan, A. A., Chataigner, C., Le Mort F., Chabot, J., Brochier, J.-E., Balasescu, A., Radu, V., & Hovsepyan, R., (2010). The settlement of Aknashen-Khatunarkh, a Neolithic site in the Ararat Plain (Armenia): Excavation results 2004–2009. *Tüba-Ar, 13,* 187–220.
Ballin, T. B. (2008). *Quartz Technology in Scottish Prehistory.* Scottish Archaeological Internet Reports (SAIR) 26.
Bellot-Gurlet, L., Le Bourdonnec, F. X., Poupeau, G., & Dubernet, S. (2010). Raman microspectroscopy of western Mediterranean obsidian glass: One step towards provenance studies? *Journal of Raman Spectroscopy, 35,* 671–677.
Beyin, A. (2010). Use-wear analysis of obsidian artifacts from later Stone Age shell midden sites on the Red Sea Coast of Eritrea, with experimental results. *Journal of Archaeological Science, 37,* 1543–1556.
Beyries, S. (1982). *Comparaison de traces d'utilisation sur différentes roches siliceuses* (pp. 235–240). Louvain: Studia Praehistorica Belgica 2.
Bracco, J.-P., & Morel, P. (1998). Outillage en quartz et boucherie au Paléolithique supérieur: quelques observations expérimentales. In J.-P. Brugal, L. Meignen, & M. et Patou-Mathis (Eds.), *Économie préhistorique: les comportements de subsistance au Paléolithique* (pp. 387–395). Sophia Antipolis: A.P.D.C.A.
Bradley, R. (1986). Microwear analysis (Tougs, Burra Isle, Shetland). *Glasgow Archaeological Journal, 13,* 1–43.
Broadbent, N. D., & Knutsson, K. (1975). An experimental analysis of quartz scrapers. Results and applications. *Fornvannen, 70,* 113–128.
Caneva, I., Lemorini, C., & Zampetti, D. (1996). Lithic technology and functionality through time and space at Çayönü. In S. K. Kozlowski & H. G. K. Gebel (Eds), *Neolithic chipped stone industries of the fertile crescent, and their contemporaries in adjacent regions, studies in early near eastern production, subsistence, and environment 3* (pp. 385–402). Berlin: Ex Oriente.
Clemente Conte, I. (1995/2008). *Instrumentos de trabajo líticos de los yámanas (canoeros-nómadas de la Tierra del Fuego): una perspectiva desde el análisis funcional.* Tesis doctoral, Universitat Autònoma de Barcelona. Published in 2008 in: Publicaciones de la Universidad Autónoma de Barcelona. http://www.tdx.cat/TDX-0415108-171300.
Clemente Conte, I. (1997). *Los instrumentos líticos de Túnel VII: una aproximación etnoarqueológica.* Madrid: Col. Treballs d.Etnoarqueologia, 2, UAB—CSIC.
Clemente Conte, I., & Gibaja Bao, J. F. (2009). Formation of use-wear traces in non-flint rocks: The case of quartzite and rhyolite. Differences and similarities. In F. Sternke, L. J. Costa, & L. Eigeland (Eds.), *Non-flint raw material use in prehistory: Old prejudices and new directions* (pp. 93–98). Oxford: Archaeopress. (Proceedings of the XV. Congress of the U.I.S.P.P. BAR International Series, 1939).
Corruccini, J. A. (1985). Moisture and the formation of obsidian striations. *Lithic Technology, 14,* 33–35.
Delagnes, A., Wadley, L., Villa, P., & Lombard, M. (2006). Crystal quartz backed tools from the Howiesons Poort at Sibudu Cave. *Southern African Humanities, 18*(1), 43–56.
Derndarsky, M., & Ocklind, G. (2001). Some preliminary observations on subsurface damage on experimental and archaeological quartz tools using CLSM and dye. *Journal of Archaeological Science, 28,* 1149–1158.
Driscoll, K., & Menuge, J. (2011). Recognising burnt vein quartz artefacts in archaeological assemblages. *Journal of Archaeological Science, 38,* 2251–2260.
Feinberg, J. M., Johnson, C., & Frahm, E. (2009). A database of obsidian magnetic properties for archaeological sourcing. GSA joint annual meeting, GSA abstracts with programs.
Fullagar, R. (1986). Use-wear on quartz. In G. Ward (Ed.), *Archaeology at ANZAAS* (pp. 191–197). Canberra: Canberra Archaeological Society.

Fullagar, R. (1991). The role of silica in polish formation. *Journal of Archaeological Science, 18,* 1–24.
Gibaja, J. F., Clemente, I., & Mir, A. (2002). Análisis funcional en instrumentos de cuarcita: el yacimiento del paleolítico superior de la Cueva de la Fuente del Trucho (Colungo, Huesca). In I. Clemente, R. Risch, & J. F. Gibaja (Eds.), *Análisis funcional. Su aplicación al estudio de las sociedades prehistóricas. British Archaeological Reports (International series)* (Vol. 1073, pp. 79–86). Oxford: Hadrian.
Gibaja, J. F., Clemente, I., & Carvalho, A. F. (2009). The use of quartzite tools in Prehistory. Some examples from the Portuguese Neolithic. In M. Araujo Igreja & I. Clemente Conte (Eds.), *Recent functional studies on non flint stone tools: Methodological improvements and archaeological inferences* (p. 41). Portugal: Fundação para a Ciencia e Tecnologia (Ministerio da Ciencia e da Tecnologia) IGESPAR Ministerio da Cultura.
González Urquijo, J. E., & Ibáñez Estévez, J. J. (1994). *Metodología de análisis funcional de instrumentos talaldos en sílex*. Bilbao: Cuadernos de Arqueología 14, Universidad de Deusto.
Greiser, S. T., & Sheets, P. D. (1979). Raw materials as a functional variable in use-wear studies. In B. Hayden (Ed.), *Lithic use-wear analysis* (pp. 289–296). New York: Academic.
Gyria, E. Y., & Plisson, H. (2009). *О преимуществах применения программы Helicon Focus в археологической трасологии*, Helicon Focus. http://www.photo-soft.ru/focus_trasologiya.html.
Hay, C. A. (1977). Use-scratch morphology: A functionally significant aspect of edge damage on obsidian tools. *Journal of Field Archaeology, 4,* 491–494.
Hayden, B. (Ed.). (1979). The Ho Ho classification and nomenclature committee report. In B. Hayden (Ed.), *Lithic use-wear analysis* (pp. 133–135). New York: Academic.
Huang, Y., & Knutsson, K. (1995). Functional analysis of middle and upper paleolithic quartz tools from China. *Tor, 27,* 7–46.
Huet, B. (2006). *De l'influence des matières premières lithiques sur les comportements technoéconomiques au Paléolithique moyen: l'exemple du Massif armoricain (France)*. PhD, Université de Rennes 1.
Hurcombe, L. (1992). *Use wear analysis and obsidian: Theory, experiments and results. (Sheffield Archaeological Monographs 4)*. Sheffield: J. R. Collis.
Ibáñez, J. J., González Urquijo, J., & Rodríguez Rodríguez, A. (2007). The evolution of technology during the PPN in the Middle Euphrates: A view from use-wear analysis of lithic tools. In L. Astruc, D. Binder, & F. et Briois (Eds.), *Technical systems and near eastern PPN communities* (pp. 153–165). Antibes: Editorial APDCA.
Ibáñez, J. J., González Urquijo, J., & Rodríguez Rodríguez, A. (2008). Analyse fonctionnelle de l'outillage lithique de Mureybet. In J. J. Ibáñez (Ed.), *Le site néolithique de Tell Mureybet (Syrie du Nord). En hommage à Jacques Cauvin. BAR Internacional Series* (Vol. 1843(I), pp. 363–405). Oxford: Archaeopress.
Iovino, M. R. (1996). La Funzione dell'ossidiana: un approccio sperimentale al problema. *Origini, 20,* 71–108.
Kamminga, J. (1982). *Over the edge*. Occasional Papers in Anthropology, 12, University of Queensland, Australia.
Kay, M. (1996). Microwear analysis of some Clovis and experimental chipped stone tools. In G. Odell (Ed.), *Stone tools: Theoretical insights into human prehistory* (pp. 315–344). New York: Plenum.
Kazaryan, H. (1993). Butchery knives in the Mousterian Sites of Armenia. In P. Anderson, S. Beyries, M. Otte, & H. Plisson (Eds.), *Traces et Fonction: Les Gestes Retrouvés* (pp. 79–85). Liège: ERAUL, No. 50, Université de Liège.
Keeley, L. H. (1980). *Experimental determination of stone tools uses. A micro-wear analysis. Prehistory, archaeology and ecology series*. Chicago: The University of Chicago Press.
Keeley, L., & Toth, N. (1981). Microwear polishes on early stone tools from Koobi Fora, Kenya. *Nature, 293,* 464–465.
Knight, J. (1991). Vein quartz. *Lithics, 12,* 37–56.

Knutsson, K. (1986). SEM analysis of wear features on experimental quartz tools. *Early Man News, 9/10/11*, 35–46.
Knutsson, K. (1988a). *Patterns of tool use: Scanning electron microscopy of experimental quartz tools*. Aun 10. Societas Archaeologica Upsaliensis, Uppsala.
Knutsson, K. (1988b). Chemical etching of wear features on experimental quartz tools. In S. L. Olsen (Ed.), *Scanning electron microscopy in archaeology. BAR International Series* (Vol. 452, pp. 117–153). Oxford: Tempus Reparatum.
Knutsson, K., & Lindé, K. (1990). Post-depositional alterations or wear marks on quartz tools, preliminary observations on an experiment with aeolian abrasion. In M. R. Séronie-Vivien & M. y Lenoir (Eds.), *Le silex de sa genèse à l'outil* (pp. 607–618). Bordeaux: Cahiers du Quaternaire, 17, Éd. C.N.R.S.
Knutsson, K., Dahlquist, B., & Knutsson, H. (1988). Patterns of tool use. The microwear analysis of the quartz and flint assemblage from the Bjurselet site, Vasterbotten, Northern Sweden. In S. Beyries (Ed.), *Industries Lithiques. Tracéologie et Technologie* (Vol. 411, pp. 253–294). Oxford: BAR International Series.
Kononenko, N. (2011). Experimental and archaeological studies of use-wear and residues on obsidian artefacts from Papua New Guinea. *Technical Reports of the Australian Museum, Online, 21*, 1–244.
Kononenko, N., Bedford, S., & Reepmeyer, C. (2010). Functional analysis of late Holocene flaked and pebble stone artefacts from Vanuatu, Southwest Pacific. *Archeology in Oceania, 45*, 13–20.
Lazuén, T., Fábregas, R., Lombera, A., & Rodríguez, X. P. (2011). La gestión del utillaje de piedra tallada en el Paleolítico Medio de Galicia. El nivel 3 de Cova Eirós (Triacastela, Lugo). *Trabajos de Prehistoria, 68*(2), 7–28.
Leipus, M. (2006). *Análisis de los modos de uso prehispánicos de las materias primas líticas en el Sudeste de la Región Pampeana: Una aproximación funcional*. Tesis Doctoral no publicada. Facultad de Ciencias Naturales y Museo, UNLP.
Leipus, M., & Mansur, M. E. (2007). El análisis funcional de base microscópica aplicado a materiales heterogéneos. Perspectivas metodológicas para el estudio de las cuarcitas de la región pampeana. In C. Bayón, et al. (Eds.), *Arqueología en las Pampas* (pp. 179–200). Buenos Aies: Sociedad Argentina de Antropología.
Lemorini, C. (2000). *Reconnaître des tactiques d'explotation du milieu au paléolithique Moyen. La contribution de l'analyse fonctionelle. Étude fonctionelle des industries lithiques de Grotta Breuil (Latium, Itale) et de la Combette (Bonnieux, Valcluse, France)*. BAR S858. Archaeopress, Oxford.
Lewenstein, S. (1981). Mesoamerican obsidian blades: An experimental approach to function. *Journal of Field Archaeology, 8*, 175–188.
Lewenstein, S. (1991). Edge angles and tool function among the Maya: A meaningful relationship? In T. Hester & H. Shafer (Eds.), *Maya stone tools* (pp. 207–217). Madison: Prehistory.
Lombard, M. (2011). Quartz-tipped arrows older than 60 ka: Further use-trace evidence from Sibudu, KwaZulu-Natal, South Africa. *Journal of Archaeological Science, 38*, 1918–1930.
Mansur, M. E. & Lasa, A. (2005). Diversidad artefactual VS especialización funcional. Análisis del IV componente de Túnel I (Tierra del Fuego, Argentina). *Magallania (Chile) 33* (2), 69–91.
Mansur, M. E. (1982). Microwear analysis of natural and use striations: New clues to the mechanisms of striation formation. *Studia Praehistorica Belgica, 2*, 213–234.
Mansur, M. E. (1999). *Análisis funcional de instrumental lítico: problemas de formación y deformación de rastros de uso*. In Actas Del XII Congreso Nacionalde Arqueologia Argentina, La plata, pp. 355–366.
Mansur-Franchomme, M. E. (1987). *El análisis funcional de artefactos líticos*. Buenos Aires: Cuadernos Serie Técnica 1, Instituto Nacional de Antropología.
Mansur-Franchomme, M. E. (1988). *Tracéologie et technologie: quelques données sur l'obsidienne. Industries Lithiques. Tracéologie et Technologie* (Vol. 411, pp. 29–47). Oxford: BAR International Series.
Moncel, M. -H., Borel, A., Lombera, A., Sala, R., & Deniaux, B. (2008). Quartz et quartzite dans le site de Payre (MIS 7 et 5, Ardèche, France): données techno-économiques sur la gestion de roches locales au Paléolithique moyen. Comptes Rendus. *Palevol, 7*, 441–451.

Odell, G. H. (1983). Problèmes dans d'étude des traces d'utilisation. Traces d'utilisation sur les outils néolithiques du Proche Orient. Travaux de la maison de l'orient n° 5, pp. 17–24.

Pant, R. K. (1989). Etude microscopique des traces d'utilisation sur les outils de quartz de la Grotte de l'Arago, Tautavel, France. *L'Anthropologie, 9*(3), 689–704.

Plisson, H. (1985). *Etude fonctionelle des outillages lithiques préhistoriques par l'analyse des micro-usures: recherche méthodologique et archéologique*. Thèse de Doctorat présentée à l'Université Paris I.

Plisson, H. (1986). Analyse des polis d'utilisation sur le quarzite. *Early Man News, 9/10/11*, 47–49. (Tübingen).

Plisson, H. & Mauger, M. (1988). Chemical and mechanical alteration of microwear polishes: an experimental approach. *Helinium XXVIII 2*, 3–16.

Plisson, H., & Lompré, A. (2008). Technician or researcher? A visual answer. In L. Longo & N. Skakun (Eds.), *"Prehistoric Technology" 40 years later: Functional studies and the Russian legacy*. BAR (Vol. 1783, pp. 503–508). Oxford: Archaeopress.

Poupeau, G., Le Bourdonnec F. X., Dubernet, S., Scorzelli, R. B., Duttine, M., & Carter, T. (2007). Tendances actuelles dans la caractérisation des obsidiennes pour les études de provenance. *Archéosciences, 31*, 79–86.

Rodríguez Rodríguez, A. C. (1993a). *La industria lítica de la isla de La Palma. Cuevas de San Juan, un modelo de referencia*. Tesis Doctoral (1990), en microfichas. Secretariado de Publicaciones de la Universidad de La Laguna.

Rodríguez Rodríguez, A. C. (1993b). *Analyse fonctionnelle des outillages lithiques en basalte de l'île de La Palma (Iles Canaries)*. Prémiers résultats. Actes du Colloque Le Geste Retrouvé á Liege 1990. ERAUL 50, pp. 295–301.

Rodríguez Rodríguez, A. C. (1997). Primeras experiencias de análisis funcional en los instrumentos de basalto tallado de Canarias. El ejemplo del material prehistórico de la isla de La Palma. *Vegueta, 3*, 29–46.

Rodríguez Rodríguez, A. C. (1998). Traceología de las obsidianas canarias. Resultados experimentales. *El Museo Canario LIII, 53*, 21–58.

Rodríguez Rodríguez, A. C. (1999). The reconstruction of ancient leather technology or how to mix methodological approaches. *Urgeschichtliche Materialhefte, 14*, 99–110.

Rodríguez Rodríguez, A. (2009). Use-wear analysis on volcanic grainy rocks: Problems and perspectives. The exemple of Canary Island. Material. In M. de Araújo & I. Clemente (Eds.), *Recent functional studies on non flint stone tools: Methodological improvements and archaeological inferences*. Lisboa: CD Publication, 26–45.

Semenov, S. A. (1957). *Pervobitnaya Tejnika*. Materiali y Isledovania po Arjeologuii SSSR. n° 54. Moskva. Traducción al inglés: Prehistoric Technology. Cory, Adams and Mackay, London. 1964.Traducción al castellano: Tecnología Prehistórica (Estudio de las herramientas y objetos antiguos a través de las huellas de uso). Akal Editor. Madrid. 1981.

Semenov, S. A. (1972). Obsidian knives from burials in the crater of Ngorongoro Volcano. *Kratie soobschenia Instituta arkheologii, 131*, 31–35. (in Russian).

Setzer, T. J. (2004). *Use-wear experiments with Sardinian Obsidian: Determining its function in the neolithic*. PhD Master of Arts, Department of Anthropology, College of Arts and Sciences University of South Florida.

Sussman, C. (1985). Microwear on quartz: Fact or fiction? *World Archaeology, 17*(1), 101–111.

Sussman, C. (1987). Résultats d'une étude des microtraces d'usure sur un échantillon d'artefacts d'Olduvai (Tanzanie). *L'Anthropologie, 91*, 375–380.

Sussman, C. (1988). *A microscopic analysis of use-wear polish formation on experimental quartz tools* (Vol. 395). Oxford: BAR International Series.

Tallavaara, M., Manninen, M. A., Hertell, E., & Rankama, T. (2010). How flakes shatter: A critical evaluation of quartz fracture analysis. *Journal of Archaeological Science, 37*, 2442–2448.

Toselli, A., Pijoan, J., & Barceló, J. A. (2002). La descripción de trazas de uso en materias primas volcánicas:Rresultados preliminares de un análisis estadístico descriptivo. In I. Clemente, R. Risch, & J. Gibaja (Eds.), *Análisis Funcional. Su aplicación al estudio de sociedades prehistóricas. BAR International Series* (Vol. S1073, pp. 65–79). Oxford: Archeopress.

Tringham, R. C., Cooper, G., Odell, G., Voytek, B., & Whitman, A. (1974). Experimentation in the formation of edge damage: A new approach to lithic análisis. *Journal of Field Archaeology, 1,* 171–196.

Tykot, R. H., Iovino, M. R., Martinelli, M. C., & Beyer, L. (2006). *Ossidiana da Lipari: le fonti, la distribuzione, la tipologia e le tracce d'usura.* Atti del XXXIX Riunione Scientifica dell'Istituto Italiano di Preistoria e Protostoria: Materie prime e scambi nella preistoria italiana, Firenze, 25–27 November 2004, pp. 592–597.

Vaughan, P. C. (1981). Microwear analysis of experimental flint and obsidian tools. *Staringia, 6,* 90–91. (Third international flint symposium).

Vaughan, P. C., & Perlès, C. (1983). Pièces lustrées, travail des plantes et moisson à Franchti (Grèce). In M. C. Cauvin (Ed.), *Traces d'utilisation sur les outils néolithiques du Proche-Orient* (pp. 209–222). Lyon: CNRS.

Chapter 6
Keys to the Identification of Prehension and Hafting Traces

Veerle Rots

6.1 Introduction

After the pioneering years (Keeley 1980; Odell 1980; Semenov 1964), use-wear analysis has gradually developed towards a valued method within prehistoric research for identifying stone tool use. Prehensile wear (i.e., wear resulting from the friction with the hand or hafting arrangement during use) enjoyed less attention in the early days, aside from some notable exceptions (Odell 1981, 1994; Owen and Unrath 1989; Stordeur 1987a), largely due to the less explicit wear patterns that were assumed to result from the friction between a stone tool and its haft. Recently, prehensile wear gained renewed interest partially because hafting became an important element in discussions on the behavioural capacities of early humans (Ambrose 2001, 2010). At the same time, a more systematic examination of prehensile wear resulted in the definition of traits that allow a distinction between hand-held and hafted stone tools as well as the identification of the hafting arrangement used (Rots 2003, 2004, 2010).

Aside from the importance of being able to determine which tools were used hafted, an adequate examination of prehensile wear is also an essential part of any microwear analysis for other reasons. Firstly, it is necessary to understand all forms of wear that may be visible on a tool surface in order to understand the variability in trace features and to be able to attribute each trace to a correct cause. Secondly, it is essential for understanding the tool as a whole. The prehensile part is an undividable part of the tool; whether or not a handle was present determines how a stone tool was used and manipulated, how much pressure could have been exerted, etc. Finally, the presence or not of hafted tools within an assemblage has important

V. Rots (✉)
Service de Préhistoire, University of Liège, Quai Roosevelt 1B, 4000 Liège, Belgium
e-mail: veerle.rots@ulg.ac.be

consequences for adequately understanding a site and its context, as well as broader technological evolutions and human behavioural capacities (Ambrose 2010).

In this article I present a summary of the results from the methodological work that was performed on prehensile wear (Rots 2002a, 2010), including the main distinctive traits that allow the identification of hand-held and hafted stone tools in the archaeological record. For details regarding the importance of being able to identify hafted stone tools in archaeological assemblages I refer to Rots (2003).

6.2 Experimental Program

In order to be able to examine whether prehensile wear actually forms and whether it is sufficiently recurring in its formation and characteristics, a large-scale experimental program was set up. Attention was focused on the formation process of prehensile wear and on the variables influencing this process. Aside from being able to determine if, for instance, hafting wear forms during use and hardly during the hafting process itself, it was also possible to confirm that prehensile wear has sufficiently distinctive traits to distinguish it from wear resulting from other causes. It also proved recurring in its formation. Different dominant and secondary variables could be identified. Dominant variables consist of a tool's use and hafting mode and have a significant influence on the formation process of prehensile wear; secondary variables consist of a tool's morphology, its raw material, etc. and cause only minor variations on the trace pattern.

The experimental reference collection consists of about 600 hafted stone tools (e.g. Rots 2002a, 2010). Various hafting arrangements (juxtaposed, male, with bindings or with resin, etc.) and various hafting materials (wood, bone, antler, etc.) were used; tools were used in different craft activities for various use durations (for details, see Rots 2010). In addition, experiments with hand-held stone tools were performed, as well as specific experiments concerning various production methods, transport activities, fractures, etc. The current experimental reference set contains more than 1700 experimental pieces and it is still continuously expanding. This reference set is considered to be sufficiently large to understand the variability in trace formation following different trace causes, and to understand the variability in prehensile wear formation and patterning.

6.3 Prehensile Wear: general features

The systematic experimental program resulted in the proposition of a number of traits that allow distinguishing between different forms of prehensile wear (Table 6.1). The observation of a clear boundary in the wear traces between the used and hafted portion is an important argument for identifying hafted use. This boundary may consist of varying wear traces such as a suddenly differing polish,

6 Keys to the Identification of Prehension and Hafting Traces

Table 6.1 Microscopic wear traits that allow the distinction between hand-held and hafted tools

Trace attribute	Prehension	Hafting	
		Wrapping	"Real" handle
Boundary between use and prehensile part			
Presence	Absent	Yes (best observable on edges)	Yes (best observable on edges)
Polish	No boundary (far intrusion towards working edge)	Abrupt start of limited polish	Abrupt start of potentially different polish (differs in distribution, extension, etc.)
Scarring	No boundary	Abrupt start of different kind of scarring	Abrupt start of different kind of scarring: generally larger and more uneven in size (at limit often distinct patch)
Bright spots	No boundary	Potential boundary	Frequent boundary
Striations	Rare, no boundary	Rare, potential boundary	Rare, may mark haft boundary
Trace distribution			
Characteristics	Unequal over both edges	Equal (but boundary may be oblique)	Equal (but boundary may be oblique)
Macroscopic			
Importance	Rare	Intermediate	Frequent
Gloss	If present: general gloss, but more intense in some zones than in others	Absent	If present: spots, patches, streaks
*Location	All over tool, largely independent of microtopography	Absent	Restricted tool portion, partially dependent on tool morphology and microtopography
Scarring	Small, more or less evenly sized	Intermediate	Larger, generally uneven in size
Microscopic			
Most important trace(s)	Polish (also scarring)	Polish = rare, also scarring	Polish, scarring and bright spots
Polish			
Polish morphology	Corresponds to use polish	Depends on hafting material	Depends on hafting material
Number of polishes (all polishes)	One: use = prehension	2 or 3: use + wrapping (+ prehension polish when incomplete wrapping)	Depends on arrangement: 2 or 3: use + haft (+ bindings/wrapping/resin)
Polish location	All over tool	Restricted well-defined zone	Restricted well-defined zone
Scarring			
Scar morphology	Dominantly scalar, sliced, nibbling	Dominantly scalar, sliced, nibbling	Varied: often scalar, also trapezoidal, sliced (with variations), crushing, superposition

Table 6.1 (continued)

Trace attribute	Prehension	Hafting	
		Wrapping	"Real" handle
Scar termination	Tends to be smoother	In between	Tends to be more abrupt (i.e. for haft contact in particular)
Bright spots			
Bright spot characteristics	No real bright spots, but well-developed polish spots	Rare, generally small	Frequent, can be very large
Bright spot associations	Integrated in polish	Potentially with scarring, often isolated	Often with scarring = very significant
Striations			
Hafting striations	Insignificant	Insignificant	Insignificant
Striation orientation	Varied	Insignificant	Partially depends on action undertaken
Striation associations	None	Potentially with scarring	Very significant when associated with scarring
Rounding	Frequent	rare	Rare

an abrupt start of larger scars or a sudden scar concentration, often in association with what has been termed bright spots (Rots 2002b) or striations, etc. Given the important pressure that may be exerted on hafted stone tools in the area around the boundary, due to a lever effect, the traces in this zone are often better developed than in the remainder of the hafted part. In the case of hand-held tools, such a clear boundary is not observed; the transition between the used and hand-held portion is more gradual.

Another important factor that needs to be taken into account when examining haft boundaries is the fact that worked material particles may accumulate near the haft boundary. Following the friction during continued use, a distinct polish concentration may form just above the haft boundary. Its characteristics are determined by the worked material particles and are independent of the hafting arrangement aside from the fact that some arrangements may allow an intrusion of worked material particles due to which this polish could extend somewhat beyond the haft boundary. This was, for instance, observed for male split hafting arrangements fixed with bindings and used to hoe earth (Rots 2010).

6.3.1 Prehension Wear

Prehension is here defined as manual grasping without any intermediate wrapping or other material. Any traces that result are thus the consequence of the friction between the naked hand and the stone tool during use. Previous studies have already suggested that this friction only causes limited wear formation, mainly consisting of a light meat-like polish (Owen and Unrath 1989). In the experiments, scarring

6 Keys to the Identification of Prehension and Hafting Traces   87

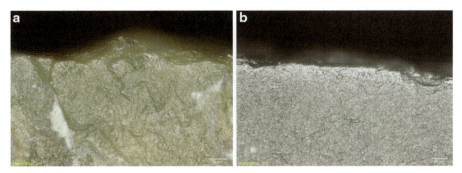

Fig. 6.1 Prehension polish determined by worked material: **a** on the ventral medial left edge of exp. 22/59, used to groove wood for 1 h (200×); **b** on the ventral proximal right edge of exp. 19/3C, used to groove dry antler for 2 h (200×)

Fig. 6.2 Explicit prehension polish on the ventral proximal right edge of exp. 19/3C, used to groove dry antler for 2 h (200×)

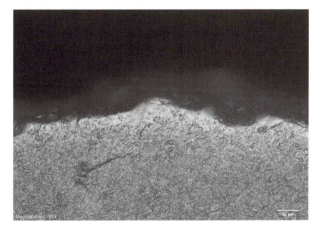

and polish were identified as the main traces that form as a result of hand-held use. While the scar presence and characteristics are quite systematic for all hand-held tools and are only determined by factors as the presence of retouch, etc. the formation of prehension polish is different. The dominant variable in the formation of prehension polish proved to be the activity that is performed, more in particular the worked material. The more "dust" comes off the worked material during use, the more this dust will quickly cover the hands and the more friction polish will result. This implies that the worked material actually determines what kind of prehension polish is produced (Fig. 6.1a, 6.1b).

In the case of "dusty" materials, such as antler, bone, schist, etc. the prehension polish is very similar to the use polish. Morphologically, it largely shows the same characteristics, only its distribution and extension do not correspond to what is expected for use-wear. In some cases, it can be so well-developed that confusion may arise if one is not aware that prehension may result in such explicit polish formation and if the distribution is not critically evaluated (Fig. 6.2). More in particular,

Fig. 6.3 Prehension polish that can be confused with transversal use motion on the ventral proximal right edge of exp. 19/3C, used to groove dry antler for 2 h (200×)

Fig. 6.4 Limited prehension polish from direct finger contact ("meat"-like polish) on the ventral medial right edge of exp. 12/6, used for cutting wet snake hide for 45 min (200×)

I would expect that confusion is sometimes possible with a transversal use motion (Fig. 6.3). One could therefore wonder whether certain tools with multiple use zones, located on the extremity and lateral edges (e.g., of blades) and for which two use motions were identified, were in reality not just hand-held tools of which the extremity was used while the polish on the lateral edges is actually a well-developed prehension polish.

In the case of "clean" activities, such as hide working without abrasives, wood working, etc. little dust from the material worked covers the hands during use and thus the prehension polish that may form is mainly caused by the friction with the flesh of the hands. It remains limited and it can be classified as a kind of meat polish (Fig. 6.4).

As a consequence, wear evidence from tool use necessarily needs to be included in the analysis when one wants to reliably identify prehension wear. The main traits of prehension wear are summarised in Table 6.1.

Fig. 6.5 Different hafting arrangements: (*left*) a juxtaposed hafting in which the stone tool is fixed on a wooden haft with bindings; (*right*) a wrapping with leather bindings

6.3.2 Hafting Wear

Hafting wear includes all wear resulting from the friction with an intermediate material, be it a wrapping of some sort, a handle or materials used for fixing the stone tool in or on a handle (Fig. 6.5). In terms of the degree of friction that may occur between the stone tool and its hafting arrangement during use, arrangements involving an actual handle will potentially cause more friction than wrappings. The handle functions as a lever, which puts a lot of stress on the stone tool unless a glue of some sort is used.

The hafting trace formation process proves to be determined by different variables and again, tool use is an important factor. A tool's motion determines the distribution of hafting traces over the hafted part. A percussion motion (hoeing, axing, etc.) results in a more or less even distribution over the whole hafted part. A scraping or grooving motion results in better developed hafting wear in the area around the haft boundary and on the most proximal part as a result of the lever effect of the handle during use. A drilling or perforating motion results in a distinction between a well-developed polish on the central part of the tool (i.e., dorsal ridges mainly) and scarring on the lateral edges. The material worked determines the intensity of the hafting traces. The more resistant the material worked, the better developed the hafting traces. As a result, hoeing wood results in better developed hafting traces

Table 6.2 Microscopic wear traits that allow the distinction between different hafting modes

Trace attribute	Juxtaposed hafting	Male split hafting	Male hafting	Wrapping
Polish				
Number of polishes	Two: haft + bindings	Two: haft + bindings	One: bindings	One: bindings; sometimes two: prehension polish
Polish frequency	Haft = bindings	Haft > bindings	Only haft	Only bindings (> prehension polish)
Polish morphology	cf. usewear	cf. usewear	cf. usewear	cf. usewear
Opposition	Dorsal versus ventral	Centre tool versus edges	No opposition	No opposition (only with butt: prehension polish)
Concentration haft polish	Ventral contact: most proximal & haft boundary	Dorsal medial ridge, bulb	Dorsal ridges, medial edges, ventral butt	None
Concentration binding polish	Dorsal contact: dorsal ridges	Edges	None	No real concentrations
Scarring				
Scar morphology				
*Sliced	Present	Present	Absent (exception: perforating, drilling)	Present
*Crushing	Poor	Poor	High	Poor
Morphological detail				
*Sliced into scalar scars	Present	Present	Absent (exception: perforating, drilling)	Present
Scar initiation				
*Straight into curved	Present	Present	Absent (exception: perforating, drilling)	Present
*Curved	Present	Present	Absent (exception: perforating, drilling)	Present
*Twisted	Present	Present	Absent (exception: perforating, drilling)	Present
Scar termination				
*Snap	Present	Present	Tends towards "rare"	Present
*Feather	Present	Present	Tends towards "rare"	Present
*Hinge	Tends towards "rare"	Tends towards "rare"	Present	Tends towards "rare"
*Step	Tends towards "rare"	Tends towards "rare"	Present	Tends towards "rare"
*Vertical	Present	Present	Tends towards "rare"	Present

Table 6.2 (continued)

Trace attribute	Juxtaposed hafting	Male split hafting	Male hafting	Wrapping
*Superposition	Tends towards "rare"	Tends towards "rare"	Present	Tends towards "rare"
Scar size	Not distinctive	Not distinctive	Not distinctive	Not distinctive
Scar depth	Not distinctive	Not distinctive	Not distinctive	Not distinctive
Scar intrusiveness				
*Intrusive scars	Present	Present	Tends towards "rare"	Present
Scar definition	Not distinctive	Not distinctive	Not distinctive	Not distinctive
Scar distribution				
*Alternating	Tends towards "rare"	Rare	Present	Absent
*Bifacial	Absent	Absent	Present	Absent
*Continuous	Rare	Rare	Present	Rare
Scar pattern				
*Crushed initiations	Rare	Rare	Present	Rare
*(Inverse) skewed saw pattern	Present	Present	Absent	Present
*Clear intrusion/notch	Rare	Rare	Present	Rare
Scar interpretability	Moderate	Moderate	High	High

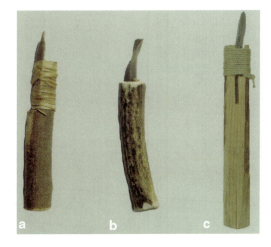

Fig. 6.6 Haft types: **a** Juxtaposed hafting; **b** male hafting; **c** male split hafting

for a given use duration than hoeing earth. Similarly, scraping bone results in better developed hafting traces for a given use duration than scraping hide.

The exact hafting arrangement determines the layout of the traces over the hafted part and some of the trace characteristics (e.g. binding scars) (Table 6.2). Three main haft types can be considered in the case of flint or other chipped stone tools (Fig. 6.6). A male arrangement (i.e. the stone tool is inserted into a hole of the

Fig. 6.7 Intense edge damage in the case of a male hafting in antler on the dorsal medial right edge of exp. 10/13, used for chiselling wood for 32 min (10×)

handle) results in the same kind of wear over the entire hafted part. A juxtaposed arrangement leads to a different pattern on the dorsal versus the ventral face. And finally, a male split arrangement (i.e. the lithic tool is inserted in a cleft of the handle) results in a different wear pattern between the centre of the stone tool and the edges (independent of the face). In addition, only a male arrangement has an important impact on the edge, which can result in intense scarring (Fig. 6.7). Of peculiar interest is the use of bindings, which are necessary in the case of juxtaposed or male split arrangements. Bindings cause the formation of a very typical scar in terms of its morphology and initiation (Fig. 6.8) that can be linked with binding use in all but one case, on the condition that a use origin can be excluded. Only when the tool is used for drilling or perforating, a similar scar type may result in the hafted area even when no bindings are used. In all other cases, it is definitely linked with bindings. Given that a use-wear analysis can easily set light on this issue, no interpretative problems should arise. The use of resin often hinders trace production, but this also depends on how the tool is extracted from its haft. When no heating is used and the resin is fractured (e.g. by percussion), very distinct friction spots are formed (Fig. 6.9). In all other cases, the absence of scarring or polish in a well-delimited area forms the most important criterion to infer resin use.

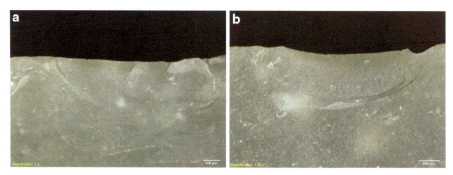

Fig. 6.8 Scarring from contact with bindings: a on the ventral medial right edge of exp. 10/17, used for chiselling wood for 40 min, fixed on a juxtaposed antler haft with dried leather bindings (applied wet) (20×); b on the ventral medial right edge of exp. 10/30, used for chiselling wood for 30 min, fixed in a male split wooden haft with leather bindings (25×)

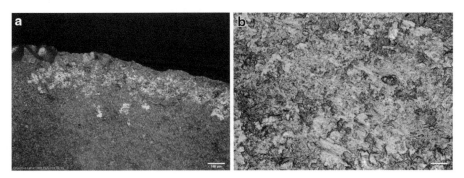

Fig. 6.9 Residual resin friction spots: **a** on the dorsal medial right edge of exp. 22/46 (100×); **b** on the ventral bulb of exp. 22/45 (200×). Both tools were used for grooving wood for 1 h, and were hafted with resin in a wooden haft

Table 6.3 Microscopic wear traits that allow the distinction between a haft made out of wood or out of hard animal matter (bone/antler)

Trace attribute	Hard animal matter	Wood
Polish		
Polish morphology	cf. usewear	cf. usewear
Typical morphology	Appears at moderate development	Appears at poor development
Polish development	Quicker moderately developed	Longer poorly developed
Polish interpretability	Slightly better interpretable	Slightly less interpretable
Polish extension	Poor presence	Moderate presence
	Tends to be concentrated on outer edge/ridge	Tends to follow microtopography
Scarring		
Scar initiation	Narrow = present	Narrow = absent
Scar termination	Abrupt	Non-abrupt
Scar definition	Moderate to well	Ill to moderate
Bright spots		
Bright spot amount	Few to moderate	Few
Bright spot size	Moderate	Small
Striations		
Striation amount	Few to moderate	Few
Striation orientation	Perpendicular	Not preferential
Rounding		
	Insignificant	Insignificant

The hafting material determines the morphology of the traces and polish proves to be most significant, while scarring can be used as supportive evidence (Table 6.3). Interpretations are based on the same criteria as in the case of use-wear, on the condition that the small differences in trace characteristics (e.g. distribution) mentioned above are taken into account. Overall, hafting polishes are not extremely well-developed. The best-developed areas are generally located on the ridges and when tools are used for at least 30 min, they are generally diagnostic (Figs. 6.10, 6.11, 6.12).

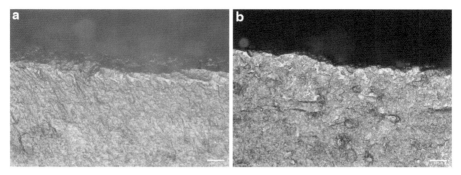

Fig. 6.10 Polish from a contact with a wooden haft: **a** poorly developed wood haft polish on the dorsal proximal ridge of exp. 1/2, used for hoeing wood for 2 min (200×); **b** well-developed wood haft polish on the dorsal medial ridge of exp. 1/1, used for hoeing wood for 30 min (200×). Both tools were fixed on a juxtaposed wooden haft with leather bindings

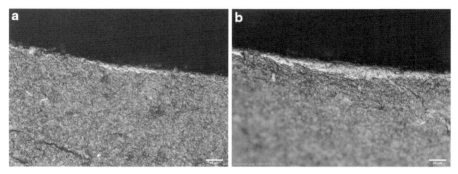

Fig. 6.11 Polish from a contact with an antler haft: **a** poorly developed antler haft polish on the dorsal proximal ridge of exp. 10/26; **b** well-developed antler haft polish on the dorsal proximal ridge of exp. 10/26 (200×). The tool was used for hoeing wood for 2 min and it was fixed on a juxtaposed antler haft with vegetal bindings

Fig. 6.12 Polish from the contact with vegetal bindings on the dorsal medial ridge of exp. 9/4, used for hoeing earth for 4 h, fixed on a juxtaposed wooden haft with lime tree bindings (200×)

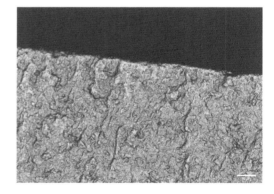

6.4 Step-By-Step Analytical Procedure

In order to aid the inexperienced analyst in an examination of prehensile wear, a systematic analytical procedure is proposed here. This procedure was previously published in comparable form in Rots (2010). It needs to be stressed that a close examination of prehensile wear necessitates a personal experimental reference collection as one cannot only base oneself on published pictures that are always selections out of more elaborate and complex trace patterns. Published pictures serve as general reference of the kind of wear one can expect.

6.4.1 Choice of Method

The adequacy of a certain method depends on the research question. I focus here on the examination of wear traces only—residues are dealt with in chapter 1 and 11 of this volume. Nevertheless, it is evident that if the preservation conditions of the site and the assemblage are sufficient for a potential preservation of residues, the analytical approach has to be adapted accordingly. Residues need to be examined before any examination of the blanks for wear traces can take place. After all, an examination of wear traces necessitates a manipulation of the blanks which may contaminate the residues, and cleaning may be necessary, which could remove the residues. For details on appropriate methods for residue analysis, I refer to the chapter 11 (this volume).

For wear traces, one of the following methods can be chosen depending on the available equipment and experience:

- Macroscopic analysis (no magnification, aside from perhaps a hand lens);
- Binocular stereoscopic microscope (low magnifications, generally less than 100×);
- Reflected-light microscope (high magnifications, generally between 50–500×), bright-field illumination;
- Scanning electron microscope;
- Confocal microscope.

When experienced, a macroscopic analysis may be appropriate for a first and superficial evaluation of the presence of hafted tools within an assemblage. It is, however, not suitable for more detailed identifications, independent of one's experience with prehensile wear. An examination with a binocular stereoscopic microscope and a reflected-light microscope differ both in the required analytical time and the type of results that can be expected. Hafting arrangements are often identifiable under low magnification; hafting materials are not, aside from perhaps their relative hardness. An analysis under high magnification is more time-consuming, but it allows for more exact hafting material identifications. Choosing between both depends on the raw material, the available equipment, the size of the tool sample to be analysed, the questions to be addressed and the required detail. The most suitable procedure is one that combines both approaches, as both have their advantages and shortcomings. In my opinion, the most successful procedure is gradual in nature; it starts from lower magnifications on a larger tool sample up to high magnifications on a smaller tool sample. This seems to combine the better of two worlds: sufficiently large samples and sufficient detail for a selection of tools. Where relevant, a scanning electron microscope can be used for more detailed examinations of selected samples (Anderson-Gerfaud 1980). It is far more cumbersome to use it for a systematic analysis of large tool samples. A confocal microscope, even though it is promising (Evans and Donahue 2008), has not yet proven its potential for improving prehensile wear identifications.

6.4.2 Relevant Initial Observations

At the start of the analysis, a general macroscopic examination provides a first insight in the assemblage.

6.4.2.1 Preservation Quality

The preservation quality of the archaeological material needs to be evaluated beforehand. It has been mentioned that polish and scarring are the most dominant trace types in the case of prehensile wear. Aside from those, also bright spots (Rots 2002b), striations and rounding may form. The presence of a macroscopically visible alteration or patination reduces or even excludes the chances of being able to rely on polish formation for reliable hafting inferences. As long as the edges are not abraded or smoothened due to post-depositional factors, scarring may still merit a close examination. Nevertheless, one should always try to rely on a combination of different trace types. Even when an assemblage may appear well-preserved macroscopically, a microscopic examination may prove otherwise. The occurrence of bright spots in a random distribution all over the tool (whether or not in association with an alteration polish, rounding, etc.) is crucial as this excludes bright spots from being used as evidence for arguing hafting. Also striations and rounding may have a post-depositional origin.

Next to post-depositional factors, also excavation may cause trace formation, mainly scarring and striations. As most traces are the result of contact with metal equipment, they are quite well distinguishable.

When alterations prove to be absent or minimal, a detailed examination of prehensile wear can take place without many problems. It is evident that well-preserved assemblages are always preferable. When alterations occur, the certainty level and the potential detail of the identifications decrease accordingly. Extra care should then be taken with certain trace types, such as polish and bright spots in particular. Thanks to the importance of trace patterning in the case of hafting, tools with explicit hafting wear may still be identifiable in spite of significant alterations. In most cases, no further detail can however be provided.

6.4.2.2 Raw Material Coarseness

On the whole, traces are less explicit on coarse-grained flints. This implies that macroscopic glosses tend to be rare, that polishes are generally somewhat less developed and bright spots more restricted in number and that scarring tends to be somewhat more abrupt in termination. Certainty levels may be slightly lower on a macroscopic level and perhaps also under low magnification.

6.4.2.3 Retouch

Retouch is an important feature to take into account as it reduces the possibilities of a straightforward identification of hafting, in particular on a macroscopic level, as it limits the chance of scarring (Odell 1981). Coarse retouch presents the greatest problem, while limited or fine retouch should not cause too much problems. Use scars are not to be confused with retouch; generally speaking, retouch tends to be more regular in morphology and more continuous in distribution, retouch scars also show a clear initiation often with crushing around the initiation point, etc.

6.4.2.4 Morphology

While some morphological features (transversal cross-section, butt protrusion, etc.; see Rots 2010) may influence the trace distribution or the location of trace concentrations, other features may be suggestive of hafting (e.g., tangs, notches) (Ferring 1975; Rots 2002c, 2005; Stordeur 1987b; Tillet 1995). The transversal convexity is particularly important for the location of the best-developed polishes. Ridges should be examined at their "flattest" and thus more prominent side first as the best-developed traces are to be expected there. The longitudinal curvature determines the ease of hafting, the amount of contact between the tool's face and the haft, and the necessity to remove the bulb of percussion (see Rots 2005 for an archaeological example). Male arrangements are less flexible, what the stone tool morphology concerns, than juxtaposed arrangements. Important longitudinal curves may limit the contact surface between tool and haft and determine the location of trace concentrations. The presence of tangs, notches, etc. does not *prove* that tools were used hafted, but they may be suggestive of the hafting arrangement once indubitable hafting wear is observed.

6.4.2.5 Fractures

Fractures may comprise of relevant information with regard to hafting. On average, hafted tools fracture more easily during use than hand-held ones. During resharpening, potential fractures may also be influenced by the presence of a handle (e.g., (Van Peer et al. 2008). In order to evaluate whether a fracture is hafting-related,

Fig. 6.13 Intense edge damage associated with a hafting fracture on the ventral proximal fracture edge of exp. 10/16, used to chisel wood for 30 min, fixed on a juxtaposed wooden haft with dried leather bindings (applied wet) (8×)

its location, initiation, termination and associated scarring need to be examined. Intense associated scarring is for instance indicative of a hafting cause (Fig. 6.13).

6.4.3 Tool Use

Tool use is a dominant variable in the formation of hafting traces, therefore, it is essential that tool use is known—if the used portion is preserved—in order to allow reliable hafting inferences.

6.4.3.1 Used Tool Portion

The typological working edge as well as every other potentially functional edge needs to be examined for suggestive macro-/microscopic use evidence, like scarring, polish, rounding of the outer edge, etc. The occurrence of more than one used portion is important in view of hafting. A haft limits the flexibility of stone tool use by selecting one part for use and by securing the other part. Unless when hafted tools are turned around in their haft for another use session, hafted tools generally have just one used portion. Different use zones could thus be an argument against hafting if one is certain that all traces are caused by the direct contact with the material worked in use. The identification of the used portion allows one to assess where a potential haft could be located approximately.

6.4.3.2 Distribution of Use-Wear Traces, i.e. Centralised or Not

A microscopic examination is most appropriate for adequately evaluating the use-wear distribution. Its extension is important with regard to the prehensile mode. For instance, a centralised use-wear distribution is indicative of hafting (Beyries and Rots 2008) even though it needs to be combined with an actual observation of hafting traces. Only a hafting arrangement that prevents the lateral inclination of a stone tool during use can cause a strictly centralised use-wear distribution (i.e., lateral hafting). It is mainly relevant for scraping activities. A decentralised use-wear distribution (independent of the degree of de-centralisation) may be the result of either hand-held or hafted use.

6.4.3.3 Worked Material and Use Motion

A magnification is required for an adequate evaluation of the exact worked material and use motion. The worked material is important for evaluating what kind of traces to expect in the case of hand-held use: processing schist, wood, bone/antler, may potentially result in a well-developed prehension polish. Some use motions exclude hand-held use (e.g., hoeing, axing). The combination of worked material and use motion gives an idea about what to expect for the hafting trace intensity and the general hafting trace pattern in the case of hafted use (see above). Knowledge on the exact tool use may also allow the exclusion of certain hafting arrangements or tool positions.

6.4.3.4 Relative Use Duration

An assessment of the minimal use duration allows an evaluation of the trace development to be expected for prehension or hafting wear. Only the last use cycle can be assessed based on use-wear given that resharpening at least partially removes these traces. Well-developed prehensile wear may consequently indicate a longer complete use cycle of the tools.

6.4.4 Hafted or Not?

The most important argument for distinguishing hafted and hand-held tools is the occurrence of some kind of boundary in the trace pattern, which only forms on hafted tools and which can consist of a number of traces:

- A suddenly differing polish distribution, extension and/or morphology. In contrast to a use-wear polish, a hafting polish generally lacks a real impact on the edge;

- An abrupt start of marked scarring or of a different kind of scarring. The scarring around the haft boundary is often more intense and larger than on the remaining hafted edges. It is generally uneven in size and it may form a patch;
- The (sudden) occurrence of bright spots and/or striations;
- An association of scarring and bright spots, or scarring and striations. These kinds of associations provide a strong argument in view of hafting.

A boundary that is observable on a macroscopic level is equally valid to one identified on a microscopic level, but the argument gains in strength if it is confirmed on different levels. An increase in magnification allows the observation of more traces, but there is a loss in overview, which should not be neglected given the importance of patterning for hafting. A low magnification analysis is therefore often very suitable for identifying potential haft boundaries. A number of additional traits that allow a distinction between hand-held and hafted tools are listed in Table 6.1.

6.4.5 Which Hafting Arrangement was Used?

For the determination of the hafting arrangement, adequate macroscopic data are rare and one should only rely on microscopic data (low or high power). Only general traits are included here, more details can be found in the included tables.

The *haft type* is interpreted based on a comparison between the traces on the dorsal face and those on the ventral face, between the traces in the centre of the tool and those on the edges (Table 6.2). If traces (polish morphology and scarring intensity in particular) differ between both faces, a juxtaposed haft is most likely. If traces are similar, a male-type arrangement is more likely. If there is no real impact on the edges, and if the traces on the edges differ from what is observed in the centre of the tool (e.g., ridges), a male split arrangement is most likely. When the traces on the ridges are not well developed, a distinction between a juxtaposed and male split haft may be hampered. For a distinction, one needs to focus on the polish intrusion on the edges in comparison with the tool morphology. When polish intrudes in lower zones, a contact with a binding material may be more likely given its softer nature. Obviously, one also needs to pay attention to differences that may be caused by the protrusion or not of the edges from their haft (i.e., for juxtaposed and male split hafting arrangements). When a stone tool is smaller than its haft, less scarring will form than when the edges protrude, given the lack of protection. In the same way, the influence of the bindings on the formation of edge polish will increase when edges protrude from their haft.

The *tool placement*, *direction* and the *orientation of the active part* can be derived based on the location of the used portion and the exact location of use-wear traces. Hafting traces are of secondary importance.

The *haft material* is more difficult to derive, given that dry wood is used for hafting and that it does not differ much in hardness in comparison to bone and antler. Nevertheless, distinctive elements concern differences in polish morphology and extension and in some scar characteristics (see Table 6.3): given its harder nature, antler results in a less intrusive polish and into more abrupt scarring than wood.

6 Keys to the Identification of Prehension and Hafting Traces

Table 6.4 Microscopic wear traits that allow a distinction between different types of bindings

Trace attribute	Leather bindings	Wet leather/intestines	Vegetal bindings
Polish			
Polish morphology	cf. usewear, but slightly brighter	cf. usewear	cf. usewear
Polish development	Tends to be moderate to important	Tends to be poor	Tends to be important
Polish linkage	Tends to be moderate to high	Tends to be low	Tends to be high
Polish extension	Several extensions, preferentially border and inner surface	Tends to be concentrated on outer edge	Tends to be distributed along microtopography
Polish interpretability	Tends to be moderate	Tends to be low	Tends to be high
Scarring			
Scar morphology			
*Sliced scars	Present	Present	Frequent, except when retouch
*Crushing	Present	Present	Absent, except when retouch
Scar intiation			
*Straight into curve	Present	Present	Present, except when retouch
*Curved	Present	Present	Present
*Twis ted	Present	Present	Present, except when retouch
Scar termination			
*Superposition	Frequent	Present	Rare, except when retouch
Scar definition	Not significant	Minor tendance to frequent well-defined scars	Minor tendance to frequent well-defined scars

The use of *bindings* is inferred based on the occurrence of very typical scars that were grouped under the category "binding scars": sliced and sliced into scalar scars mainly, with a curved or bent initiation (see Table 6.1, 6.4, Fig. 6.8). These scars occur in isolation or in small patches, and they are often most explicit around the haft boundary. A few causes must be excluded beforehand if these scars are to be used as evidence:

1. On a general morphological level, use and prehension may lead to similar scars, but these differ in location and distribution, etc.;
2. Male-hafted tools (direct contact) used in rotation may show similar scarring on the hafted edges not linked to the use of bindings. Next to scarring evidence, also polish characteristics may be used; polish (if sufficiently developed) is particularly useful for a distinction between different binding materials (see Table 6.4).

A *wrapping* reduces the amount of friction and thus also the trace intensity (see Table 6.5). *Resin* may prevent all trace formation, although some very typical and distinct resin polish spots may form (see Table 6.6, Fig. 6.9).

Table 6.5 Microscopic wear traits that allow the identification of the use of a (leather) wrapping

Trace attribute	Wrapping
Macroscopic	
Scarring	Decrease
Gloss	Decrease
Microscopic polish	
Polish morphology	Mixed polish
Polish development	Not significant
Polish extension	Slightly more extensive (and intrusive)
Microscopic scarring	
Number of damaged tool part	Decrease (significant)
Scar intensity	Minor decrease
Scar morphology	
*Sliced	Minor decrease (insignifcant)
*Nibbling	Increase
*Crushing	Decrease (significant)
*Elongated	Absent (needs confirmation)
Scar initiation	
*Narrow	Decrease
Scar termination	
*Non-abrupt (snap, feather)	Increase
*Abrupt (hinge, step)	Decrease
*Superposition	Decrease
Rounding	Minor increase

Table 6.6 Microscopic wear traits that allow the identification of resin use

Trace attribute	Resin use
POLISH	
nr of polished tool parts	important reduction
polish attribution	resin friction polish (other polishes are extermely rare)
polish extension	on surface or on border & inner surface
SCARRING	
nr of damaged tool parts	reduction
scar morphology	not significant
scar termination	increase in hinge terminations
scar size	reduction of very large scars
BRIGHT SPOTS	
bright spot attribution	resin friction (systematically)
bright spot cause	extraction from the haft mainly
STRIATIONS	
striation attribution	often to resin friction
striation cause	often to extraction from haft

6.5 Conclusion

The experimental program allowed the identification of traits that permit a distinction between hand-held and hafted stone tools in archaeological assemblages. Based on the described traits, prehensile wear should be recognisable and interpretable, and clues regarding the exact hafting arrangement used can be obtained. Nevertheless, a personal experimental reference collection remains essential during the analysis and one should not only rely on published pictures. This counts for all use-wear identifications. The interrelation between traces and trace types as well as detailed distributions and extensions are not easy to grasp in just a few pictures. When performing experiments, attention should be devoted to task completion instead of trace production in order to reconstruct the prehistoric use situation as reliable as possible.

I would like to stress that in spite of the efforts needed for integrating prehensile wear in larger functional studies, it is worth the investment given the importance of hafting for inferences regarding technological evolutions and past human behaviour and its complexity. In addition, it completes the understanding of the causes that may lead to wear formation and of the wear distribution and patterning on archaeological stone tools.

Acknowledgements I am indebted to the Research Foundation of K.U.Leuven and the Foundation for Scientific Research (FWO and FNRS-FRS) for supporting this research. I sincerely thank the *Chercheurs de la Wallonie* attached to the *Préhistosite de Ramioul* for performing the experiments on which this research is based.

References

Ambrose, S. H. (2001). Paleolithic technology and human evolution. *Science, 291,* 1748–1753.
Ambrose, S. H. (2010). Coevolution of composite-tool technology, constructive memory, and language. Implications for the evolution of modern human behaviour. *Current Anthropology, 51,* S135–S147.
Anderson-Gerfaud, P. (1980). A testimony of prehistoric tasks: Diagnostic residues on stone tool working edges. *World Archaeology, 12,* 181–193.
Beyries, S., & Rots, V. (2008). The contribution of ethnoarchaeological macro- and microscopic wear traces to the understanding of archaeological hide-working processes. In L. Longo & M. Della Riva (Eds.), *Proceedings of the congress "Prehistoric technology: 40 years later. Functional studies and the Russian legacy".* Verona, Italy, 20–23 April 2005, pp. 21–28.
Evans, A. A., & Donahue, R. E. (2008). Laser scanning confocal microscopy: A potential technique for the study of lithic microwear. *Journal of Archaeological Science, 35,* 2223–2230.
Ferring, C. (1975). The Aterian in North African prehistory. In F. Wendorf & A. E. Marks (Eds.), *Problems in prehistory: North Africa and the Levant* (pp. 113–126). Dallas: Southern Methodist University Press.
Keeley, L. H. (1980). *Experimental determination of stone tool uses: A microwear analysis.* Chicago: University of Chicago Press.
Odell, G. H. (1980). Toward a more behavioral-approach to archaeological lithic concentrations. *American Antiquity, 45,* 404–431.
Odell, G. H. (1981). The mechanics of use-breakage of stone tools: Some testable hypotheses. *Journal of Field Archaeology, 8,* 197–209.

Odell, G. H. (1994). Prehistoric hafting and mobility in the North-American midcontinent-examples from Illinois. *Journal of Anthropological Archaeology, 13,* 51–73.

Owen, L. R., & Unrath, G. (1989). Microtraces d'usures dues à la préhension. *l'Anthropologie, 93,* 673–688.

Rots, V. (2002a). *Hafting traces on flint tools: Possibilities and limitations of macro- and microscopic approaches.* Leuven: Katholieke Universiteit Leuven.

Rots, V. (2002b). Bright spots and the question of hafting. *Anthropologica et Praehistorica, 113,* 61–71.

Rots, V. (2002c). Are tangs morphological adaptations in view of hafting? Macro- and microscopic wear analysis on a selection of tanged burins from Maisières-Canal. *Notae Praehistoricae, 114,* 61–69.

Rots, V. (2003). Towards an understanding of hafting: The macro- and microscopic evidence. *Antiquity, 77,* 805–815.

Rots, V. (2004). Prehensile wear on flint tools. *Lithic Technology, 29,* 7–32.

Rots, V. (2005). Wear traces and the interpretation of stone tools. *Journal of Field Archaeology, 30,* 61–73.

Rots, V. (2010). *Prehension and hafting wear on flint tools. A methodology.* Leuven: Leuven University Press.

Semenov, S. A. (1964). *Prehistoric technology. An experimental study of the oldest tools and artefacts from traces of manufacture and wear.* London: Cory, Adams and Mackay.

Stordeur, D. (1987a). *La main et l'outil: manches et emmanchements préhistoriques.* Lyon: Maison de l'Orient Méditerranéen.

Stordeur, D. (1987b). Manches et emmanchements préhistoriques: quelques propositions préliminaires. In D. Stordeur (Ed.), *La main et l'outil: manches et emmanchements préhistoriques* (pp. 11–34). Lyon: Maison de l'Orient Mediterranéen.

Tillet, T. (1995). *Recherches sur l'Atérien du sahara méridional (bassins Tchadien et de Taoudenni): Position, chrono-stratigraphique, définition et étude comparative.* L'homme méditerranéen, Mélanges offerts à Gabriel Camps Professeur émérite de l'université de Provence, P.U.P., pp. 29–56.

Van Peer, P., Rots, V., & Vermeersch, P. M. (2008). A wasted effort at the quarry. Analysis and interpretation of an MSA lanceolate point from Taramsa-8, Egypt. *Paleoanthropology, 2008,* 234–250.

Chapter 7
Current Analytical Frameworks for Studies of Use–Wear on Ground Stone Tools

Laure Dubreuil, Daniel Savage, Selina Delgado-Raack, Hugues Plisson, Birgitta Stephenson and Ignacio de la Torre

7.1 Introduction

This chapter serves as a discussion of the framework currently used in use–wear studies of ground stone tools. What we present here is an update of an earlier paper (Dubreuil and Savage 2013), with revisions and contributions from other scholars on the topics of use–wear analysis and research design, raw material analysis, the equipment used in use–wear analysis and photography, residue analysis, as well as the framework developed at naked eye and high magnifications.

L. Dubreuil (✉) · D. Savage
Department of Anthropology, Trent University, Life and Health Sciences Building Block C, 2140 East Bank Dr. Peterborough, Peterborough, ON K9J 7B8, Canada
e-mail: lauredubreuil@trentu.ca

D. Savage
e-mail: danielsavage@trentu.ca

S. Delgado-Raack
Human Development in Landscapes, Christian-Albrechts Universität Kiel,
Johanna-Mestorf-Straße 2-6, 24118 Kiel, Germany
e-mail: sdelgadoraack@hotmail.com

H. Plisson
UMR 5199 PACEA, PPP Bâtiment B18, University of Bordeaux I,
Avenue des Facultés, 33405 Talence cedex, France
e-mail: hugues.plisson@u-bordeaux1.fr

B. Stephenson
In the Groove Analysis Pty, Ltd., 16 Charlane Avenue, Indooroopilly,
4068 Brisbane, QLD, Australia
e-mail: itg.analysis@gmail.com

I. de la Torre
Institute of Archaeology, University College London,
31-34 Gordon Square, London WC1H 0PY, UK
e-mail: i.torre@ucl.ac.uk

The category of "ground stone tools" (GST) encompasses objects which were manufactured and/or used according to motions such as percussion, pounding, pecking, grinding, abrasion, polishing, etc. The terms "macrolithic tools" or "non-flint implements" have also been proposed as synonyms for this category (e.g., Adams et al. 2009). Common GST types include hammerstones, abraders, grinding tools (e.g., grinding slabs/querns/metates used in conjunction with handstones/manos), as well as pounding (e.g., mortars and pestles) and cutting (axes and adzes) implements.

Large scale syntheses by Wright (1992b) in Southwest Asia, Adams (2002) in the American Southwest, and de Beaune (2000) in Europe, have shown that GST assemblage composition often varies substantially through time and according to geographic area. From a chronological perspective, tool types such as cupmarks, anvils, hammerstones, and pounders appear well represented in early prehistory (e.g., Leakey 1971; Willoughby 1987; Goren-Inbar et al. 2002; Mora and de la Torre 2005). Whereas sets of grinding slabs—handstones (also known as metates and manos) and other grinding implements make their earliest appearance in South Africa (e.g., McBrearty and Brooks 2000; Klein 2009, p. 537; Henshilwood et al. 2011) early in the Middle Stone Age (dated approximately between 300 ka and 50 ka following Klein 2009). Mortars and pestles emerged later, and some of the earliest manifestations are seen during the Upper Paleolithic period in Europe (43–11 ka, following Klein 2009, p. 666) and the Early Epipaleolithic (23.0–14.6 ka cal. BP, following Maher et al. 2011) in Southwest Asia (e.g., Semenov 1964, p. 134; Bar-Yosef 1980; Wright 1992, 1994; de Beaune 2004). Ground stone assemblages tend to become larger and more varied during the terminal Pleistocene–Early Holocene (for instance at Natufian and Jomon sites), a period which coincided with the development of semisedentary communities. Precursors of edge-ground tools, such as axes and adzes, often viewed as characteristic of the Neolithic period, can also be found in such contexts. Recent studies suggest that they appear even earlier in Australia (Geneste et al. 2012) and Japan (Takashi 2012). The subsequent proto-historic and historic periods coincide with major developments in GST technologies, including those related to metallurgy, the stabilization of querns into a solid platform, the invention of the hopper mill and rotary quern, as well as presses for the extraction of oil, and the development of water and wind-milling industries (e.g., Lidström-Holmberg 1998; Curtis 2001; Alonso Martinez 2002; Treuil 2002; Delgado-Raack and Risch 2008).

Semenov's (1957) pioneering work on use–wear included an analysis of axes, adzes, mortars, pestles, and abraders. However, unlike chipped stone implements, studies aimed at exploring use–wear formation on ground stones only expanded in the decades following the publication in 1964 of the English translation of Semenov's book. The aim of the present chapter is to discuss the methodological framework currently employed to study use–wear on ground stones, with a focus on noncutting types of GST. Some parallels in the characteristics of use–wear formation do exist between noncutting (e.g., hammerstones, abraders, polishers, grinding, and pounding implements) and cutting (e.g., knifes, axes, and adzes) GSTs, as they can be made of the same types of raw materials. However, their mode of operation differs significantly, which has a major impact on use–wear development. For similar reasons, use–wear formation on stone beads and pendants, which are sometimes included in the ground stone category, is not discussed in this paper. Before reviewing the methodological framework, we will first discuss the approach to research design for studies of GSTs.

7.2 GST Analysis: Use–wear Approach and Research Design

GST studies play a key role in investigating major anthropological questions, including the emergence of early hominid technology and complex cognitive abilities, the transition from foraging to farming, the rise of symbolic behavior, and hierarchical social organization as well as gender construction. Understanding the function of the GST is often central to these studies.

A few examples of such studies are briefly reviewed here. For instance, it has been recently suggested that percussive technology (hammerstones and anvils) might have been inherited from a human–chimpanzee clade (e.g., Mercader et al. 2007). The hypothesis that percussive technology could be a precursor to more complex stone knapping techniques is also under investigation (e.g., Carvalho et al. 2008; Haslam et al. 2009; McGrew 2010; Bril et al. 2012). Comparative technological and functional analysis of early hominin and modern primate percussive tools is one of the main avenues of research to explore these hypotheses.

For the Middle Stone Age or Middle Paleolithic, GST technology has been particularly discussed in the perspective of the origins of complex or "modern" behavior. In these contexts, ground stone analysis is critical for investigating the emergence of symbolism because of the common association of these tools with ochre remains (e.g., McBrearty and Brooks 2000; Van Peer et al. 2003; d'Errico et al. 2009; d'Errico and Stringer 2011). Functional analysis of GSTs is of major importance for better understanding the use of ochre and ocher processing techniques.

Moving forward in time, studies of Natufian GSTs demonstrate the importance of functional analysis for investigating the transition from foraging to farming. The Natufian corresponds to a transitional phase between hunter–gatherer and farmer adaptations in the Southern Levant. During this period, a significant increase in the relative abundance and typological diversity of GSTs is observed (e.g., Bar-Yosef 1980, 1981; Wright 1992a, 1994). These trends are often said to support the assumption of intensified plant exploitation during the Natufian period; however, direct evidence of this intensification is scarce, given the generally poor preservation of macrobotanical remains in Epipaleolithic contexts (e.g., Zohary et al. 2012; Miller 1991; Weiss et al. 2004; Dubreuil and Rosen 2010). Consequently, functional analyses of grinding implements are of prime importance for investigating potential changes in plant exploitation during the Natufian (see for instance, Dubreuil 2004, 2008, 2009; Dubreuil and Plisson 2010). These analyses are also essential for testing some of the most influential hypotheses proposed to explain the origins of farming, such as the broad spectrum revolution (Flannery 1969, 1973), or the development of socio-economic competition and feasting (Hayden 1990, 2004, 2009; Hayden et al. 2013). Hence, GSTs are key artifacts to explore major transformations associated with the development of farming communities, including changes in subsistence as well as in the social organization of production and consumption, and the development of socio-economic inequality and hierarchy (Wright 2000, 2014; Belfer-Cohen and Hovers 2005; Rosenberg 2008; Dubreuil and Plisson 2010). As underlined by Risch (2008), functional analysis is an important tool to investigate the social organization of labour, a decisive factor in the economic development of societies and of the production of surpluses.

At the site level, Adams (2002, pp. 46–56) lists a number of research questions which can be investigated through the study of GSTs, including: settlement continuity, duration and intensity; food processing activities and intensity of use; manufacturing or craft activities which took place at a site, as well as group affiliation. Several aspects of the GST assemblages can be analyzed to investigate these questions, such as the size of the tools, the numbers of tools and working surfaces, and the investment in tool manufacture, including the presence of comfort features (any feature which makes the tool more comfortable to use, Adams 2002, p. 19) as well as their spatial distribution (Delgado-Raack 2013). In general, and as with the larger anthropological issues mentioned earlier, identifying the function of GSTs plays a central role for investigating "site level" questions.

In archeology, the functional approach generally includes the complimentary fields of use–wear and residue analysis (Rots and Williamson 2004). For instance, use–wear analysis can provide information about the way a tool was used, while residue analysis can identify the processed material to a greater degree of precision. Kinetics is an important and often overlooked aspect, which can only be fully assessed by combining the use–wear approach with morphological analysis. The tool morphology provides essential data on the way the tool is operated, as the form is intrinsically linked to kinetics. However, ground stone tool morphology should be regarded as being mediated by various parameters, not only its function (Horsfall 1987). Moreover, as stressed by Sigaut (1991), there is commonly a range of kinetics a specific tool can be associated with. Sigaut (1991) draws on the example of a knife, noting that there are various ways of cutting depending on both, how the tool is held and moved. For example, a knife can be used to peel or cut, but can also be used as a screwdriver. In prehistoric chipped stone technology, the burin is a good example of a tool type once thought to have a single function, but which has been found to be associated with various kinetics, including engraving, grooving, scraping, boring, splitting (Plisson 2006), not to mention misidentified bladelet cores and other burin like artefacts. With regard to GSTs, a striking example of such functional variability is the use of handstone-like tools without a lower grinding slab to process hide (Adams 1988; Dubreuil and Grosman 2009). As will be discussed later, use–wear is a particularly useful approach to unravel the way a tool was used, as it allows assessing the working parts of the tools, the manner of prehension or handling, and the direction of the motion.

It is important to underline here that determining the matter processed and the kinetics only gives a partial definition of the technical function of the tool. According to Sigaut (1991), to fully understand the function of a tool, we need not only unravel the matter processed and the kinetics but also answer the following questions: who used the tool, for what, and when? The question "for what?" is at least partly related to the issue of intentionality, which includes not only the action (for instance, a mortar was used with a pestle operated according to a combination of pounding and grinding motion to reduce acorn into smaller particle) but also its purpose (for a family meal or for a party). Clearly, a comprehensive description of the function of a prehistoric tool, as defined here, is beyond the reach of our current analytical methods. Nevertheless, some key elements can be assessed, especially by combining functional studies with other approaches such as morphological, technological, typological, and spatial analysis.

What follows is an example of how use–wear studies and spatial data can be combined to explore the "for what" questions presented above. GSTs are sometimes found associated with graves. Ethnographic studies indicate that tools associated with graves can hold different meanings. These tools may, for instance, represent personal possessions, gifts, debt payments, offerings, or may reflect the funerary ritual itself (e.g., Ucko 1969; Binford 1971; Carr 1995). At the Natufian site of Hilazon, various types of GSTs were found associated with burials (Dubreuil and Grosman 2013). Among them, a small abrader shows wear patterns similar to those observed on pebbles used as pottery burnishers, yet pottery production does not appear until a much later period in the region. However, the burial pit in which the abrader was found was plastered with clay, which suggests the possibility that this abrader was used in the preparation of the burial pit into which it was later interred. In general, the spatial context can provide crucial data for understanding the function, context of use, discard behavior, and symbolic aspects of the ground stone implements (e.g., Lidström Holmberg 1998, 2004; Tsoraki 2007; Wright 2008, 2014; Roda Gilabert et al. 2012; Buonasera 2013; Delgado-Raack 2013).

Finally, it should be emphasized that the use–wear approach allows assessing the kinetics and the processed material corresponding not just to the last stage of utilization of the tool, but earlier stages as well. In fact, when traces are preserved, a wider range of utilization phases, including manufacture, hafting, and manipulation can be investigated using the use–wear approach. Identifying these phases, and reconstructing the history of each implement is an important step contributing to our understanding of the artifact function as defined by Sigaut (1991), and ultimately of past technological, economic, social, and symbolic systems. Nevertheless, the use–wear approach cannot be dissociated from a more general, technological study of archeological stone tools, as first conceived by Semenov (1964, see also Risch 2008). In this perspective, establishing the "sequence of wear" and the "life history" of artifacts is particularly helpful.

7.3 The Tool Life History and the Sequence Of Wear

The life history of a GST can encompass several stages (e.g., Nierlé 1983; Wright 1992; Dubreuil 2002; Adams 2002; Baysal and Wright 2005; van Gijn and Verbaas 2009; Dubreuil and Savage 2013) including: raw material procurement; manufacture; primary, secondary use etc.; recycling; discard; and lastly, postdepositional processes (see Table 7.1).

The reconstruction of the life history of a tool partly relies on the ability of the analyst to identify various types of wear on a tool and to organize them in a sequence according to their relative chronology. This can be achieved by looking for zones where different types of wear overlap. However, reconstructing the life history of an artifact based on use–wear is complex, as some of the stages of use can be difficult to isolate. In particular, distinguishing multifunctional from multiple-use or reused objects (sensus Adams 2002; Table 7.1) is challenging when distinct types of nonoverlapping wear are identified on an artifact. Using broader categories (e.g., evidence of multiple use or evidence of recycling) appears often more appropriate.

Furthermore, short-term use, and some cases of multiple uses (as discussed later), will be difficult to detect. These limitations have to be taken into account while interpreting the results. Accordingly, it is important to compare several tools of the same type in order to expose general trends or patterns within a GST assemblage. Through an understanding of the life history of the variety of tools from a site, it is possible to characterize a GST assemblage by the relative proportion of ad-hoc and manufactured tools, the investment in the manufacture of the different tool types, the relationship between tool morphologies and function, the specialization and standardization of the tool categories, as well as curation and recycling behavior (e.g., Dubreuil 2002, 2008, 2009).

In order to assess the life history of an artifact, one must determine whether the aspects of the surface and wear result from manufacture, use, curation, or postdepositional processes. An important step toward the resolution of this problem is the use or creation of an experimental reference collection. Our understanding of use–wear formation on GSTs depends heavily on experiments.

7.4 The Reference Collections

The creation of a "natural reference collection" of raw materials is an essential step for use–wear studies of GSTs. In particular, this reference collection should aim at documenting the aspects of fresh, eroded, or water-worn surfaces and breakage planes. This will help in sorting between the implements that have been manufactured and/or used from the unused (or too briefly used) items. Observation of "natural surfaces" can also help in identifying postdepositional alterations, which may affect the archeological material. For example, Mansur (1997) draws on characteristics of natural alteration of quartz resulting from dissolution phenomena to

Table 7.1 Ground stone tool life history

Stages	Definition—comments
I: Raw material choice and procurement	The tool efficiency is largely determined by raw material properties, so the choice of the raw material is an important aspect for discussing tool function. Furthermore, the type of procurement (e.g., whether it is collected as a pebble or an eroded block or extracted from a quarry) has an impact on the manufacture process
II: Manufacture	This step is absent for ad-hoc implements
III: Primary utilization	The function the artifact was initially designed for
IV: Secondary utilization	Artifacts used for several tasks are frequently referred to as "multifunctional" or as "multiple tools." Adams (2002) differentiated between single use, reuse (when the tool is employed in a second activity that does not alter the design of the tool), and multiple-use (when several areas of the surface are used in distinct activities)
V: Recycling	According to Schiffer and Skibo (1987), recycling necessitates a reshaping of the tool for a new utilization. This definition corresponds to Adams (2002) "redesigned tools" category. For Adams, recycling implies changing the type of use as, for instance, when a ground stone tool is incorporated into the wall of a structure
VI: Discard	In theory, discard can happen at various stages during and after manufacture, and is the process by which stages I–IV become apparent within a single archeological assemblage. Exhausted, or worn out, tools which are no longer usable can be identifiable by thinning or perforation of the tool at the working surface, or breakage of the tool. Ground stone tools may be placed in specific discard contest such as grave. The "killing", or intentional breakage, of ground stone tools placed in grave has been reported ethnographically (Adams 2008) and the issue is discussed in light of specific archeological examples in Adams (2008), Van Gijn and Verbaas (2009), Stroulia and Chondrou (2013), and Wright (2014). Arguments favoring intentional breakage can be based on recurrent fracture patterns found in an assemblage. Other indices may also be used such as the localization, numbers, and arrangements of fracture scars
VI: Post-depositional processes	After discard, postdepositional processes such as breakage or weathering may affect the shape and surfaces of an implement

identify postdepositional alteration on GST from the Beagle Channel region. Experiments aimed at exploring how postdepositional processes may affect use–wear are yet to be developed for GST. This is partly related to the significant amount of time required for the production and use of these experimental tools. However, experiments with a tumbling mill and basalt fragments have allowed for a better understanding of wear related to soil movement (Dubreuil 2002, p. 228).

The wear resulting from the production of an experimental tool should be examined and described in detail before its use. This is particularly important for investigating the manufacturing process which has been used to produce an archeological tool. Furthermore, as underlined in the definition of the GST, these implements can be manufactured and used by similar action (e.g., pecking, pounding, grinding, and polishing). Differentiating use–wear related to manufacture from those related to use is a critical issue in GST analysis.

Experiments with GSTs have focused primarily on manufactured, rather than ad-hoc implements (see Tables 7.2 and 7.3). Most frequently, experiments were performed with grinding implements such as handstones and grinding slabs, as well as different kinds of abraders. In addition, use–wear on ethnographic tools has been examined in a variety of studies (e.g., Hayden 1987; Hampton 1997; Clemente et al. 2002; Rodriguez Rodriguez et al. 2004, 2006; Cunnar 2007; Liu et al. 2010; Procopiou et al. 2011). Ethnographic studies indicate that GSTs can be used over long periods of time, in some cases, for generations (e.g., Runnels 1981; Hayden 1987; Horsfall 1987; Ertug-Yaras 2002; Baudais and Lundström-Baudais 2002; Delgado-Raack and Rich 2009; Hamon and Le Gall 2013). Consequently, it is not always feasible to document the fullest extent of wear development on experimental tools. However, tools such as grinding slabs and handstones require regular maintenance, accomplished by pecking the working surface to restore the abrasive qualities which initially made it desirable as a grinding tool. These maintenance cycles remove previous traces of wear, refreshing the surface for wear development to begin anew.

Several types of experimental programs can be undertaken (e.g., Keeley 1980; Plisson 1991), including mechanized or manual, and exploratory or systematic approaches (when parameters which may affect use–wear formation are controlled as much as possible). Most experiments with GST involve manual approaches, as it is not possible to fully reproduce manual motions with a machine, and kinetics is an important aspect affecting use–wear formation. Manual approaches can serve to assess the feasibility and efficiency of the action performed with tools. Assessing tool productivity is very important, and has been attempted in a few studies (e.g., see discussion in Wright 1994; Menasanch et al. 2002; Samuel 2010; Valamoti et al. 2013).

Manual experiments can be used to evaluate the capacity of an experimental tool to perform a certain task, and to compare the efficiency of different tools or different raw materials. Although quantification is needed, this more qualitative approach is particularly crucial to explore past technical systems. For instance, drawing on the example of the technology associated with cereal exploitation, assessing GST efficiency with manual experiments can provide insight into the chaine operatoire of plant processing, by helping assessing the most viable techniques for dehusking, grinding, and pounding the material in different states (e.g., fresh, dry, grilled, and soaked), or to produce a variety of products (e.g., gruel, flour, and beer-alcohol).

A few mechanized experiments have been conducted as well, often with a focus on the analysis of material behavior using material science approaches (e.g., Procopiou et al. 1998; Procopiou 2004; Delgado-Raack et al. 2009). These approaches are particularly important for our understanding of wear formation processes.

7 Current Analytical Frameworks for Studies of Use–Wear on Ground Stone Tools

Activity	Raw material of the active and/or passive tool(s)	References
Grinding, pounding (with upper and lower implements)		
Grinding maize	Medium-grained quartzite and granitic stones, vesicular basalt, sandstone	Wright (1993); Kamp (1995); Adams (1999)
Grinding cereals (e.g., wheat, spelt barley, millet)	Granatiferous mica schist, conglomerate, gabbro, wood (olive, oak, almond), metapsammite, basalt, compact sandstone, quartzitic sandstone, fine-grained sandstone	Procopiou (1998); Menasanch et al. (2002); Risch (2002); Dubreuil (2002); Zurro et al. (2005); Hamon (2007); Delgado-Raack (2008); Verbaas and van Gijn (2008); Hamon and Plisson (2008); Bofill et al. (2013)
Pounding cereals	Basalt	Dubreuil (in prep)
Grinding linseed	Quartzitic sandstone	Verbaas and van Gijn (2008)
Grinding sunflower seeds	Medium-grained quartzite, granitic stone, sandstone, vesicular basalt	Adams (1999)
Grinding amaranth seeds	Medium-grained quartzite, granitic stone	Adams (1999)
	Medium-grained quartzite, sandstone	Adams (1999)
	Vesicular basalt	Adams (1999)
Grinding nuts	Basalt	Dubreuil (2002); Bofill et al. (2013)
Grinding acorns	Basalt, quartzitic sandstone	Dubreuil (2002); Hamon and Plisson (2009)
Pounding acorns	Basalt	Dubreuil (in prep)
Grinding mustard seeds	Basalt	Dubreuil (2002)
Grinding legumes (e.g., fenugreek, feva beans, lentils)	Basalt	Dubreuil (2002); Bofill et al. (2013)
Pounding lentils	Basalt	Dubreuil (in prep)
Pounding rosemary	Basalt	Dubreuil (in prep)
Grinding meat	Basalt	Dubreuil (2002)
Pounding meat	Basalt, quartzitic sandstone, compact sandstone	Hamon and Plisson (2009); Dubreuil (in prep)
Grinding fish	Basalt	Dubreuil (2002)
Crushing bone, cartilage and marrow	Compact altered sandstone, quartzitic sandstone, calcareous sandstone	Hamon and Plisson (2009)
Grinding pottery clay, pot sherds	Medium-grained quartzite, compact sandstone	Adams (1989); Cunnar (2007); Hamon (2007)
Temper grinding ("chamotte", cooked bone and flint)	Compact sandstone	Hamon (2007)
Grinding calcite	Compact sandstone, calcareous sandstone	Hamon and Plisson (2009)
Grinding ochre and processing pigment	Basalt, compact sandstone, medium-grained sandstone	Logan and Fratt (1993); Dubreuil (2002); Hamon (2006); Verbaas and van Gijn (2008)

Table 7.3 List and references of experiments that include a functional analysis of abraders, polishers, and ad-hoc implements. (Source: Dubreuil and Savage 2013)

Activity	Raw material of the tool	References
Abrading, polishing (active or passive use)		
Bone sharpening, bone abrasion and bone tool polishing	Fine-grained sandstone, quartzitic sandstone, basalt	Adams (1989, 1993); Dubreuil (2002); Cunnar (2007); Hamon (2007); Verbaas and van Gijn (2008)
Antler tool polishing	Quartzitic sandstone	Hamon (2007); Verbaas and van Gijn (2008)
Wood smoothing and abrasion	Medium-grained quartzite, basalt, quartzitic sandstone	Adams (1989, 1993); Kamp (1995); Dubreuil (2002); Cunnar (2007); Hamon (2007)
Stone against stone abrasion, stone polishing	Basalts, fine-grained sandstone, quartzitic sandstone, amphibolites, tuff, rhyolites, other (unspecified)	Mansur (1997); Dubreuil (2002); Hamon (2007); Cunnar (2007); Verbaas and van Gijn (2008); Bofill et al. (2013)
Limestone bead polishing	Quartzitic sandstone	Hamon (2007)
Ochre abrasion	Basalt	Dubreuil (2002)
Flint axe polishing	Quartzitic sandstone, sandstone	Hamon (2007); Cunnar (2007)
Shell Working	Medium-grained quartzite, basalt, compact sandstone	Adams (1989, 1993); Dubreuil (2002); Hamon (2007); Bofill et al. (2013)
Ceramic (modelling, burnishing)	Quartzitic sandstone and other (unspecified)	Kamp (1995); Hamon (2007); Cunnar (2007); Van Gijn and Lammers-Keijsers (2010)
Hide processing	Medium-grained quartzite, basalt, sandstones (several types), metamorphic stones, limestone, siltstone, greenstone, other	Adams (1988, 1993); Gonzalez and Ibanez (2002); Hamon (2007); Delgado-Raack (2008); Dubreuil and Grosman (2009); Hamon and Plisson (2008); Cristiani et al. (2012); Bofill and Taha (2013); Bofill et al. (2013)
Metal working	Gabbro, quartzitic sandstone	Delgado-Raack and Risch (2009)
Experiments with hammerstones, pitted stones, anvils, spheroids and unmodified pebbles		
Working stone: direct and indirect percussion, abrasion	Limestone, siltstone, greenstone, basalt, quartzite	Willoughby (1985); Hayden (1987); de Beaune (1993, 1997); Reid and Pritchard-Parker (1993); de Beaune and Pinçon (2001); Goren-Inbar et al. (2002); Poissonnier (2002); Cristiani et al. (2012); Roda Gilabert et al. (2012); de la Torre et al. (2013)
Direct and indirect percussion on bone	Limestone, basalt, quartzite	de Beaune (1997); de la Torre et al. (2013)
Pounding mineral matter	Quartzite	Willoughby (1987); Sajnerova-Duskova et al. (2009)
Pounding vegetal matter	Quartzite, limestone, basalt, sandstone	Dodd (1979); Willoughby (1987); Goren-Inbar et al. (2002); Ramos (2005); Revedin et al. (2010); Gilabert et al. (2012); de la Torre et al. (2013)
Pounding meat	Quartzite	de la Torre et al. (2013)

7.5 Use–wear Formation Processes and Raw Material Analysis

7.5.1 Use–wear Formation Processes

From a tribological point of view, wear can be defined as "a continuous damage process of surfaces, which are in contact with a relative movement" (Shizu and Ping 2012, p. 263). Drawing on tribology, Adams (2002, pp. 27–33) defines four processes of wear formation for GST: adhesive wear, which results from the attraction between contacting surfaces at the atomic level (Bahadur 2012, pp. 6–2); fatigue wear, the crushing and fracturing of rock grains by the pressure of contact; abrasive wear, the gouging and scratching of a soft surface by the asperities of a harder surface; and tribochemical wear, a buildup of chemical reaction products created through the interaction of the two surfaces.

Each process leaves distinct patterns on the surface of the stone which can be used to reconstruct the contact environment associated with the use-context of the tool (Adams et al. 2009; Table 6.2). Adhesive wear is notable for the manner in which it interacts with other wear processes (Adams 2002, p. 29). For example, grains removed by adhesion become abrasive agents within the contact environment, which accelerates the development of abrasive wear patterns. Fatigue and abrasive wear are additional reductive processes that are associated with cracks, fractures, striations, and gouges. The heat produced by friction accelerates the chemical processes responsible for tribochemical wear, which may become visible as a reflective polish on the surface of the rock (see for instance in Fig. 7.7).

Two models of use–wear formation have dominated the discussion of use–wear analysis on flint tools. While the role of abrasive processes in use–wear formation has been widely acknowledged, the extent to which adhesive or tribochemical wear comes into play is debated (e.g., Diamond 1979; Kamminga 1979; Anderson 1980; Meeks et al. 1982; Unger-Hamilton 1984; Mansur-Franchomme 1986; Yamada 2000, pp. 47–62; Anderson et al. 2006; Christensen 1998; Astruc et al. 2003; Evans and Donahue 2005). In general, tribological approaches, and more specifically, multiscale analysis using continuous wavelengths (Vargiolu et al. 2007; Procopiou et al. 2011, 2013; Bofill et al. 2013), as well as residue analysis, may be needed to fully understand these wear formation processes. The analysis of the mechanical properties of the various raw materials used for making GSTs can also greatly contribute to our understanding of use–wear formation processes

7.5.2 The Physical and Mechanical Properties of Stones (Selina Delgado-Raack)

The types of rock commonly used in the making of GSTs can be described as aggregates of mineral particles, in which grains or crystals of very different compositional nature and size coexist. These characteristics diverge from those found in the chipped stone industry, where siliceous or vitreous materials such as flint, chert, or obsidian are typically used. These rocks tend to be fine grained and much more homogeneous.

A detailed description of GST raw materials is crucial for functional analysis, because several properties of the rock affect the efficiency of a tool and the formation of use–wear. A number of publications have discussed this aspect, especially for grinding artifacts such as handstones and grinding slabs (Shoumacker 1993, pp. 165–176; Procopiou 1998; Baudais and Lundström-Baudais 2002, pp. 155–180; Santallier et al. 2002, pp. 15–29; Schneider 2002, pp. 31–53; Milleville 2007; Schneider and LaPorta 2008, pp. 19–40). However, lithic properties have only recently been fully integrated in functional studies. Mechanical tests using industrial machines, in which rocks are subjected to wear under controlled conditions, have allowed for the evaluation of the mechanical behavior of a variety of rocks in certain wear systems (e.g., Delgado-Raack 2008; Delgado-Raack et al. 2008, 2009). It is important to emphasize that these trials are not intended to replicate work processes as they actually happened in prehistory. Following these studies, Table 7.4 summarizes the petrographic variables which can potentially influence the mechanical behavior of rock, while providing a basis for raw material description.

The importance of mechanical tests lies on their ability to systematically and objectively characterize the physical reaction of a rock in a controlled environment. We focus here on GSTs operating by what is called in physics, "kinetic friction" or "dynamic friction," that is the force produced when one solid body moves tangentially over another with which it is in contact (Blau 1996, p. 18). In systems in which wear is generated through frictional processes, the physical reaction of a rock can be characterized by its abrasive capacity. The abrasive capacity results from the combination of two independent variables: (1) the ability of a rock to develop surface roughness and (2) the resistance against friction, measured by volume loss.

The mechanical tests carried out so far demonstrate that the physical reaction of a rock depends primarily on the mechanical system (Table 7.5), which is to say that raw materials react differently to friction, percussion, cutting, drilling, etc. Accordingly, rocks that are hard to cut will not necessarily be the most difficult to knap, and the easiest rocks to knap will not necessarily be easy to polish.

Mechanical tests have also shown that a combination of several petrographic features needs to be considered when examining wear processes (Table 7.5). Wear processes are regarded here as being related to the physical reaction of the rock, or, as discussed previously, its abrasive capacity determined by its surface roughness as well as its resistance to friction. In general, the compositional homogeneity of a rock reduces surface roughness, while the quantity of quartz favors it. Quartz is one of the most abundant and hardest minerals in nature. However, it often coexists in rocks with other softer minerals. This heterogeneity can lead, under certain mechanical system, to the development of surface roughness. Rock porosity and hardness are features that can

Table 7.4 Main petrographic features that potentially can influence the mechanical behavior of the rock

Generic petrographic feature	Specific petrographic feature	Description	Technique
Mineralogic properties	Predominant minerals	Percentage	Polarised light microscope (thin section) and density charts; also XRD
	Accessory minerals	Presence/Absence	Idem
	Compositional homogeneity	High (1–2 minerals) Medium (3–4 minerals) Low (>4 minerals)	–
Structural properties	Fabric	Isotropic Anisotropic: Planar Linear Plano-linear	Polarised light microscope (thin section)
Textural properties	Apparent (bulk) density	$\rho_a = \dfrac{M_o}{V}$ where M_o is the dry weight (g) and V is the volume (cm^3)	Bascule and ruler
	Real density	$\rho_r = \dfrac{M_o}{V - v^i\left(M_s^i - M_o\right)}$ where M_o is the dry weight (g), V is the volume (cm^3), M_s^i is the weight in saturation of substance i, and v_i is the specific volume of the saturating substance i (cm^3/g).	Saturating substance (water, aluminum, helium, etc.) vacuum pump, bascule, ruler
	Open porosity	$\phi = 1 - \dfrac{\rho_a}{\rho_r}$	Also microscope (thin section) and density charts

Table 7.4 (continued)

Generic petrographic feature	Specific petrographic feature	Description	Technique
	Maximum grain size	Micron (μ)	Scale incorporated into the eyepiece of the microscope
	Minimum grain size	Micron (μ)	
	Homogeneity of grain size	Equigranular Inequigranular (Varitextured) Bimodal Seriate	Polarised light microscope (thin section)
	Cohesion	High (minerals are hold in crystallisations of quartz or phyllosilicate) Low (minerals are interconnected by carbonate)	
	Weighted average of microhardness	$$\bar{H} = \frac{(h_a \cdot \%a) + (h_b \cdot \%b) + \cdots + (h_n \cdot \%n)}{100}$$ where $a, b, \ldots, n$ are minerals contained in the rock, $\%a, \%b, \ldots \%n$ are percentages of each mineral and $h_a, h_b, \ldots h_n$ are the absolute values of microhardness in the Gpa scale	Gpa absolute hardness chart (Broz et al. 2006, pp. 135–142)
	Angularity	High/ Anhedral Medium/ Subhedral Low/ Euhedral	Polarised light microscope (mince section)
Other physic features	Alteration	Presence/ Absence	Polarised light microscope (mince section)
	Matrix	Detritic Micaceous Cement Volcanic glass	Polarised light microscope (mince section) Hydrochloric acid
General classification of the rock			

7 Current Analytical Frameworks for Studies of Use–Wear on Ground Stone Tools

Table 7.5 Petrographic features that influence physical behavior of the rocks, as observed in a series of mechanical tests conducted in industrial machines (Delgado-Raack et al. 2009, p. 1828 and Table 7.3). In the PEI test, the surface is put under frictional wear of several steel balls of milimeter size, which oscillate some revolutions per minute. In the Dorry test, the lithic surface wears through the rotating contact of a steel track. In both tests, several grams of abrasive (corundum) are added. X = proportional relationship; 1/X = inverse relationship

	Frictional wear by oscillating steel balls (PEI)		Frictional wear by rotating steel track (DORRY)	
	Roughness	Volume lost	Roughness	Volume lost
Compositional homogeneity	1/X	1/X	1/X	
Quartz	X		X	X
Angularity		1/X		
Apparent density	1/X	1/X		1/X
Open porosity	X	X		
Weighted average of microhardness			X	X
Cohesion		1/X		1/X

positively influence the development of surface roughness under certain mechanical system. Conversely, density can be detrimental to this feature. Similarly, the resistance against friction, the second parameter characterizing the physical reaction of a rock, mainly depends on the density of the rock and on the cohesion of the constituent particles.

Other mechanical parameters, such as flexion, also highlight that mechanical behavior of rocks depends on a combination of petrographic features. In this case, high porosity, the presence of anisotropy, and heterogeneous grain sizes are characteristics which adversely affect the resistance to flexion.

Mechanical tests of the type described above and especially their application to GSTs analysis are still in an initial stage, although their potential regarding both functional analysis of GST and economic studies of past societies is remarkable (e.g., Bradley et al. 1992, pp. 223–233; Delgado-Raack et al. 2008, 2009).

Indeed, in-depth knowledge of the petrographic properties of rocks can contribute greatly to the functional interpretation of use–wear traces. As indicated above, the results obtained in mechanical analysis highlight the role of some petrographic variables in the physical behavior of the rock, and therefore, in the development of wear traces. For instance, high lithological cohesion can favor the development of sinuous reliefs, while constant surface renewal in less cohesive materials will, under similar wear conditions, result in irregular reliefs (Fig. 7.1). Given the complex causal relationship between the characteristics of the raw material a tool is made of, the properties of the other materials involved in the tool operation (i.e., the matter processed, eventually a complementary tool), the kinetics, and wear processes, taking into account the petrographic features of the rock, are crucial. In addition, the study of rock properties allows addressing the concept of tool efficiency. Some analyses have shown that the optimal mechanical solution is not always the one that was

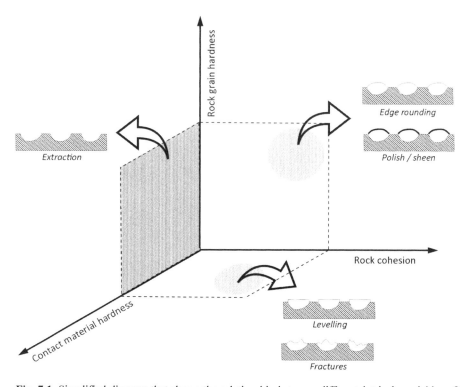

Fig. 7.1 Simplified diagram that shows the relationship between different intrinsic variables of rocks and the contact material in a frictional system, always under the assumption that the mineralogical composition is uniform. (S. Delgado-Raack)

actually chosen, indicating that considerations other than productivity could be acting in some cases, such as territorial control for instance. This has been discussed for example for the Neolithic axe trade in England (Bradley et al. 1992, pp. 223–233) and the Bronze Age grinding tool production in South-East Iberia (Delgado-Raack et al. 2008, 2009). Hence, when the analysis of the mechanical properties of rocks is combined with the study of raw material procurement, of the spatial distribution of technical equipments, and of the social contexts of their use, it is possible to better characterize the production systems, to discuss the social access to resources, and their management in past societies.

Detailed description of the raw material following the framework outlined in Table 7.4 is therefore regarded here as an essential preliminary step in use–wear analysis.

Before discussing the frameworks currently used for describing use–wear, cleaning procedures and residue analysis, as well as methods for observation, macro- and microphotography will be first discussed in the next section.

7.6 Methods of Preparation, Observation and Documentation

7.6.1 Cleaning Procedure

The effectiveness of different cleaning procedures has been compared experimentally (Dubreuil 2002, 2004). The cleaning techniques examined included: rinsing with water, with water and detergent using a gentle toothbrush, cleaning with hydrogen peroxide of different concentrations, and rinsing with pure acetone. Washing with detergent using a gentle brush was generally found sufficient both for low and high magnification analysis. Even with experiments involving the processing of greasy materials such as nuts, meat, or fish, the use of hydrogen peroxide or acetate was not found to be necessary. A soft brush was needed however to remove the residues which have accumulated in the interstices. It is important to note the aspect of residues and their distribution within the surface before cleaning the experimental objects. However, following Evans and Donahue (2005), more aggressing cleaning techniques may be preferred in order to remove as much of the remaining residue as possible, especially when investigating use–wear formation processes (see also Byrne et al. 2006).

The desire for clear observation must be weighed against the preservation of residues related to the use of the tool. Ochre remains represent an obvious example; when such residues are present, the object should not be cleaned, and the use–wear approach must be adapted to this specific situation by focusing on the visible part of the stone surface, and by taking into account the distribution and aspect of the residues (e.g., Logan and Fratt 1993; Dubreuil and Grosman 2009).

Ideally, a strategy for residue analysis should be designed before cleaning the archeological implements, and even earlier during field work, as taking sediment samples from around the tool can be of critical importance (e.g., Procopiou et al. 2002; Piperno 2006, p. 84). Although a discussion of residue analysis is beyond the scope of this chapter, an overview of the type of residues that can be investigated on GST is important to assess cleaning procedures.

7.6.2 Residues Analysis: An Overview (Birgitta Stephenson)

The matrices and voids associated with ground surfaces such as grindstones, handstones, grinding surfaces, and mortars provide an ideal environment for the trapping of residues (e.g., Buonasera 2005; Quigg 2003; Stephenson 2011, p. 78). It has been demonstrated that oily and or fatty films will penetrate grinding surfaces without much effort, and that the depth of penetration is determined by the porosity of the surface (Stephenson 2011). In the case of other residues such as phytoliths, starches, ochre, collagen, and resin, the mechanical actions which accompany grinding and pounding force residues into the interstitial spaces. Depth in this case varies according to the duration of action. While attrition of the stone surface caused by subsequent processing can remove some of these impacted residues, a large percentage may remain and survive below the active working surface. These become overwritten by layers of additional residues thereby creating a debris trail and a history of grinding activity. Due to differing molecular weights and differential residue preservation, however, currently it is not possible to determine the sequence of residue layering (Langejans 2010).

Until recently, identifying microresidues has primarily relied upon nondestructive high power reflected light microscopy approaches (e.g., Prinsloo et al. 2014). A number of recent investigations have combined use–wear studies with the mapping of residues across the tool surfaces (see Hogberg et al. 2009; Lombard 2005, 2008) to determine residue distribution and particular wear. This approach has been recently implemented in ground stone analysis (e.g., Stephenson 2011, 2012; Fullagar and Stephenson 2012). In the case of complete tools such as grindstones, mortars, and handstones or in-situ features such as bedrock GST, a handheld digital microscope is useful to examine the surface of the tool and assist with the selection of residue sampling points. Experimental work on grooved artefacts has demonstrated that in addition to the cross-sectional center of a groove, residues build up across the shoulders and the lip of the groove (Field et al. 2009; Stephenson 2011). The distribution of residues varies with the materials being ground and work is being currently undertaken to identify particular signature of grinding patterns (Smith 2004). It can be supposed that, given the nature of grinding and pounding, residues should rarely be confined to the working surface and may be found on nearby nonworked areas (as documented for instance for scrapers by Rots and Williamson 2004).

Residue preservation mechanisms are an important issue that remain poorly understood (Langejans 2010; Buenasera 2013; Portillo et al. 2013). Some studies have demonstrated that residues can survive across GST surfaces for prolonged periods of time in certain context (e.g., Del Pilar Babot and Apella 2003; Fullagar and Jones 2004; Piperno et al. 2004, 2009; Revedin et al. 2010; Liu et al. 2011; Nadel et al. 2012; Portillo et al. 2013). Residue analysis involves the identification of surviving residues which commonly include organic remains such as plant (e.g., starch, raphides, phytoliths, and pollen) and animal (e.g., blood, bone, hair, and collagen), as well as inorganic matters (e.g., vivianite, aragonite, and ochre).

Sampling for phytoliths and starch usually requires the collection of sediments from the stone's surface, as well as several rinses with an ultrasonic device (e.g., Piperno et al. 2004, 2009; Pearsall et al. 2004; Rumold 2010; Portillo et al. 2013). Lipids and other amorphous residues may also be extracted from GSTs (e.g., Formenti and Procopiou 1998; Christensen and Valla 1999; Del Pilar Babot and Apella 2003; Buonasera 2007, 2012, 2013) by collecting residues from the surface, from within interstices, or by drilling into the stone (e.g., Procopiou et al. 2002; Del Pilar Babot and Apella 2003; Buonasera 2007, 2013). Successful residue extraction from ground surfaces has been also obtained by employing a series of ultra purified water lifts across the ground surface to extract residues trapped in the matrix (Stephenson 2011; Fullagar and Stephenson 2012). This procedure allows a detailed sampling of residues across the tool surface. Using a variable volumetric pipette, aliquots of ultra purified water are applied to selected sample points. Preferred points are porous and include natural fissures, cracks, and pitted areas. Initially, water aliquots are left to soak with the process being repeated a number of times depending on the porosity of the stone. A second pipette is used to agitate the lift surface area and to draw back and expel the ultra purified water through the matrix. This is repeated a number of times until a sample of the water containing lifted residues is drawn up and placed in an eppendorf tube for later microscopic examination.

Another method used successfully by archeologists to examine grinding tool residues and microwear involves the use of Polyvinyl Siloxane (PVS) peels (e.g., Fullagar and Wallis 2011). PVS peels allow for high resolution "negative" impressions or moulds of the ground surface which can be examined using incident light microscopy to show polish, striations, and other use–wear features. In some instances, residues ripped from the ground surface can be observed across the PVS peel. An injector gun or dispenser with a cartridge and an applicator is used to apply the Polyvinyl Siloxane to the surface and is left to dry for approximately 10 min before removing with tweezers and storing in a plastic bag for later microscopic examination (Fullagar and Stephenson 2012).

Regardless of the type of residue in question, sampling should be done before cleaning, although in the case of phytoliths at least, some can still be recovered afterward (Piperno 2006, p. 84).

Until recently, identifying and interpreting residues has relied heavily on morphological characteristics. The visual diagnostic properties of some residues however, can be altered when their structural bonds are broken due to the mechanical forces associated with processing and alterations associated with cooking which cause residues to become ambiguous. Likewise, environmental influences such as water can cause residues to swell and become amorphous, making them more difficult to identify. As such, contemporary microscopic residue analysis approaches benefit greatly from the use of multiple lines of evidence. The recent introduction of the biochemical staining of lifted residues in conjunction with microscope residue analysis studies has helped identify these altered and/or ambiguous residues (see Stephenson 2012). A number of class specific stains have been developed to identify particular residues and includes stains for lignin, starch, alkaloids, collagen, lipids, and keratin (Haslam 2004; Smith 2004; Lamb and Loy 2005; Barton 2007; Torrence 2006; Crowther 2009; Stephenson 2011).

Fourier transform infrared spectroscopy (FTIR) provides a further line of evidence for residue identification. FTIR allows broad categories of residues like protein to be identified to species level (Prinsloo et al. 2014). Cross-over immunoelectrophoresis (CIEP) techniques have also been employed with some success to identify protein residues to the family level (Yost 2008). This process makes use of antigen–antibody reactions but is limited by similar serum protein antigenic determinations (Prinsloo et al. 2014). This may occur between distinctly and closely related animals alike and may lead to equivocal residue determinations. Other protein detection methods which have been used in archeological tool investigations include radioimmune assay (RIA) and enzyme-linked immunosorbent assay (ELISA) to varying degrees of success (Prinsloo et al. 2014).

As with use–wear observations, it is important to consider that not all residues are related to use (Odell 2001, p. 56); for instance, the depositional context, particularly in grassland environments, may skew the results of starch and phytolith analyses (Haslam 2009). Similarly, weathering can distort or remove residues, and poor preservation conditions can markedly bias the quantity and type preserved (Briuer 1976). It is necessary to compare densities of residues from nonground areas and from adhering soils to ascertain the use-relatedness of observed residues. Importantly, use–wear and residue analysis are complementary and inform each other to assess tool function. The additional lines of residue analysis described here help increase the accuracy and robusticity of derived determinations.

7.6.3 A Multiple Scale Approach

This section reviews the widely used, as well as emerging approaches and equipment for use–wear analysis of GSTs. It is argued that all of these approaches should be regarded as complementary, as they each focus on specific aspects of use–wear. A holistic analysis builds on the use of all of these approaches in addition to unaided eye observations (discussed in Sect. 7.1) which represent a crucial step in use–wear analysis.

As illustrated by the pioneering work of Jenny Adams (1988, 1989, 1994), research on use–wear formation on noncutting GSTs has largely focused on observations at low magnifications (traditionally up to 80× using a stereomicroscope). Although less developed, analyses at high magnifications (traditionally 50–500× with a metallographic microscope) are, however, becoming increasingly common. Regarding observations with metallographic microscopes, the use of a differential interference contrast, or Nomarski system, is indispensable to distinguish use–wear features on microcrystals which are hardly visible below 400× magnification (Plisson and Lompré 2008; Adams et al. 2009). Long working distance objectives (LWD) are more convenient for analyzing irregular rough surfaces and give a better depth of field.

Because GST can be of various sizes, large microscope stands with an extendable boom are generally necessary for the analysis of large implements. Portable digital microscopes are particularly useful for the study of deep mortars and bedrock features. High resolution casts of dental elastomer or acetate can also be used with microscopes which are unable to accommodate the original object (Adams et al. 2009). However, elastomer casts tend to leave greasy stains on the artifact which are difficult to remove, a problem which is not encountered with the acetate. However, acetate casts are more fragile and tend to deform.

Other analyses have also been carried out on GST, including for instance, the use of SEMs (scanning electronic microscopes, e.g., Dubreuil 2004; Cunnar 2007; Bofill et al. 2013), rugosimeters (e.g., Procopiou et al. 1998; Procopiou 2004; Delgado-Raack et al. 2009), interferometry, and confocal microscopy (Bofill 2012; Bofill et al. 2013). Generally, due to time and budget constraints, SEM and confocal microscopy, as well as rugosimetry and interferometry, are used only for the study of small samples and/or to address specific questions such the processes of use–wear formation, or quantification of wear.

Geographic Information System (GIS) methods can also help in quantifying and recording use–wear patterns. Recently, de la Torre et al. (2013) explored the potential of GIS tools to characterize battering damage in experimental anvils used for a variety of tasks (meat pounding, bipolar flaking, bone breaking, plant processing, and nut cracking). Photographs of the battered anvils were georeferenced in a local Cartesian system, and the distribution of use–wear was mapped over the pictures. This enabled calculating the perimeter, area, and relative position of battering features observed in the anvils, as well as their density, size, orientation, and shape. These data were used to calculate indices on the percentage of the anvil area covered by use–wear, the areas with more intense battering, the density of use–wear, the mean shapes of battering marks, and to obtain a large number of indices related to the spatial patterning of marks (e.g., distance of battering traces to the center and edge of the anvil, elongation of battering clusters, etc). While de la Torre et al. (2013) based their spatial analysis on 2D variables derived from georeferenced photographs, new developments in 3D scanning reconstruction can be used to develop high resolution digital elevation models (DEMs) of GST surfaces, which expand the analytical potential of GIS for use–wear studies. More details on 3D modeling and photogrammetry are provided in the next section.

7.6.4 Documenting Use–wear (Hugues Plisson)

The wear analysis of ground tools involves various observation and recording techniques for covering a large range of relevant criteria, from the morphology of the whole working surface (see for instance, Fig. 7.8) to the wear of individual microscopic crystals (for instance, Fig. 7.6), to say nothing of residues. There is probably more emphasis on both ends of the magnification scale than for chipped stone artifacts, which is particularly appropriate for digital imaging. The development of digital photography has not only provided a more convenient means of taking basic images, but it has also allowed the production of new types of images which were unthinkable in the times of the film camera.

Contrary to the extravagant claims of magnification promoted by advertisers of so called "digital microscopes" (their figures are based in fact on enlargement to a 15 in. screen rather than the sensor plane), digital photo recording at macro- and microscopic scales has not overturned the laws of optics. Therefore, before attempting microphotography, it is necessary to have a good understanding of all the basic parameters which determine the quality of an optical image (Plisson 1989, 2014, in press). This is becoming even more critical as magnification increases. It is also important to select the appropriate equipment:

Fig. 7.2 Macroscopic detail of an experimental sandstone abrader used for shaping bone needles. Wild M7 stereoscope with 1 × achromatic objective at 9 × visual magnification (3:1 on the sensor plane, since for photography only the center of the frame is used). Crop (45 % of 10 million pixels) of a postprocessed raw file from a Nikon D80 SLR camera fixed via a Wild phototube with a Nikon MDC 10 × projective lens (the best optical coupling). *Left bottom*: enlarged residue. Scale 4 mm, graduation 1 mm. (H. Plisson)

- The large sensors of SLR cameras have both higher resolution and better dynamic range than the very small sensors found in the video cameras designed for the microscopes. SLR cameras are, in addition, far more versatile.
- The optical geometry used in stereoscopic observation is far from being optimal for photography. Consequently, an SLR camera with a 50 or 60 mm macrolens produces better images than when fixed to a binocular microscope (Figs. 7.2 and 7.3). In practice, with a DX format sensor (15 × 25 mm), the frame at 1:1 magnification of the macrolens is the same as seen in direct observation with a Leica MZ6 or Nikon SMZ2B stereoscope at 8 × with 10 ×/21 oculars (note that magnification is not calculated in the same way for macrophotography as it is for observation with a microscope). With additional rings or macro bellow, it is possible to reach 5:1. However, beyond 3:1, it is more convenient to replace the macrolens with a 4 or 5 × microscope objective (finite design) or the whole extension device and the macro objective with a 200 m telezoom to which is fixed a microscope objective (infinite design) (Fig. 7.4 and Littlefield 2010). The telephoto objective acts like the tube lens of the microscope. In any case, the resolution of the photography depends on the stability and rigidity of the stand.
- At higher magnification, or when a specific illumination is needed (bright field, dark field, etc.), there is no other solution than to attach the camera to the microscope. Ideally apochromatic objectives (corrected across all frequencies

Fig. 7.3 Same macroscopic detail as Fig. 7.2. Leitz Elmar f=5 cm 1:3,5 1951 objective on a bellow with 15 mm extension (=3:1 magnification). Crop (45% of 10 million pixels) of a postprocessed raw file from a Nikon D80 SLR camera. *Left bottom*: enlarged residue. Scale 4 mm, graduation 1 mm. (H. Plisson). Both photos have been equally postprocessed; the difference being purely optical. The second image would be even sharper with a modern objective designed for photomacrography

of white light) are highly recommended, but they are very expensive. In practice, the differential interference contrast system (Figs. 7.5, 7.6, and 7.7), which is indispensable for distinguishing use–wear on microcrystals, also reduces the chromatic aberration of more common achromatic lenses.

Once the optical and photographic equipment has been adequately chosen, digital tools can be explored. They are of three types: software for remote shooting, image processing, and image analysis. The first two are discussed here as they are directly related to the structure and quality of the images produced.

Remote shooting software allows the control of the SLR camera from a computer, a tablet or a smartphone, and direct monitoring of the frame and focus. Most of the camera adjustments can be manipulated on screen. Automation of the shots with specific parameters is also possible, including progressive, step by step changes in focus, which produces a vertical scan of the sample.

Two varieties of image processing software are discussed here: conversion programs for processing raw image files into standard formats (jpg, tif, etc.), and composition programs which combine several images into one.

Raw format is the digital equivalent of the film negative, and each SLR camera has its own raw format, which encodes the image in 12, 14, or 16-bit color depth (e.g., Verhoeven 2010). Any adjustment of the image quality made before shooting (contrast, sharpness, color balance, saturation, etc.) can be afterward corrected or canceled when operating in raw format, which is not the case in jpg or tif. Moreover,

Fig. 7.4 Microscopic detail of pyrite grains encrusted in the crushed active edge of a Neolithic lighter (Mikolas burial cave, France). Shot with a long working distance Olympus LMPlanFL 10×/0.25 microscope objective coupled to a 70–300 mm telephoto zoom lens (*left side*). Postprocessed 16 million pixels single raw photo from a Nikon D7000 SLR Camera. On a BH2 microscope, the frame would cover 0.95 mm of the object. Scale 1 mm, graduation 100 µm. (H. Plisson)

Fig. 7.5 Micro wear of a quartz crystal of a sandstone handstone used to process dry hide. Single shot taken at 500× (50×/0.50 objective) from an acetate print, with a 5.3 million pixels Nikon D1X SLR camera on an episcopic DIC bright field microscope. (H. Plisson)

12, 14, or 16-bit encoding gives a larger contrast range than the 8-bit encoding of the jpg format, since more information is recorded.

With virtual imaging, we are entering into the digital dimension of photography: it is possible to create a representation that is no longer the direct transposition of an optical image, but a mathematical construction based on the analysis of a series of photos (Figs. 7.6, 7.7, 7.8, and 7.9). Three applications involving this third dimension are particularly useful for use–wear analysis. They are based on two principles: the treatment of several photos taken under (i) a single axis (focus stacking) or (ii) different axes (photogrammetry).

Fig. 7.6 Same microscopic detail as Fig. 7.5. Digital stacking with Helicon Focus of 16 shots taken at 500× (50×/0.50 objective) from an acetate print, with a Nikon D1X 5.3 million pixels SLR camera on an episcopic DIC bright field microscope. Scale 100 μm, graduation 1 μm. (H. Plisson)

Fig. 7.7 Micropolish on the grains of a basalt handstone used to process dry hide. Digital stacking with Helicon Focus of 9 shots taken at 500× (50×/0.50 objective) from an acetate print, with a Nikon D1X 5.3 million pixels SLR camera on an episcopic DIC bright field microscope. Scale 100 μm, graduation 1 μm. (H. Plisson)

Focus stacking (also called z-stacking, depth of field stacking, multifocus, or focal plane merging) enhances the depth of field of 2D views (Figs. 7.5 and 7.6). This is particularly interesting in photomicrography (e.g., Thiéry and Green 2012), especially when working with high-magnification lenses. Focus stacking can also provide 3D reconstructions, the resolution of which depends on the number and regularity of shots (Fig. 7.8). Photogrammetry refers only to 3D and enables reconstructing an entire volume (Pierrot-Deseilligny and Clery 2011; Fig. 7.9). It works by assigning absolute coordinates to individual points in a sequence of images taken from many angles. In practice, both solutions are complementary because they have opposite requirements; whereas photogrammetry needs a wide depth of field, image stacking requires a narrow depth of field. Consequently, the only modus operandi at high magnification is focus stacking, while photogrammetry is relevant at low magnification and for whole objects. The inconvenience of focus stacking is that the steps between each shot must be equal and that the Z axis has to be calibrated according to the shooting condition (Berejnov 2009). Photogrammetry is less constraining than focus stacking for acquiring the set of photos: the shots just need to overlap each other and cover the whole surface or the object while taken from different angles, with a difference of 10–20° between each shot. Lighting has to be very dull and spatially uniform, with little shadow, but shooting distance can vary.

There is a large variety of programs for remote shooting, focus stacking, and photogrammetry, from free and open source to very expensive and commercial, as

Fig. 7.8 3D modeling by focus stacking (21 shots) made with Helicon Focus of an experimental bone point shaper (14 × 9.3 cm). *Top*: with photographic texture. *Down*: comparison without texture between a photogrammetric model of the same object (*left*) and the stacked model (*right*). With object of this size, the large depth of field restricts the vertical resolution. (H. Plisson)

well as an increasing choice of reasonably priced products, plus online services for photogrammetry:

- Among the remote programs, Helicon Remote from Helicon Soft, is certainly the most complete and flexible; Helicon Remote is compatible with Canon and Nikon cameras and also with stepper motors, and is available for Windows, Mac, and Android 3.1+. For PC users, a worthwhile alternative for remote bracketing and monitoring is provided by ControlMyNikon, while DslrDashboard and DSLR Controller (Canon only) are two valuable solutions with Android tablets and smartphones.
- The most commonly used softwares for focus stacking are Combine Z (freeware, but PC only), Zerene Stacker, and Helicon Focus; Photoshop can also give good results, but without the large range of options and functions provided by Helicon Focus, which is the most comprehensive software package.
- A free licensed package (Bundler, CMVS, and PMVS2 for point cloud extraction, coupled with Meshlab for meshing and texturing), with various integrated interfaces (SFMToolKit, VisualSFM), has been critical for the development of photogrammetry in archeology. However, the initial learning curve of these

7 Current Analytical Frameworks for Studies of Use–Wear on Ground Stone Tools   131

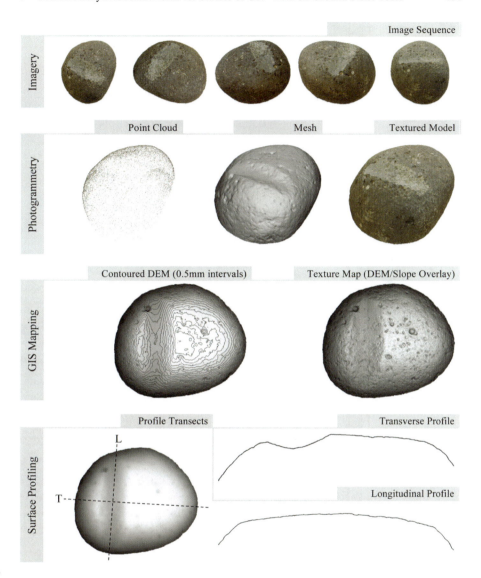

Fig. 7.9 The application of photogrammetry and GIS to the study of GST surfaces. Workflow: *1* high density point cloud processed with VisualSFM. *2* point cloud cleaned, cropped, rotated, and scaled using Meshlab. *3* point cloud data prepared for GIS in Microsoft Access. *4* surface maps and profiles produced in GRASS GIS. *5* mesh and textured models produced with Agisoft Photoscan. (D. Savage)

software packages may be a barrier to their adoption. Free web services are now available, but with the exception of Arc3D, they still do not provide sufficient 3D resolution for detailed analysis. Today, the easiest and most efficient solution is provided by Agisoft, with the inexpensive standard edition of photoscan for Windows, Mac OS, or Linux.

In the use–wear analysis of ground stone tools, both techniques are quite indispensable: photogrammetry for characterizing the deformation of the working surface and focus stacking, combined with acetate cast which reduces flare (Plisson and Lompré 2008; Adams et al. 2009) for documenting microwear polishes on microscopic crystals. The development of 3D scanning and photogrammetry, allowing 3D reconstruction of an artifact, is of major importance for investigating a largely overlooked aspect of use–wear formation: overall morphological changes through use. We will discuss these changes in the following section on unaided eye analysis before reviewing low and high magnification analysis.

7.7 Use–wear Analysis: Framework for Unaided Eye, Low, and High Magnifications Analysis

7.7.1 Unaided Eye Analysis

In general, observations with the unaided eye are crucial in use–wear analysis of GSTs. Substantial information can be gathered with the naked eye, and many features are best observed and described at this scale. For instance, overall morphological changes constitute an important manifestation of wear, and more generally of the tool's life history, which can be observed without the use of magnification.

Overall Morphological Changes Morphological changes related to use can include alteration of the working surface profile (becoming more concave, convex, or flat), the creation of facet(s), cupholes, or groove(s), and can lead to the transformation of the overall shape of the object as, for instance, more surfaces are put into use. Only a few experimental programs have explored this aspect so far (e.g., Adams 1993; Delgado-Raack and Risch 2009; de la Torre et al. 2013; Stroulia and Dubreuil 2013). It is therefore premature to suggest a framework for analyzing those changes and only general observations are discussed here.

Changes to the initial morphology of the tool are strongly correlated with the way the tool is used (its kinetics as well as the use of a complementary tool; Adams 1993; Lidström Holmberg 2004). Gaining a better understanding of morphological changes through use is particularly important for the analysis of tool kinetics, and is critical for investigating the development of certain grinding systems, such as those associated with the concavo-convex configuration of grinding slab working surfaces (e.g., Delgado-Raack and Risch 2009; Stroulia and Dubreuil 2013). Yet, overall morphological changes are also correlated to a number of factors including the type of matter processed and the intensity and length of use.

Maintenance and recycling strategies are also important. Maintenance strategies can, for instance, involve the pecking of the surface, and if the working surface has become too deep, the removal of the edges by flaking. Ultimately, those morphological changes can result in the recycling of a tool. Therefore, a better understanding of morphological change is crucial for investigating the life history of an artifact. In addition, at a more methodological and practical level, understanding morphological changes through use can provide important data for the definition of tool types, which are often based on morphological characteristics.

Analyzing morphological changes can greatly benefit from approaches such as GIS or 3D modeling, as those changes may be difficult to record accurately using traditional tools. For example, precise surface profiles or contours can be arduous to acquire by profile gauge. Instead, this can be accomplished by combining 3D modeling techniques with GIS tools, traditionally employed in landscape analysis, can also be used to convert the 3D output from a photogrammetry application into a digital elevation model (DEM), a continuous raster plane within which is embedded the elevation data for the surface of the artifact (Fig. 7.9). DEMs produced both before and after an experiment can be compared to precisely measure any morphological changes. The GIS approach offers a number of advantages over traditional 3D viewing software. A DEM of the surface of an artifact can be contoured and profiled with greater precision than can be achieved with a profile gauge. Furthermore, a contoured elevation map embeds accurate 3D data into a 2D image, something no traditional photographic technique can accomplish. First order derivatives, such as slope maps, can be used to examine the extent of leveling or grain rounding across the surface of the stone, and perhaps, to even quantify some of these use–wear criteria. However, the GIS approach has its limitations as well. Since a raster map can only have a single cell for any set of XY coordinates, only one nonoverlapping face of a tool may be analyzed at a time. Accordingly, any extraneous points which lie either above or below the desired surface can cause spikes and other anomalies when the point cloud is rasterized by the GIS. The point-cloud must therefore be carefully cleaned (using Meshlab or an equivalent) prior to importing it into the GIS. Nevertheless, GIS is a powerful tool for analyzing surfaces, and its application to use–wear analysis is still exploratory in nature.

7.7.1.1 Unaided Eye Observations and Tool Kinetics

In addition to the analysis of the morphological changes, unaided eye observations also provide a scheme for implementing study at low and high magnifications. The identification of the working part(s) of a tool, the modes of prehension, or the resting surfaces are generally initiated during unaided eye observations. At this stage, it is also possible to assess the kinetic motions involved in the use of the tool. In this respect, Leroi-Gourhan's classification of tool motions (1971, but see also Nierlé 1983; de Beaune 1989, 2004) provides a useful analytical framework (Table 7.6). Henceforth, we will use the terminology presented in Table 7.6. Most relevant for our discussion is the distinction between percussion and abrasion or thrusting percussion, which describes the way force is applied to the processed matter, and the distinction between active and passive tools. In this section, we will discuss use–wear patterns observed at naked eyes on tools used by percussion and by abrasion.

Table 7.6 Description of a tool motion according to Leroi-Gourhan's principles

Stages	Definition – comments
I: Raw material choice and procurement	The tool efficiency is largely determined by raw material properties, so the choice of the raw material is an important aspect for discussing tool function. Furthermore, the type of procurement (e.g., whether it is collected as a pebble or an eroded block or extracted from a quarry) has an impact on the manufacture process.
II: Manufacture	This step is absent for ad hoc implements
III: Primary utilization	The function the artifact was initially designed for
IV: Secondary utilization	Artifacts used for several tasks are frequently referred to as "multifunctional" or as "multiple tools." Adams (2002) differentiated between single use, reuse (when the tool is employed in a second activity that does not alter the design of the tool), and multiple-use (when several areas of the surface are used in distinct activities).
V: Recycling	According to Schiffer and Skibo (1987), recycling necessitates a reshaping of the tool for a new utilization. This definition corresponds to Adams (2002) "redesigned tools" category. For Adams, recycling implies changing the type of use as, for instance, when a ground stone tool is incorporated into the wall of a structure;
VI: Discard	In theory, discard can happen at various stages during and after manufacture, and is the process by which stages I - IV become apparent within a single archaeological assemblage. Exhausted, or worn out, tools which are no longer usable can be identifiable by thinning or perforation of the tool at the working surface, or breakage of the tool. Ground stone tools may be placed in specific discard contest such as grave. The 'killing', or intentional breakage, of ground stone tools placed in grave has been reported ethnographically (Adams, 2008) and the issue is discussed in light of specific archaeological examples in Adams (2008), Van Gijn and Verbaas (2009), Stroulia and Chondrou (2013), Wright (2014). Arguments favoring intentional breakage can be based on recurrent fracture patterns found in an assemblage. Other indices may also be used such as the localization, numbers and arrangements of fracture scars.
VI: Post-depositional processes	After discard, post-depositional processes such as breakage or weathering may affect the shape and surfaces of an implement.

7.7.1.2 Use–wear on Percussive Tools

Noncutting GSTs used by percussion, such as hammerstones or anvils, are associated with impact marks, scars, or breakage as well as abrasion patches. The impacts can be concentrated, forming specific features such as cupholes. Fewer experiments have been performed for percussion tools (Table 7.2) than for tools used by abrasion or thrusting percussion, but they have nonetheless shown variation in use–wear patterns associated with different use-contexts. Macroscopically, these variations encompass the morphology of the impacts, fractures, and abrasion patches as well as the extension, localization, and morphology of the active zone (e.g., Chavaillon 1979; Dodd 1979; Hayden 1987; Willoughby 1987; de Beaune 1989, 1997, 2000; Reid and Pritchard-Parker 1993; Wilke and Quintero 1994, 1996; Goren-Inbar et al. 2002; Poissonier 2002; Mora and de la Torre 2005; Roda Gilabert et al. 2012; de la Torre et al. 2013). The wear pattern characteristics produced on percussion tools, such as impact depth and morphology, are especially sensitive to the raw material properties of both the upper and lower implements.

Recent experiments with quartzite anvils from Olduvai Gorge (de la Torre et al. 2013) contribute to characterizing use–wear in Early Stone Age pounding tools. In these experiments, the abrasion patches produced on the working surface of the quartzite anvils were negligible due to the resistant structure of quartzite crystals. On softer materials, including many igneous and sedimentary rocks, abrasion patches eventually deepen to pits, as observed in chimpanzee stone tool assemblages (Carvalho et al. 2008).

According to experimental results (de la Torre et al. 2013), bone cracking as well as meat and vegetable pounding produces shallow battering (impact) marks; however, bipolar knapping causes significant crystal damage due to the massive load produced by contact between two equally hard elements—the core and the anvil. Thus, crushed areas in bipolar anvils are normally caused by the strong loading force of the core against the passive pounder when the core is hit by the hammer. Repeated contact between the core and the anvil, plus occasional missed blows of the hammer against the anvil, produces abundant deep impact marks over the working surface of the passive pounder. Distance between active (hammer) and passive (anvil) elements during the pounding process is also important to explain battering; for example, strikes are not strong during meat and plant pounding, and therefore, it could be expected that battering marks would be negligible when compared to more forceful percussive tasks. However, during meat and plant pounding, distance between the pounders becomes progressively shorter as the material is processed, producing impact marks on the working surface of active and passive percussion tools.

Impact marks are less common during bone breaking and nut cracking, where the elements being processed are thick and elastic, which dissipates the force of impact. In contrast, both bone and nut cracking cause abrasion on the working surface of anvils, produced by the friction of the nuts and bones against the passive pounder. In addition, since bone cracking is often performed with the bone placed at an angle to the edge of the anvil, damage to the edges, in the form of scarring and rounding, is often observed (de la Torre et al. 2013).

Breakage patterns are relevant in characterizing battered tools, as fracturing of both the active and passive pounder can produce a variety of lithic debris, and modify the morphology of the tools. Experiments aimed at replicating Early Stone Age pounding tools (de la Torre et al. 2013) found that most of the fragments come from the edge of the tools, particularly edges with an angle of <90°. These byproducts are not complete flakes, and only rarely do they feature a striking platform. Instead, they have either very thin sections or irregular thick profiles. Many preserve remnants of the anvil edges, creating a characteristic triangular section (de la Torre et al. 2013). These experimental results support the interpretation of some archeological assemblages from Olduvai Gorge as the byproduct of battering activities (Mora and de la Torre 2005; de la Torre and Mora 2010). Others, such as that shown in Fig. 7.10, bear abundant impact marks produced by unknown pounding tasks

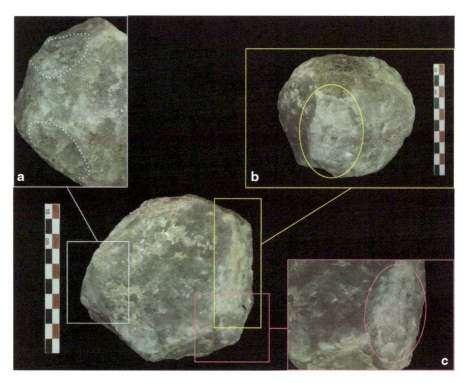

Fig. 7.10 Quartzite battered artifact from TK Lower Floor, an approx. 1.3 million-year-old assemblage from Olduvai Gorge (Tanzania). A) Edge scarring. B) Battering (impact marks). Leakey collections, Museum of Dar-es-Salaam, Tanzania. (I. de la Torre)

and use–wear analysis. Both of archeological and experimental assemblages (de la Torre et al. 2013) can help to disentangle the activities involved in their production.

Generic or poorly developed use–wear is also described in some experiments with percussion tools. For instance, in bone breakage experiments with quartz hammerstones, as described by de la Torre et al. (2013) and also observed in another study (pers.obs., L.D), most of the macroscopically visible impact marks are mainly created when the hammerstone accidentally strikes the anvil. In general, the issue of generic or weakly developed use–wear is most pronounced with expedient tools used for short periods of time.

To the unaided eye, there may be some similarities between the wear patterns created by abrasion and percussion. As noted in some experiments (e.g., Poissonnier 2002), percussive tools used for pecking can develop regularized and beveled surface facets. These facets, produced here by repeated, shallow impacts, are similar to those typically associated with abrasion activities.

7.7.1.3 Use–wear on Tools Used By Abrasion or Thrusting Percussion

The use–wear patterns developed by abrasion, or thrusting percussion, can be described as a leveling or smoothing of the microrelief on the active surface of a GST. As argued by Semenov (1964, p. 66), the high and low elevations of the surface topography of a stone generally present a "hole and bump kind of appearance." On a surface manufactured by pecking, the asperities often look like irregular domes or peaks. The topography of pecked surfaces varies mainly according to the type of raw material, the morphology of the hammerstone's working edge, the force applied, and the angle of impact. When a pecked tool or an implement with an irregular surface is used for grinding or abrading, contact with the processed matter and/or the complementary tool is more extensive on the highest points of the surface, leading to the formation of plateaus and leveled areas. These traces may develop discontinuously across the surface, forming a reticular pattern.

The characteristics of the low and high topography are significant parameters for describing use–wear variation on ground stone implements used for abrasive activities. In this respect, the abundance of plateaus or leveled areas on the working surface, as well as the size, morphology, and roughness of these features, are important variables. Experiments suggest that variation in the low and high aspects of the topography depends on several parameters such as the type of raw material, the techniques of manufacture, the way the tool was used, the processed matter, and the duration of use (see for instance, Dubreuil and Savage 2013, Fig. 7.2).

On GSTs used in abrasive tasks, in addition to the characteristics of low and high topography, striations and reflective patch(es) may also be visible to the unaided eye. Subsequent observations with the microscope and stereomicroscope generally test the hypotheses made at this scale. It should be underlined that most of the criteria defined for use–wear analysis at the stereoscopic and microscopic scales focus on tools used by abrasion. We will focus in the following section on the frameworks established for describing use–wear more than on the criteria used at low and high magnification to assess the tool kinetics and the matter processed. Some of the reasons beyond this are related to the variability found among the different raw materials used for making the GSTs and also to the fact that we would like to encourage the use of a reference collection. As for the unaided observations, comparisons between various zones of the tool, and if possible natural surfaces, are also important to identify and analyze use–wear pattern on an archeological tool.

7.7.2 Low Magnification Analysis

The framework developed by several scholars to study use–wear at low magnification has recently been discussed (Adams et al. 2009). The outline of this framework and additional comments are provided here (Table 7.7). Main characteristics for use–wear description include the aspect of the topography, changes on individual grains, surface reflectivity, and linear traces. Most GSTs are made of raw materials

Tables 7.7 Framework at low magnifications

Activity	Raw material of the active and/or passive tool(s)	References
Grinding, pounding (with upper and lower implements)		
Grinding maize	Medium-grained quartzite and granitic stones, vesicular basalt, sandstone	Wright, 1993; Kamp, 1995; Adams, 1999
Grinding cereals (e.g., wheat, spelt barley, millet)	Granatiferous mica schist, conglomerate, gabbro, wood (olive, oak, almond), metapsammite, basalt, compact sandstone, quartzitic sandstone, fine-grained sandstone	Procopiou, 1998; Menasanch et al. 2002; Risch, 2002; Dubreuil, 2002; Zurro et al., 2005; Hamon, 2007; Delgado-Raack, 2008; Verbaas and van Gjin, 2008; Hamon & Plisson, 2008; Bofill et al., 2013
Pounding cereals	Basalt	Dubreuil, in prep.
Grinding linseed	Quartzitic sandstone	Verbaas and van Gjin, 2008
Grinding sunflower seeds	Medium-grained quartzite, granitic stone, sandstone, vesicular basalt	Adams, 1999
Grinding amaranth seeds	Medium-grained quartzite, granitic stone	Adams, 1999
	Medium-grained quartzite, sandstone	Adams, 1999
	Vesicular basalt	Adams, 1999
Grinding nuts	Basalt	Dubreuil, 2002; Bofill et al. 2013
Grinding acorns	Basalt, quartzitic sandstone	Dubreuil, 2002; Hamon & Plisson, 2009
Pounding acorns	Basalt	Dubreuil, in prep.
Grinding mustard seeds	Basalt	Dubreuil, 2002
Grinding legumes (e.g., fenugreek, feva beans, lentils)	Basalt	Dubreuil, 2002; Bofill et al. 2013
Pounding lentils	Basalt	Dubreuil, in prep.
Pounding rosemary	Basalt	Dubreuil, in prep.
Grinding meat	Basalt	Dubreuil, 2002
Pounding meat	Basalt, quartzitic sandstone, compact sandstone	Hamon & Plisson, 2009; Dubreuil, in prep.
Grinding fish	Basalt	Dubreuil, 2002
Crushing bone, cartilage and marrow	Compact altered sandstone, quartzitic sandstone, calcareous sandstone	Hamon & Plisson, 2009
Grinding pottery clay, pot sherds	Medium-grained quartzite, compact sandstone	Adams, 1989; Cunnar, 2007; Hamon, 2007
Temper grinding ("chamotte", cooked bone and flint)	Compact sandstone	Hamon, 2007
Grinding calcite	Compact sandstone, calcareous sandstone	Hamon & Plisson, 2009
Grinding ochre and processing pigment	Basalt, compact sandstone, medium-grained sandstone	Logan and Fratt, 1993; Dubreuil, 2002; Hamon, 2006; Verbaas and van Gjin, 2008

which are composed of a fine matrix or groundmass in which larger grains are imbedded. Important criteria for describing use–wear at low magnifications concern the changes observed in the morphology of these larger grains. In general, the presence/absence of wear traces on individual grains and the prevalence of these traces across the surface are two important parameters for characterizing use–wear.

In addition to the features mentioned in Table 7.7, several parameters can be used to further characterize the wear traces on individual grains, such as linear traces and surface reflectivity, particularly their incidence on low and high topography; the distribution of wear traces on the surface (e.g., sparse, covering, and concentrated); their density (e.g., separated, adjacent, and connected); their morphology in section and degree of roughness (especially for leveling), and the orientation of the traces (especially for linear traces and pits created by grain removal).

The analytical framework used for describing use–wear must be adapted to the sample that is analyzed. Depending on the variability observed, some aspects will require greater attention than others. Even though the procedure for recording use–wear patterns may vary, the use of common terminology and conceptual frameworks, such as the one presented in this and earlier studies (e.g., Adams et al. 2009) is strongly suggested in order to facilitate the diffusion of the results.

In the framework presented above, the description of wear patterns on the largest grains is critical to use–wear description, and is one of the main criteria used for assessing the properties of the processed matter. An obvious limitation of this system is its application to the study of fine-grained raw materials, whose constituent minerals are too small to be observed under the stereomicroscope. This is the case, for instance, with some varieties of basalt (Dubreuil 2002) and limestone (pers.obs., L.D). In this situation, observations at higher magnifications may provide a viable alternative.

7.7.3 High Magnification Analysis

Investigations at high magnification have focused primarily on micropolish formation. However, other use–wear characteristics are important at this scale as well. These characteristics, presented in Table 7.8, are similar to those investigated at low magnifications. For instance, they include the description of microrelief as well as wear present on the largest grains. Additional criteria are proposed in Table 7.8 to characterize the linear traces at high magnification as well as specific features, such as abraded areas (regularized surfaces with a rough or granular texture and low reflectivity).

An application of this approach is provided in the following example, which illustrates the importance of considering mechanics while interpreting use–wear patterns. The four experiments discussed here, a subset of a larger grooved stone experimental program, focus on the use–wear variability produced by processing bone tools with grooved abraders of both sandstone and basalt. In the first set of experiments, a rotating group of volunteers was asked to grind the shaft of a deer

Table 7.8 Framework at high magnifications

Wear characteristic	Description
The aspect of the topography	Describes whether the topography is uneven, sinuous or leveled, the texture of the surface (rough or smooth), and variation of these factors across the surface of the object
Wear traces on individual grains	Focuses on the damage present on the large grains when clearly distinguishable from the groundmass, most particularly the presence and relative abundance of microfracture, edge rounding, and leveling. In general, the framework outlined at low magnification can be used at high magnification to describe this aspect of use-wear (e.g., relative abundance, density, distribution, etc.)
Linear traces	The framework used at low magnification can be employed at high magnification as well to describe these features. Additional parameters significant at a microscopic scale (following the framework developed for flint tools e.g., Semenov 1964; Keeley 1980; Mansur-Franchomme 1986) include: their reflectivity, whether or not the traces appear abrasive or additive on the surface, the texture of the bottom (rough, smooth, and granulated), and the aspect of the side or ridge Among the linear features observed on flint implements, Keeley (1980, pp. 23–24) includes abrasion tracks, which are defined as broad, deep, and typically short, traces with multiple parallel tracks. The author notes that these traces are associated with a variety of contexts, including manufacture. On basalt ground stone tools, these features were found mostly in association with the manufacture of the surface by pecking, and have been referred to as "impact marks" in previous works (Dubreuil 2002, p. 219)
Abraded areas	Abraded areas are defined here as even, regularized surfaces with a rough or granular texture and low reflectivity. These features are specifically associated with abrasion against a hard, rough surface. It should be noted that our definition differs from Mansur (1997), who attributed these features to postdepositional processes. Abraded areas can be described based on their density (separated, adjacent, and connected), dimension and localization
Surface reflectivity (polish or sheen)	As for low magnification analysis, arbitrary levels of reflectivity can be defined

metapodial to a smooth, even surface, using a reciprocal stroke with the bone held parallel to the base of the groove. The second round of experiments simulated the manufacture of a bone awl by grinding the end of a metapodial fragment at an angle to the base of the groove. Each experiment was performed for a total of 4 h and 15 min.

These use mechanics differ in terms of the pressure applied to the stone as well as the size and morphology of the bone surface making contact with the groove. Abrading a bone shaft along the base of the groove is mostly a horizontal process; with the metapodial held at its free end to the side of the groove, at no point does the bone sit directly between the hand and the stone. By contrast, the higher angle

7 Current Analytical Frameworks for Studies of Use–Wear on Ground Stone Tools 141

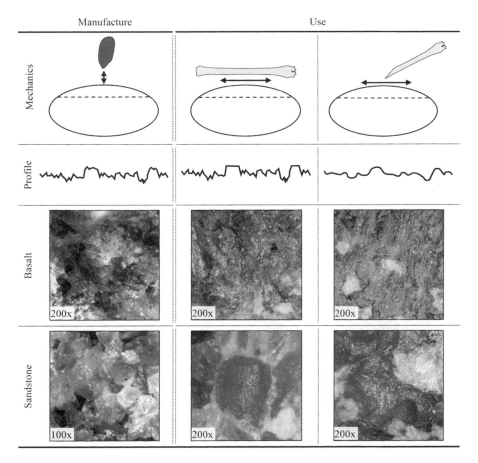

Fig. 7.11 Illustrating the effects of kinetics on wear development. Even though both experiments used the same materials, grinding a bone point caused more dramatic leveling of the basalt and sandstone crytals. Furthermore, the ability of the bone point to follow the topography of the stone caused these wear patterns to be more widely distributed across the surface. (D. Savage)

of attack required for point manufacture involves direct pressure into the groove base, and accordingly, more force spreads across a smaller area. These factors are reflected by the resulting microscopic use–wear patterns, which manifest similarly on both the sandstone and basalt raw materials (Fig. 7.11).

Both experiments resulted in the erosion of the highest peaks of the crystal grains, flattening the asperity of the groove surface, best observed at high magnifications. This effect, which Adams et al. (2009) term leveling, is expressed most dramatically by the point manufacture experiments. These experiments leveled the crystals of both the sandstone and basalt grooves. In the case of the sandstone groove, the result is a network of interconnected plateaus, with only shallow interstices remaining between the quartz grains; similarly, the microtopography of the basalt groove was leveled to an even, continuous surface. Furthermore, the narrow tip of the metapodial fragment traced the existing contour of the basalt groove, equally affecting both the high and low topography, as well as rounding off the margins of the vesicles (the sandstone groove was very flat to begin with). The end result is a topographic profile which can be described as smooth and sinuous.

By contrast, the leveling produced by the shaft abrasion experiments is both, less pronounced and restricted to small, isolated patches of the surface. The length of the metapodial shaft causes it to act as a bridge between the peaks of the microtopography, transforming them into isolated plateaus while leaving most of the groove surface untouched. The crystals on these peaks show some leveling, though the effect did not reach to the bottom of the interstices, and therefore, the grains remain individually distinct. On the sandstone abrader, these interstices became filled with compacted bone powder, which was burnt yellow by frictional heat.

Investigating micropolish formation on GSTs remains a major goal of use–wear analysis at high magnifications. Some studies have shown that raw materials differ in their susceptibility to the development of micropolish. For instance, through experiments, Fullagar and Field (1997) noted that "polish development on weakly cemented sandstone is limited in extent by the constant abrasion of quartz grains." Similarly, Liu et al. (2010) report greater polish development on diabase compared to sandstone.

Yet, well-developed micropolish has also been observed on experimental and archeological GSTs, sometimes with characteristics similar to those seen on flint implements (e.g., plant micropolish). The framework established for the description of micropolish on flint (e.g., Keeley 1980; Anderson-Gerfaud 1981; Vaughan 1981; Plisson 1985; Mansur-Franchomme 1986; Van Gijn 1990) can be adapted to GST analysis. The system developed by Plisson (1985) was mostly used here, however it is important to underline that the terminology used in this study is different. Accordingly, it is suggested to characterize micropolishes based on their localization, their distribution on the surface (e.g., sparse, covering, and concentrated), their density (e.g., separated, adjacent, and connected), orientation, dimensions, and microtopographic context. Microtopographic context refers here to the distribution relative to a number of characteristics of the stone, including: the position on the high and low topography; specific features, such as abraded, rounded, and leveled areas; or even certain types of minerals. Furthermore, micropolish should be described with respect to its morphology in cross-section (irregular, domed, or flat); texture (rough, fluid, or smooth); contours (limits can be sharp or diffuse); structure, which describes variation in the distribution of the micropolish (e.g., separated, closed, or connected); and the presence of special features (for instance striations or pits). It should be noted that variation in the morphology and texture may occur within a micropolish, so that micropolish formations can be described, for instance, as flat/domed or fluid/smooth. The vertical extension, opacity, and brightness are also important features to consider when characterizing micropolish on GST. The vertical extension of the micropolish which can be more or less invasive in the microtopography is often related to the micropolish development in the sense that weakly developed micropolish tends to be superficial. Figure 7.12 provides examples of the criteria used for describing micropolish morphology for features observed on experimental and archeological grooved abraders.

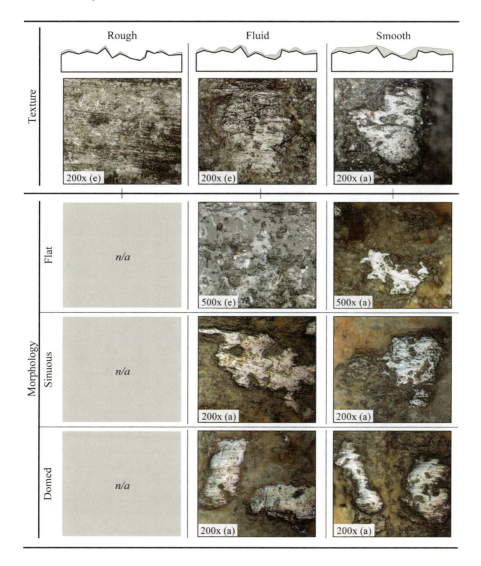

Fig. 7.12 Visual examples of the micropolish criteria outlined in this chapter. Imagery draw from an assortment of archeological (*a*) and experimental (*e*) basalt tools. (D. Savage)

Experiments have shown that the characteristics of micropolish vary as a function of the kinetics and matter involved in a processing task, however, this variation may only be apparent when the micropolish has become sufficiently well developed (e.g., Field and Fullagar 1997; Dubreuil 2004; Dubreuil and Grosman 2009; Cunnar 2007; Verbaas and Van Gijn 2008; Van Gijn and Verbaas 2009; Dubreuil and Plisson 2010; Bofill et al. 2013). Figure 7.13 illustrates distinct types of micropolish

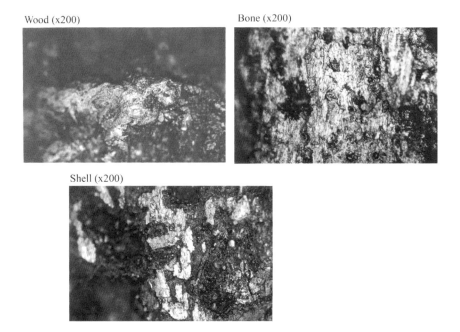

Fig. 7.13 Distinct types of micropolish found on basalt abraders

observed on basalt abraders. Each object was used as a passive implement for 210 min, the worked material being rubbed onto the surface in a back-and-forth motion. Definition of micropolish types associated with specific use context is developing (e.g., Field and Fullagar 1997; Cunnar 2007; Van Gijn and Verbaas 2009; Dubreuil and Grosman 2009, 2013; Bofill et al. 2013), however more experiments are required to better understand micropolish variability.

Even where the entire surface is used, micropolish formation may be restricted to a small area of the working surface or even to a single crystal. On implements such as grinding slabs and handstones, zones of micropolish are often discontinuous on the working surface or present, as described in Liu et al. (2010), as a reticular pattern. A striated type of polish, probably related to an "abrasive background," and caused by contact with the opposing grinding tools, has been described by several authors (e.g., Field and Fullagar 1997 on sandstone, Dubreuil 2002 on basalt; Fig. 7.14). These features present some similarities with use–wear found on abraders used to process hard materials, especially stones (Dubreuil 2002, 2004). On basalt grinding implements, this micropolish can be described as flat, striated, superficial on the topography, translucent to opaque, and reflective.

On basalt implements at least, the micropolish found on abraders and polishers generally shows greater morphological variation than that observed on grinding-slabs and handstones. This can be explained by the presence on grinding-slabs and

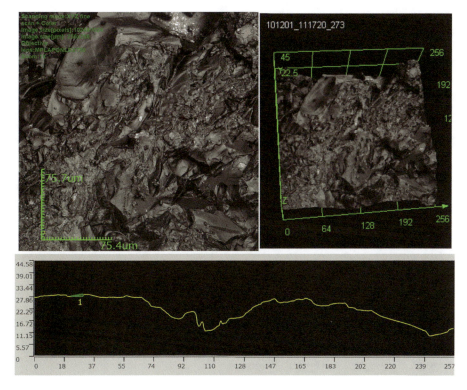

Fig. 7.14 Detail of the working surface of an experimental handstone used for grinding dry naked wheat (Fig. 3a From a quoted article of Hamon and Plisson 2008) and cross section. Olympus LEXT OSL4000 laser confocal microscope with 50× objective. Measurement in pixel and micrometer. (Hugues Plisson)

handstones of the aforementioned "abrasive background." As well, diagnostic micropolish seems to develop faster on abraders and polishers. Along the same lines, it is interesting to note that well-developed prehension wear is commonly found on GST. This type of micropolish is apparent on all aspects of the microrelief, and can be described as bright, opaque, rather thick, domed, and smooth.

7.8 Conclusion

Use–wear approaches are critical in ground stone studies, including in the first steps of the analysis, since tool description and classification already incorporate information about wear patterns. Obviously, use–wear approaches can also provide significant data on the function of a ground stone tool. Functional hypotheses based on ground stone tools play a major role in the interpretation of key anthropological events, including the emergence of early hominid technology and complex cognitive abilities, the transition from foraging to farming, and the rise of symbolic behavior and hierarchical social organization, and gender construction.

The main objective of use–wear analysis is to unravel the function of a tool by assessing both its kinetics and the material(s) processed. Use–wear analysis generally allows the identification of broad, more of less inclusive, categories of processed materials (e.g., soft, hard or stone, bone, wood, etc.), and in some cases, the state in which this matter was processed (for instance, dry or damp). In this respect, residue analysis can permit a more precise determination. A wide range of organic and nonorganic residues, as well as methods of sampling and identification, are currently being investigated. Residue and use–wear approaches are complementary, especially considering that use–wear is needed to assess the kinetics of the tool. Kinetics is an important, often disregarded aspect of tool function; the kinetics of a processing task indicates how the tool was operated, and therefore, how the material was transformed.

Assessing the kinetics and the processed material(s) only represents part of the definition of the function of a tool, the more "technical" part. A comprehensive definition would require unraveling for what purpose(s) the identified activity was performed and by whom the tool was operated (Sigaut 1991). While this is beyond the scope of the use–wear approach alone, these issues can nevertheless be approached by combining use–wear and spatial analysis. Furthermore, the use–wear approach not only allows investigating a tool's function but its entire life history as well. To this end, use–wear analysis can provide significant data on tool manufacture, specialization, recycling, and discard behaviors.

Use–wear analysis relies to a great extent on experiments. Experiments which have been carried out with ground stone objects cover a wide range of tool types, raw materials, and tasks. Nevertheless, only a limited fraction of ground stone variability has been explored so far. Replication of experiments and blind tests—two approaches that are important for strengthening the analytical framework of use–wear analysis—are still too few.

The available experimental evidence indicates that use–wear characteristics vary, among other factors, according to the type of processed matter and the kinetics of the processing task. The integration of observations made with the unaided eye, as well as at low and high magnifications, is ideal because it increases the accuracy of use–wear interpretations. Depending on the type of rock and modes of use, one scale of observation may be more informative than another.

Observations with unaided eyes are particularly important as many features are best observed and described at this scale, including morphological changes resulting from use, such as the formation of cupholes, facets, grooves, or any other alteration to the working surface. Morphological changes are a significant manifestation of the use, maintenance, and recycling of a tool, however, they remain understudied. Analysis of these morphological changes can greatly benefit from the development of GIS and 3D modeling approaches reviewed in this chapter. Unaided observations often provide a scheme for implementing study at low and high magnifications, and enable the identification of the working part(s) of a tool, the modes of prehension, or the resting surfaces.

Regarding low magnification analysis, a synthesis of experiments carried out by several scholars has led to the creation of a general analytical framework, which is applicable to a wide range of raw materials and tools (Adams et al. 2009). However, as emphasized above, this framework is of limited value for fine-grained raw materials.

As suggested in this chapter, observations at high magnifications can be used to further investigate those made at low magnifications; however, the analysis of micropolish has been privileged at this scale. Experiments have shown that the formation of well-developed micropolish is not assured, even after a relatively long period of utilization. For instance, rocks with loose and easily dislodged minerals may prevent the formation of micropolish. When present, micropolish is not necessarily evident on the entire working surface, but can be limited to small areas or to single mineral grains. A number of studies have documented the development of diagnostic micropolish both on experimental and archeological ground stone objects. It is suggested here that the system developed in chipped stone analysis for the description of micropolish can be adapted to GST study. More experiments are required in order to define the micropolish morphological characteristics associated with specific use contexts.

New advances in use–wear analysis, including the use of electronic and confocal microscopy, as well as tribological approaches, will likely provide more precise information on certain aspects of use–wear on GSTs, especially with regard to the quantification of use–wear characteristics and the investigation of formation processes. These two dimensions are critical for improving the use–wear analysis of ground stone implements.

Acknowledgments The authors would like to thank Maria Bofill, Hara Procopiou, and Roberto Risch for their comments on early drafts of the manuscript. Funding for this research was provided by the Fondation Fyssen (LD), the Trent University Archaeological Research Center (DS), the Social Sciences and Humanities Research Council of Canada (LD and DS), and Lascarbx for the project "Tracéologie tridimensionnelle" (HP). IT acknowledges funding provided for this research by the Leverhulme Trust (IN-052) and the European Research Council (Starting Grants—283366). BS acknowledges The University of Queensland (UQ), School of Social Science, and In the Groove Analysis Pty Ltd (Brisbane, Australia).

References

Adams, J. L. (1993). Technological development of manos and metates on the Hopi mesas. *Kiva, 58,* 331–344.
Adams, J. (1994). The development of prehistoric grinding technology in the point of pines area, east-central Arizona. Ph.D Thesis, University of Arizona, Arizona.
Adams, J. L. (1988). Use-wear analyses on manos and hide-processing stones. *Journal of Field Archaeology, 15*(3), 307–315.
Adams, J. L. (1989). Methods for improving ground stone analysis: Experiments in mano wear patterns. In D. S. Amick & R. P. Mauldin (Eds.), *Experiments in lithic technology* (pp. 259–276). Oxford: Archaeopress.
Adams, J. L. (1999). Refocusing the role of food-grinding tools as correlates for subsistence strategies in the U.S. Southwest. *American Antiquity, 64*(3), 475–498.

Adams, J. L. (2002). *Ground stone analysis : A technological approach*. Salt Lake City: University of Utah Press.

Adams, J. L. (2008). Beyond the broken. In Y. M. Rowan & R. Z. Smith (Eds.), *New approaches to old stones: Recent studies of ground stone artifacts* (pp. 213–229). London: Equinox Publishing Ltd.

Adams, J. L., Delgado, S., Dubreuil, L., Hamon, C., Plisson, H., & Risch, R. (2009). Functional analysis of macro-lithic artefacts: A focus on working surfaces. In F. Sternke, L. Eigeland, & L. J. Costa (Eds.), *Non-flint raw material use in prehistory: Old prejudices and new directions* (pp. 43–66). Oxford: Archaeopress.

Alonso Martinez, N. (2002). Le moulin rotatif manuel au nord-est de la Péninsule ibérique: Une innovation technique dans le contexte domestique de la mouture des céréales. In H. Procopiou & R. Treuil (Eds.), *Moudre et Broyer* (pp. 111–127). Paris: CTHS.

Anderson, P. C. (1980). A testimony of prehistoric tasks: Diagnostic residues on stone tool working edges. *World Archaeology, 12*(2), 181–194.

Anderson, P. C., Georges, J.-M., Vargiolu, R., & Zahouani, H. (2006). Insights from a tribological analysis of the tribulum. *Journal of Archaeological Science, 33*(11), 1559–1568.

Anderson-Gerfaud, P. (1981). *Contribution méthodologique à l'analyse des microtraces d'utilisation sur les outils préhistoriques*. Bordeaux: Institut de Préhistoire et de Géologie du Quaternaire, Université de Bordeaux I.

Astruc, L., Vargiolu, R., & Zahouani, H. (2003). Wear assessments of prehistoric instruments. *Wear, 255*(1–6), 341–347.

Bahadur, S. (2012). Wear: A synoptic view. In G. Totten (Ed.), *Handbook of lubrification and tribology* (pp. 6–90). Boca Raton: Taylor & Francis.

Bar-Yosef, O. (1980). Prehistory of the Levant. *Annual Review of Anthropology, 9*(1), 101–133.

Bar-Yosef, O. (1981). The Epi-Palaeolithic complexes in Southern Levant. In M. C. Cauvin & P. Sanlaville (Eds.), *Préhistoire du Levant. Chronologie et organisation de l'espace depuis les origines jusqu'au VIème Millénaire* (pp. 389-408). Editions du CNRS.

Barton, H. (2007). Starch residues on museum artefacts: Implications for determining tool use. *Journal of Archaeological Science, 34*(10), 1752–1762.

Baudais, D., & Lundström-Baudais, K. (2002). Enquête ethnoarchéologique dans un village du nord-ouest du Népal. In H. Procopiou & R. Treuil (Eds.), *Moudre et Broyer, I Méthodes* (pp. 155–180). Paris: CTHS.

Baysal, A., & Wright, K. I. (2005). Cooking, crafts and curation: the ground stone artefacts from Çatalhöyük. In I. Hodder (Ed.), *Excavations at Çatalhöyük, Volume 5. Changing materialities at Çatalhöyük: Reports from the 1995–1999 seasons* (pp. 313–324). Cambridge: British Institute for Archaeology at Ankara.

Belfer-Cohen, A., & Hovers, E. (2005). The ground-stone assemblages of the Natufian and Neolithic Societies in the Levant—A brief review. *Journal of the Israel Prehistoric Society, 35*, 299–308.

Berejnov, V. (2009). Rapid and inexpensive reconstruction of 3D Structures for Micro-Objects Using Common Optical Microscopy. arXiv.org, 2024. http://arxiv.org/abs/0904.2024.

Binford, L. R. (1971). Mortuary practices: Their study and their potential. In J. A. Brown (Ed.), *Approaches to the social dimensions of mortuary practices* (pp. 6–29). Michigan: Society for American Archaeology.

Blau, P. J. (1996). *Friction science and technology*. New York: Dekker.

Bofill, M. (2012). Quantitative analysis of use-wear patterns: A functional approach to study grinding stone tools. In Broadening horizons 3: Conference of young researchers working in the Ancient Near East (pp. 63–84). Barcelona: Universitat Autonoma de Barcelona.

Bofill, M., & Taha, B. (2013). Experimental approach to hide-processing task combining the use of bone and basalt tools: The Neolithic case of Tell Halula (Middle Euphrates Valley, Syria). In R. Palomo, R. Piqué, & X. Terradas (Eds.), *Experimentacion in arqueologia* (pp. 45–55). Girona: Serie Monografica del MAC.

Bofill, M., Procopiou, H., Vargiolu, R., & Zahouani, H. (2013). Use-wear analysis of near eastern prehistoric grinding stones. In P. C. Anderson, C. Cheval, & A. Durand (Eds.), *Regards croisés sur les outils liés au travail des végétaux* (pp. 225–242).

Bradley, R., Meredith, P., Smith, J., & Edmonds, M. (1992). Rock physics and the neolithic axe trade in great britain. *Archaeometry, 34*(2), 223–233.

Bril, B., Smaers, J., Steele, J., Rein, R., Nonaka, T., Dietrich, G., Biryukova, E., Hirata, S., & Roux, V. (2011). Functional mastery of percussive technology in nut-cracking and stone-flaking actions: Experimental comparison and implications for the evolution of the human brain. *Philosophical Transactions of the Royal Society B, Biological Sciences, 367*(1585), 59–74.

Briuer, F. L. (1976). New clues to stone tool function: Plant and animal residues. *American Antiquity, 41*(4), 478–484.

Broz, M. E., Cook, R. F., & Whitney, D. L. (2006). Microhardness, toughness, and modulus of Mohs scale minerals. *American Mineralogist, 91*(1), 135–142.

Buonasera, T. (2005). Fatty acid analysis of prehistoric burned rocks: A case study from central California. *Journal of Archaeological Science, 32*(6), 957–965.

Buonasera, T. (2007). Investigating the presence of ancient absorbed organic residues in groundstone using GC-MS and other analytical techniques: A residue study of several prehistoric milling tools from central California. *Journal of Archaeological Science, 34*(9), 1379–1390.

Buonasera, T. (2012). Expanding archaeological approaches to ground stone: Modeling manufacturing costs, analyzing absorbed organic residues, and exploring social dimensions of milling tools, Ph.D. University of Arizona, Tucson, Dissertation.

Buonasera, T. (2013). Extracting new information from old experiments: GC/MS analysis of organic residues in aged experimental grinding tools. *SAS Bulletin, 36*(1), 2–7.

Byrne, L., Ollé, A., & Vergès, J. M. (2006). Under the hammer: Residues resulting from production and microwear on experimental stone tools. *Archaeometry, 48*(4), 549–564.

Carr, C. (1995). Mortuary practices: Their social, philosophical-religious, circumstantial, and physical determinants. *Journal of Archaeological Method and Theory, 2*(2), 105–200.

Carvalho, S., Cunha, E., Sousa, C., & Matsuzawa, T. (2008). Chaînes opératoires and resource-exploitation strategies in chimpanzee (Pan troglodytes) nut cracking. *Journal of Human Evolution, 55*(1), 148–163.

Chavaillon, J. (1979). Essai pour une typologie du matériel de percussion. *Bulletin de La Société Préhistorique Française, 76*(8), 230–233.

Christensen, M. (1998). Processus de formation et caractérisation physico-chimique des polis d'utilisation des outils de silex. Application à la technologie de l'ivoire. *Bulletin de La Société Préhistorique Française, 95,* 183–202.

Christensen, M., & Valla, F. R. (1999). Pour relancer un débat : que sont les pierres à rainure du Natoufien Proche-Oriental? *Bulletin de La Société Préhistorique Française, 96*(2), 247–252.

Clemente, I., Risch, R., & Zurro, D. (2002). Complementariedad entre analisis de residuos y trazas de uso para la determinacion functional de los instrumentos macroliticos: su aplicacion a un ejemplo etnografico del pais Dogon (Mali). In I. Clemente, R. Risch, & J. Gibaja (Eds.), *Analisis Funcional. Su Applicacion al Estudio de Sociedades Prehistoricas.* Oxford: BAR.

Cristiani, E., Lemorini, C., & Dalmeri, G. (2012). Ground stone tool production and use in the Late Upper Palaeolithic: The evidence from Riparo Dalmeri (Venetian Prealps, Italy). *Journal of Field Archaeology, 37*(1), 34–50.

Crowther, A. (2009). Investigating Lapita subsistence and pottery use through microscopic residues on ceramics: Methodological issues, feasibility and potential, Ph.D Dissertation, School of Social Science, University of Queensland, Brisbane.

Cunnar, G. E. (2007). The production and use of stone tools at the Longshan period site of Liangchengzhen, China, Ph.D Dissertation, Yale University, Yale.

Curtis, R. I. (2001). *Ancient food technology.* Leiden: Brill.

D'Errico, F., & Stringer, C. B. (2011). Evolution, revolution or saltation scenario for the emergence of modern cultures? *Philosophical Transactions of the Royal Society B: Biological Sciences, 366*(1567), 1060–1069.

D'Errico, F., Vanhaeren, M., Henshilwood, C., Lawson, G., Maureille, B., Gambier, D., & Van Niekerk, K. (2009). From the origin of language to the diversification of languages: What can archaeology and palaeoanthropology say? In F. d'Errico & J. M. Hombert (Eds.), *Becoming eloquent: Advances in the emergence of language, human cognition, and modern cultures* (pp. 13–68). Amsterdam: Benjamins Publishing Company.

De Beaune, S. A. (1989). Essai d'une classification typologique des galets et plaquettes utilisés au Paléolithique. *Gallia Préhistoire, 31*(1), 27–64.

De Beaune, S. A. (1993). Approches expérimentales de techniques paléolithiques de façonnage des roches peu aptes à la taille. *Paléo, 5,* 155–174.

De Beaune, S. A. (1997). Les galets utilisés au Paléolithique supérieur : approche archéologique et expérimentale. Presented at the XXXIIème supplément à "Gallia Préhistoire," Paris: CNRS éditions.

De Beaune, S. A. (2000). *Pour une archéologie du geste. broyer, moudre, piler, des premiers chasseurs aux premiers agriculteurs*. Paris: CNRS éditions.

De Beaune, S. A. (2004). The invention of technology: Prehistory and cognition. *Current Anthropology, 45*(2), 139–162.

De Beaune, S. A., & Pinçon, G. (2001). Approche expérimentale des techniques magdaléniennes de sculpture pariétale: le cas d'Angles-sur-l'Anglin (Vienne). In L. Bourguignon, I. Ortega, & M.-C. Frère-Sautot (Eds.), *Préhistoire et approche expérimentale* (pp. 67–75). Montagnac: Editions Monique Mergoil.

de la Torre, I., & Mora, R. (2010). A technological analysis of non-flaked stone tools in Olduvai Beds I & II. Stressing the relevance of percussion activities in the African Lower Pleistocene. In V. Mourre & M. Jarry (Eds.), *Entre le marteau et l'enclume. La percussion directe au percuteur dur et la diversité de ses modalités d'application. Actes de la table ronde de Toulouse* (pp. 13–34), 15–17 March 2004.

de la Torre, I., Benito-Calvo, A., Arroyo, A., Zupancich, A., & Proffitt, T. (2013). Experimental protocols for the study of battered stone anvils from Olduvai Gorge (Tanzania). *Journal of Archaeological Science, 40*(1), 313–332.

Del Pilar Babot, M., & Apella, M. C. (2003). Maize and bone: Residues of grinding in northwestern Argentina. *Archaeometry, 45*(1), 121–132.

Delgado-Raack, S. (2008). Prácticas económicas y gestión social de recursos técnicos en la Prehistoria Reciente (III-I Milenio AC) del Mediterráneo Occidental, Ph.D Dissertation, Universitat Autònoma de Barcelona, Bellaterra.

Delgado-Raack, S. (2013). *Tecnotipología y distribución especial del material macrolítico del Cerro de la Vigen de Orce (Granada)*. Oxford: Bar 2518.

Delgado-Raack, S., & Risch, R. (2008). Lithic perspectives on metallurgy: An example from Copper and Bronze Age south-east Iberia. In L. Longo (Ed.), *"Prehistoric technology" 40 years later: Functional studies and the Russian legacy* (pp. 235–252). Verona: Museo Civico di Verona, & Universita degli Studi di Verona.

Delgado-Raack, S., & Risch, R. (2009). Towards a systematic analysis of grain processing technologies. In M. de Araujo Igreja & I. Clemente (Eds.), *Proceedings of the workshop: Recent functional studies on non flint stone tools: Methodological improvements and archaeological inferences*. Lisbon.

Delgado-Raack, S., Gómez-Gras, D., & Risch, R. (2008). Las propiedades mecánicas de los artefactos macrolíticos: Una base metodológica para el análisis funcional. In S. Rovira, M. García-Heras, M. Genery, & I. Montero (Eds.), *Actas del VII Congreso Ibérico de Arqueometría* (pp. 330–345). Madrid.

Delgado-Raack, S., Gómez-Gras, D., & Risch, R. (2009). The mechanical properties of macrolithic artifacts: A methodological background for functional analysis. *Journal of Archaeological Science, 36*(9), 1823–1831.

Deseilligny, M. P., & Clery, I. (2011). Évolution récentes en photogrammétrie et modélisation 3D par photo des milieux naturels. In S. Jaillet & E. Ployon (Eds.), *Images et modèles 3D en milieux naturels* (Vol. 12, pp. 51–66). Le Bourget-du-Lac: Edytem.

Diamond, G. (1979). The nature of so-called polished surfaces on stone artifacts. In B. Hayden (Ed.), *Lithic use-wear analysis* (pp. 159–166). New York: Academic.

Dodd, W. A. (1979). The wear and use of battered tools at Armijo Rockshelter. In B. Hayden (Ed.), *Lithic use-wear analysis* (pp. 231–242). New York: Academic.

Dubreuil, L. (in prep). Investigating Natufian mortars and pestles function: An experimental approach.

Dubreuil, L. (2002). Etude fonctionnelle des outils de broyage natoufiens: nouvelles perspectives sur l'émergence de l'agriculture au Proche-Orient, Ph.D Dissertation, Bordeaux I University, Bordeaux.

Dubreuil, L. (2004). Long-term trends in Natufian subsistence: A use-wear analysis of ground stone tools. *Journal of Archaeological Science, 31*(11), 1613–1629.

Dubreuil, L. (2008). Mortar versus grinding-slabs and the neolithization process in the Near East. In L. Longo & N. Skakun (Eds.), *"Prehistoric Technology" 40 years later: Functional studies and the Russian legacy* (pp. 169–177). Verona: Museo Civico di Verona, and Universita degli Studi di Verona.

Dubreuil, L. (2009). Functional analysis of grinding tools from the natufian site of mallaha: Toward an understanding of assemblage evolution in the levant. *The Arkeotek Journal, 3*(1), (Online Publication).

Dubreuil, L., & Grosman, L. (2009). Ochre and hide-working at a Natufian burial place. *Antiquity, 83*(322), 935–954.

Dubreuil, L., & Grosman, L. (2013). The life history of macrolithic tools at Hilazon Tachtit cave. In O. Bar-Yosef & F. R. Valla (Eds.), *Natufian foragers in the Levant: Terminal Pleistocene social changes in western Asia* (pp. 527–543). Ann Arbor: International Monographs in Prehistory.

Dubreuil, L., & Plisson, H. (2010). Natufian flint versus ground stone tools: A use-wear perspective on subsistance change. *Eurasian Prehistory, 7*(1), 45–60.

Dubreuil, L., & Rosen, A. (2010). Alternative methods for gathering: Direct and indirect evidence of plant exploitation during the Natufian. *Eurasian Prehistory, 7*(1), 3–5.

Dubreuil, L., & Savage, D. (2013). Ground stones: A synthesis of the use-wear approach. *Journal of Archaeological Science, 48*, 139–153.

Ertug-Yaras, F. (2002). Pounders and grinders in a modern central Anatolian village. In H. Procopiou & R. Treuil (Eds.), *Moudre et Broyer* (pp. 211–225). Paris: CTHS.

Evans, A. A., & Donahue, R. E. (2005). The elemental chemistry of lithic microwear: An experiment. *Journal of Archaeological Science, 32*(12), 1733–1740.

Field, J., Cosgrove, R., Fullagar, R., & Lance, B. (2009). Starch residues on grinding stones in private collections: A study of morahs from the tropical rainforests of NE Queensland. In M. Haslam, G. Robertson, A. Crowther, S. Nugent, & L. Kirkwood (Eds.), *Archaeological science under a microscope studies in residue and ancient DNA analysis* (pp. 228–238). Canberra: ANU E Press. (In honour of Thomas H. Loy).

Flannery, K. V. (1969). Origins and ecological effects of early domestication in Iran and the Near East. In P. J. Ucko & G. W. Dimbleby (Eds.), *The domestication and exploitation of plants and animals* (pp. 73–100). Chicago: Aldine Publishing Company.

Flannery, K. V. (1973). The origins of agriculture. *Annual Review of Anthropology, 2*, 271–310.

Formenti, F., & Procopiou, H. (1998). Analyse chromatographique de traces d'acides gras sur l'outillage de mouture. Contribution à son interprétation fonctionnelle. *Cahiers de l'Euphrate, 8*, 151–177.

Fullagar, R., & Field, J. (1997). Pleistocene seed-grinding implements from the Australian arid zone. *Antiquity, 71*(272), 300–307.

Fullagar, R., & Jones, R. (2004). Usewear and residue analysis of stone artefacts from the enclosed chamber, Rocky Cape, Tasmania. *Archaeology in Oceania, 39*, 79–93.

Fullagar, R., & Stephenson, B. (2012). A Functional study of grinding stones from South Flank, Pilbara, W.A. An unpublished report prepared by scarp archaeology and in the groove analysis Pty Ltd for BHP Billiton.

Fullagar, R., & Wallis, L. (2011). Usewear and phytoliths on bedrock grinding patches in North-Western Australia. In L. Russel (Ed.), Papers in Honour of Beth Gott.

Geneste, D., Plisson, H., Delannoy, J. J., & Petchey, F. (2012). The origins of ground-edge axes: New findings from Nawarla Gabarnmang, Arnhem Land (Australia) and global implications for the evolution of fully modern humans. *Cambridge Archaeological Journal, 22,* 1–17.

Gonzalez, J. E., & Ibanez, J. J. (2002). The use of pebbles in Eastern Vizcaya between 12 000 and 10 000 B.P. In H. Procopiou & R. Treuil (Eds.), *Moudre et broyer: L'interprétation fonctionnelle de l'outillage de mouture et de broyage dans la préhistoire et l'antiquité* (pp. 69–80). Paris: CTHS.

Goren-Inbar, N., Sharon, G., Melamed, Y., & Kislev, M. (2002). Nuts, nut cracking, and pitted stones at Gesher Benot Ya'aqov, Israel. *Proceedings of the National Academy of Sciences, 99,* 2455–2460.

Hamon, C. (2006). *Broyage et abrasion au Neolithique ancien. Caracterisation technique et fonctionnelle des outils en gres du Bassin parisien.* Oxford: Archaeopress.

Hamon, C. (2007). Functional analysis of stone grinding and polishing tools from the earliest Neolithic of north-western Europe. *Journal of Archaeological Science, 36,* 1502–1520.

Hamon, C., & Le Gall, V. (2013). Millet and sauce: The uses and functions of querns among the Minyanka (Mali). *Journal of Anthropological Archaeology, 32*(1), 109–121.

Hamon, C., & Plisson, H. (2009). Functional analysis of grinding stones: The blind test. In L. Longo & N. Skakun (Eds.), *"Prehistoric Technology" 40 years later: Functional studies and the Russian legacy* (pp. 29–38). Verona: Museo Civico di Verona, & Universita degli Studi di Verona.

Hampton, O. W. (1997). Rock quarries and the manufacture, trade, and uses of stone tools and symbolic stones in the Central Highlands of Irian Jaya, Indonesia: Ethnoarchaeological perspectives, Ph.D Dissertation, Texas A & M University, College Station.

Haslam, M. (2004). The decomposition of starch grains in soils: Implications for archaeological residue analyses. *Journal of Archaeological Science, 31*(12), 1715–1734.

Haslam, M. (2009). Mountains and molehills: Sample size in archaeological microscopic stone-tool residue analysis. In M. Haslam, G. Robertson, A. Crowther, S. Nugent, & L. Kirkwood (Eds.), *Archaeological science under a microscope studies in residue and ancient dna analysis in honour of Thomas H. Loy* (pp. 47–79). Canberra: ANU E Press.

Haslam, M., Hernandez-Aguilar, A., Ling, V., Carvalho, S., de la Torre, I., DeStefano, A., & Warren, R. (2009). Primate archaeology. *Nature, 460*(7253), 339–344.

Hayden, B. (1987). *Lithic studies among the contemporary highland Maya.* Tucson: University of Arizona Press.

Hayden, B. (1990). Nimrods, piscators, pluckers, and planters: The emergence of food production. *Journal of Anthropological Archaeology, 9*(1), 31–69.

Hayden, B. (2004). Sociopolitical organization in the Natufian: A view from the Northwest. In C. Delage (Ed.), *The last hunter-gatherer societies in the Near East* (pp. 263–308). Oxford: John and Erica Hedges.

Hayden, B. (2009). The proof is in the pudding. *Current Anthropology 50,* 596–601.

Hayden, B., Canuel, N., & Shanse, J. (2013). What was brewing in the Natufian? An archaeological assessment of brewing technology in the Epipaleolithic. *Journal of Archaeological Method and Theory, 20*(1), 102–150.

Henshilwood, C. S., d'Errico, F., van Niekerk, K. L., Coquinot, Y., Jacobs, Z., Lauritzen, S.-E., & Garcia-Moreno, R. (2011). A 100,000-year-old ochre-processing workshop at Blombos Cave, South Africa. *Science, 334*(6053), 219–222.

Högberg, A., Puseman, K., & Yost, C. (2009). Integration of use-wear with protein residue analysis—a study of tool use and function in the south Scandinavian Early Neolithic. *Journal of Archaeological Science, 36*(8), 1725–1737.

Horsfall, G. A. (1987). Design theory and grinding stones. In B. Hayden (Ed.), *Lithic studies among the contemporary highland Maya* (pp. 332–372). Tucson: University of Arizona Press.

Kamminga, J. (1979). The nature of use-polish and abrasive smoothing on stone tools. In B. Hayden (Ed.), *Lithic use-wear analysis* (pp. 143–157). New York: Academic.

Kamp, K. (1995). A use-wear analysis of the function of basalt cylinders. *Kiva, 61,* 109–119.

Keeley, L. H. (1980). *Experimental determination of stone tool uses: A microwear analysis.* Chicago: University of Chicago Press.

Klein, R. G. (2009). *The human career: Human biological and cultural origins* (3rd ed.). Chicago: The University of Chicago Press.

Lamb, J., & Loy, T. (2005). Seeing red: The use of Congo Red dye to identify cooked and damaged starch grains in archaeological residues. *Journal of Archaeological Science, 32*(10), 1433–1440.

Langejans, G. H. J. (2010). Remains of the day-preservation of organic micro-residues on stone tools. *Journal of Archaeological Science, 37*(5), 971–985.

Leakey, M. D. (1971). *Olduvai Gorge, Vol.3. Excavations in Beds I and II, 1960–1963.* Cambridge: Cambridge University Press.

Leroi-Gourhan, A. (1971). *L'homme et la matière* (2nd ed.). Paris: Albin Michel.

Lidström Holmberg, C. (1998). Prehistoric grinding tools as metaphorical traces of the past. *Current Swedish Archaeology, 6,* 123–142.

Lidström Holmberg, C. (2004). Saddle querns and gendered dynamics of the Early Neolithic in Mid Central Sweden. In H. Knutsson (Ed.), *Proceedings of the final coast to coast conference 1–5 October 2002 in Falköping, Sweden* (pp. 199–231). Uppsala: Uppsala University.

Littlefield, R. (2010). Infinity objective on low-end zoom telephoto works fine. http://www.photomacrography.net/forum/viewtopic.php?t=9664.

Liu, L., Field, J., Fullagar, R., Bestel, S., Chen, X., & Ma, X. (2010). What did grinding stones grind? New light on Early Neolithic subsistence economy in the middle Yellow River Valley, China. *Antiquity, 84,* 813–833.

Liu, L., Field, J., Fullagar, R., Zhao, C., Chen, X., & Yu, J. (2011). A functional analysis of grinding stones from an early Holocene site at Donghulin, North China. *Journal of Archaeological Science, 37,* 2630–2639.

Logan, E., & Fratt, L. (1993). Pigment processing at Homol'ovi III: A preliminary study. *Kiva, 58,* 415–428.

Lombard, M. (2005). Evidence of hunting and hafting during the Middle Stone Age at Sibidu Cave, KwaZulu-Natal, South Africa: A multianalytical approach. *Journal of Human Evolution, 48*(3), 279–300.

Lombard, M. (2008). Finding resolution for the Howiesons Poort through the microscope: Micro-residue analysis of segments from Sibudu Cave, South Africa. *Journal of Archaeological Science, 35*(1), 26–41.

Maher, L. A., Banning, E. B., & Chazan, M. (2011). Oasis or mirage? Assessing the role of abrupt climate change in the prehistory of the Southern Levant. *Cambridge Archaeological Journal, 21*(01), 1–30.

Mansur, M. E. (1997). Functional analysis of polished stone-tools: Some considerations about the nature of polishing. In M. A. Bustillo & A. Ramos Millan (Eds.), *Siliceous rocks and culture* (pp. 465–486). Madrid: CSIC et Université de Grenade.

Mansur-Franchomme, M. E. (1986). *Microscopie du matériel lithique préhistorique. Traces d'utilisation, altérations naturelles, accidentelles et technologiques: exemples de Patagonia.* Bordeaux: Éditions du Centre National de la Recherche Scientifique.

Mcbrearty, S., & Brooks, A. S. (2000). The revolution that wasn't: A new interpretation of the origin of modern human behavior. *Journal of Human Evolution, 39*(5), 453–563.

McGrew, W. C. (2010). In search of the last common ancestor: New findings on wild chimpanzees. *Philosophical Transactions of the Royal Society B: Biological Sciences, 365*(1556), 3267–3276.

Meeks, N. D., de G. Sieveking, G., Tite, M. S., & Cook, J. (1982). Gloss and use-wear traces on flint sickles and similar phenomena. *Journal of Archaeological Science, 9*(4), 317–340.

Menasanch, M., Risch, R., & Soldevilla, J. A. (2002). Los tecnologias del procesado de cereal en el sudeste de la peninsula ibérica durante el III y el II milenio A.N.E. In H. Procopiou & R. Treuil (Eds.), *Moudre et Broyer* (pp. 81–110). Paris: CTHS.

Mercader, J., Barton, H., Gillespie, J., Harris, J., Kuhn, S., Tyler, R., & Boesch, C. (2007). 4,300-Year-old chimpanzee sites and the origins of percussive stone technology. *Proceedings of the National Academy of Sciences, 104*(9), 3043–3048.

Miller, N. (1991). The Near East. In W. Van Zeist, K. Wasylikowa, & K. Behre (Eds.), *Progress in old world palaeoethnobotany* (pp. 133–160). Rotterdam: A.A. Balkema.

Milleville, A. (2007). "De la pierre à la meule" durant le néolithique. Circulation et gestion des matières premières entre Rhin et Rhône, Ph.D Dissertation, Université de Franche-Comté, Besançon.

Mora, R., & de la Torre, I. (2005). Percussion tools in Olduvai Beds I and II (Tanzania): Implications for early human activities. *Journal of Anthropological Archaeology, 24,* 179–182.

Nadel, D., Piperno, D. R., Holst, I., Snir, A., & Weiss, E. (2012). New evidence for the processing of wild cereal grains at Ohalo II, a 23 000-year-old campsite on the shore of the Sea of Galilee, Israel. *Antiquity, 86*(334), 990–1003.

Nierlé, M. C. (1983). Mureybet et Cheik Hassan (Syrie): outillage de mouture et de broyage (9e et 8e millénaires). *Cahiers de l'Euphrate, 3,* 177–216.

Odell, G. H. (2001). Stone tool research at the end of the millennium: Classification, function, and behavior. *Journal of Archaeological Research, 9*(1), 45–100.

Pearsall, D. M., Chandler-Ezell, K., & Zeidler, J. A. (2004). Maize in ancient Ecuador: Results of residue analysis of stone tools from the Real Alto site. *Journal of Archaeological Science, 31*(4), 423–442.

Pierrot-Deseilligny, M., & Clery, I. (2011). Évolution récentes en photogrammétrie et modélisation 3D par photo des milieux naturels. In S. Jaillet & E. Ployon (Eds.), *Images et modèles 3D en milieux naturels* (Vol. 12, pp. 51–66). Le Bourget-du-Lac: Edytem.

Piperno, D. R. (2006). *Phytoliths: A comprehensive guide for archaeologists and paleoecologists.* Lanham: AltaMira.

Piperno, D. R., Weiss, E., Holst, I., & Nadel, D. (2004). Processing of wild cereal grains in the upper palaeolithic revealed by starch grain analysis. *Nature, 430*(7000), 670–673.

Piperno, D. R., Ranere, A. J., Holst, I., Iriarte, J., & Dickau, R. (2009). Starch grain and phytolith evidence for early ninth millennium B.P. maize from the Central Balsas River Valley, Mexico. *Proceedings of the National Academy of Sciences, 106*(13), 5019–5024.

Plisson, H. (2014). 3D en kit : des solutions pour la tracéologie et au-delà. In L. Costa, F. Djindjian, F. Giligny (Eds.), *Actes des 3èmes Journées d'Informatique et Archéologie de Paris-JIAP 2012 (Paris, 1–2 juin 2012)*. Monterotondo Stazione: CNR. (Archeologia e Calcolatori).

Plisson, H. (in press). Digital photography in use-wear studies, from 2D to 3D. In R. Vergnieux, & C. Delavoie (Eds.), Virtual Retrospect 2013, Proceedings of the 5th conference. Pessac: Editions Ausonius.

Plisson, H. (1985). Etude fonctionnelle d'outillages lithiques préhistoriques par l'analyse des micro-usures: recherche méthodologique et archéologique, Ph.D Dissertation, Université de Paris I, Paris.

Plisson, H. (1989). Quelques considérations sur l'équipement optique adapté à la micro-tracéologie. *Helinium, XXIX,* 3–12.

Plisson, H. (1991). Tracéologie et expérimentation : bilan d'une situation. In Actes du colloque international "Expérimentation en archéologie" (pp. 152–160). Errance, Paris.

Plisson, H. (2006). Un burin ne sert pas à buriner mais en burinant. *Archéologiques, 2,* 23–33.

Plisson, H., & Lompré, A. (2008). Technician or researcher? A visual answer. In L. Longo & N. Skakun (Eds.), *"Prehistoric Technology" 40 years later: Functional studies and the Russian legacy* (pp. 503–508). Oxford: British Archaeological Reports Ltd.

Poissonnier, B. (2002). Pilons, broyeurs, bouchardes, marteaux et autres percuteurs : Les interprétations fonctionnelles au risque de l'expérimentation. In H. Procopiou & R. Treuil (Eds.), *Moudre et Broyer*. Paris: CTHS.

Portillo, M., Bofill, M., Molist, M., Albert, R. M. (2013). Phytolith and use-wear functional evidence for grinding stones from the Near East. In Anderson, P. C., Cheval, C., & Durand, A. (Eds.), Regards croisés sur les outils liés au travail des végétaux. An interdisciplinary focus on plant-working tools (pp. 205–218). Éditions APDCA, Antibes.

Prinsloo, L. C., Wadley, L., & Lombard, M. (2014). Infrared reflectance spectroscopy as an analytical technique for the study of residues on stone tools: Potential and challenges. *Journal of Archaeological Science, 41,* 732–739.

Procopiou, H. (1998). L'outillage de mouture et de broyage en Crète Minoenne, Ph.D Dissertation, Université de Paris I, Panthéon- Sorbonne.

Procopiou, H. (2004). Le broyage des matiéres minérales: l'apport de la tribologie à l'identification de la transformation des matières minérales. *Dossiers D'archéologie, 290,* 58–61.

Procopiou, H., Jautee, E., Vargiolu, R., & Zahouni, H. (1998). Petrographic and use-wear analysis of a quern from Syvritos Kephala. In F. Facchini, A. Palma Di Cesnola, M. Piperno, & C. Peretto (Eds.), *Actes du XIIème Congrès de l'UISPP, Forli 8–14 September 1996* (pp. 1183–1192). Forli: A.B.A.C.O.

Procopiou, H., Anderson, P., Formenti, F., & Jordi, J. T. (2002). Étude des matières transformées sur les outils de mouture: Identification des résidus et des traces d'usure par analyse chimique et par observation en microscopie optique et électronique. In H. Procopiou & R. Treuil (Eds.), *Moudre et broyer* (pp. 111–127). Paris: CTHS.

Procopiou, H., Boleti, A., Vargiolu, R., & Zahouani, H. (2011). The role of tactile perception during stone-polishing in Aegean prehistory (5th–4th millennium B.C.). *Wear, 271*(9–10), 2525–2530.

Procopiou, H., Morero, E., Vargiolu, R., Suarez-Sanabria, M., & Zahouani, H. (2013). Tactile and visual perception during polishing: An ethnoarchaeological study in India (Mahabalipuram, Tamil Nadu). *Wear, 301*(1–2), 144–149.

Quigg, J. (2003). New analytical approaches to South Texas cultural assemblages. *Journal of the Southern Texas Archaeological Association, 30*(3), 15–23.

Ramos, R. R. (2005). The function of the edge ground cobble put to the test: An initial assessment. *Journal of Caribbean Archaeology, 6,* 1–22.

Reid, D. M., & Pritchard-Parker, M. A. (1993). Preliminary results of a replicative study: Metate re-roughening, pecking, or pounding? *Proceedings of the Society for California Archaeology, 6,* 199–206.

Revedin, A., Aranguren, B., Becattini, R., Longo, L., Marconi, E., Lippi, M. M. et al. (2010). Thirty thousand-year-old evidence of plant food processing. *Proceedings of the National Academy of Sciences, 107*(44), 18815–18819.

Risch, R. (2002). *Recursos naturales, medios de producción y explotación social: Un análisis económico de la industria lítica de Fuente Álamo, (Almería), 2250–1400 antes de nuestra era.* Mainz am Rhein: Verlag Philipp Von Zabern.

Risch, R. (2008). From production traces to social organization: Towards an epistemology of functional analysis. In L. Longo & N. Skakun (Eds.), *"Prehistoric Technology" 40 years later: Functional studies and the russian legacy* (pp. 519–527). Oxford: British Archaeological Reports.

Roda Gilabert, X., Martínez-Moreno, J., & Mora Torcal, R. (2012). Pitted stone cobbles in the Mesolithic site of Font del Ros (Southeastern Pre-Pyrenees, Spain): Some experimental remarks around a controversial tool type. *Journal of Archaeological Science, 39*(5), 1587–1598.

Rodriguez Rodriguez, A. C., Jimenez Medina, A. M., & Zamora Maldona, J. M. (2004). El instrumental lítico en el trabajo de la loza tradicional: Apuntes etnoarqueologicos. In F. Morales Padron (Ed.), *Coloquio de Historia Canario-Americana* (pp. 419–436). Las Palmas de Gran Canaria: Casa de Colon.

Rodriguez Rodriguez, A. C., Jimenez Medina, A. M., Zamora Maldona, J. M., & Mangas Vinuela, J. (2006). El empleo de cantos rodados en la elaboracion de la loza tradicional de la isla de Gran Canaria, implicaciones etnoarquelogicas. *Trebals d'Etnoarqueologia, 6,* 209–225.

Rosenberg, D. (2008). Serving meals making a home: The PPNA limestone vessel industry of the Southern Levant and its importance to the neolithic revolution. *Paléorient, 34,* 23–32.

Rots, V., & Williamson, B. (2004). Microwear and residue analyses in perspective: The contribution of ethnoarchaeological evidence. *Journal of Archaeological Science, 31*(9), 1287–1299.

Rumold, C. U. (2010). *Illuminating women's work and the advent of plant cultivation in the highland Titicaca Basin of South America: New evidence from grinding tool and starch grain analyses.* Santa Barbara: University of California.

Runnels, C. N. (1981). A diachronic study and economic analysis of millstones from the Argolid, Greece, Ph.D Dissertation, Indiana University, Bloomington.
Sajnerova-Duskova, A., Fridrich, J., & Fridrichova-Sykorova, I. (2009). Pitted and grinding stones from the middle Palaeolithic settlements in Bohemia: A functional study. In F. Sternke, L. J. Costa, & L. Eigeland (Eds.), *Non-flint raw material use in prehistory: Old prejudices and new directions* (pp. 1–10). Oxford: Archaeopress.
Samuel, D. (2010). Experimental grinding and ancient egyptian flour production. In S. Ikram & A. Dodson (Eds.), *Beyond the horizon: Studies in Egyptian art, archaeology and history in honour of Barry J. Kemp* (pp. 253-290). Cairo: American University in Cairo Press.
Santallier, D., Caron, V., Gisclon, J. L., Jautee, E., & Rantsordas, S. (2002). Les qualités mécaniques des matériaux lithiques utilisés pour la confection du matériel de broyage et de mouture. In H. Procopiou & R. Treuil (Eds.), *Moudre et Broyer* (pp. 15–29). Paris: CTHS.
Schiffer, M., & Skibo, M. (1987). Theory and experiment in the study of technological change. *Current Anthropology, 28,* 595–622.
Schneider, J. S. (2002). Milling tool design, stone textures and function. In H. Procopiou & R. Treuil (Eds.), *Moudre et broyer* (pp. 31–53). Paris: CTHS.
Schneider, J., & LaPorta, P. (2008). Geological constraints on ground stone production and consumption in the Southern Levant. In Y. Rowan & J. Ebeling (Eds.), *New approaches to old stones. Recent studies of ground stone artifacts* (pp. 19–40). London: Equinox.
Semenov, C. A. (1957). *Первобытная техника*. Москва: Академия Наук СССР.
Semenov, S. (1964). *Prehistoric technology: An experimental study of the oldest tools and artefacts from traces of manufacture and wear*. (M. Thompson, Trans.). London: Cory, Adams and Mackay.
Shizhu, W., & Ping, H. (2012). *Principles of tribology*. Hoboken: Wiley.
Shoumacker, A. (1993). Apports de la technologie et de la pétrographie pour la caractérisation des meules. In P. C. Anderson, S. Beyries, M. Otte, & H. Plisson (Eds.), *Traces et fonction, les gestes retrouvés* (Vol. 1, pp. 165–176). Valbonne: Centre de Recherches Archéologiques du CNRS & Etudes et Recherches Archéologiques de l'Université de Liège.
Sigaut, F. (1991). Un couteau ne sert pas à couper mais en coupant. Structure, fonctionnement et fonction dans l'analyse des objets. In *Actes des rencontres 18-19-20 Octobre 1990: 25 ans d'études technologiques en Préhistoire. Bilan et perspectives* (pp. 21–34). Juan-les-Pins: APDCA.
Smith, M. (2004). The grindstone assemblage from Puritjarra rock shelter: Investigating the history of seed-based economies in arid Australia. In T. Murray (Ed.), *Archaeology from Australia* (pp. 168–186). Melbourne: Australian Scholarly Publishing.
Stephenson, B. (2011). In the groove: An integrated functional analysis of arid zone millstones from Queensland (Unpublished BA (Hons) Thesis). School of Social Sciences, University of Queensland, Brisbane.
Stephenson, B. (2012). Roy Hill rail corridor, chainages 25-110 and 110-136, Pilbara, Western Australia: Report on use-wear and residue analysis of a representative sample of grinding patch sites. A report prepared by ITGA for LAS.
Stroulia, A., & Chondrou, D. (2013). Destroying the means of production. The case of ground stone tools from Kremasti-Kilada, Greece. In J. Driessen (Ed.), *Destruction: Archaeological, philological and historical perspectives* (pp. 100–150). Louvain: Presses Universitaires de Louvain.
Stroulia, A., & Dubreuil, L. (2013). Design or use? Discussion of a peculiar shape among grinding tools from Kremasti-Kilada, Northern Greece. In 78th annual meeting of the Society for American Archaeology. Hawaii.
Takashi, T. (2012). MIS3 edge-ground axes and the arrival of the first Homo sapiens in the Japanese archipelago. *Quaternary International, 248,* 70–78.
Thiéry, V., & Green, D. I. (2012). The multifocus imaging technique in petrology. *Computers & Geosciences, 45,* 131–138.
Torrence, R. (2006). Description, classification and identification. In R. Torrence & H. Barton (Eds.), *Ancient starch research* (pp. 115–144). California: Left Coast Press Inc.
Treuil, R. (2002). En guise de conclusion: Mouture et sociétés, questions pour une histoire. In Treuil, R. and Procopiou, H. (Eds.), Moudre et broyer (pp. 229–235). Paris: CTHS.

Tsoraki, C. (2007). Unravelling ground life histories: The spatial organization of stone tools and human activities at LN Makriyalos, Greece. *Documenta Praehistorica, XXXIV,* 289–297.
Ucko, P. J. (1969). Ethnography and archaeological interpretation of funerary remains. *World Archaeology, 1*(2), 262–280.
Unger-Hamilton, R. (1984). The formation of use-wear polish on flint: Beyond the "deposit versus abrasion" controversy. *Journal of Archaeological Science, 11*(1), 91–98.
Valamoti, S. M., Chondrou, D., & Papadopoulou, L. (2013). Plant food processing and ground stone equipment in prehistoric Greece: An experimental investigation using seeds of einkorn and grass-pea. In P. C. Anderson, C. Cheval, & A. Durand (Eds.), *Regards croisés sur les outils liés au travail des végétaux. An interdisciplinary focus on plant-working tools* (pp. 169–187). Juan-les-Pins: APDCA.
Van Gijn, A. (1990). The wear and tear of flint: Principles of functional analysis applied to Dutch Neolithic assemblages. *Analecta Praehistorica Leidensia, 22,* 1–181.
Van Gijn, A., & Lammers-Keijsers, Y. (2010). Toolkits for ceramic production: Informal tools and the importance of high power use-wear analysis. *Bulletin de La Société Préhistorique Française, 107,* 755–762.
Van Gijn, A., & Verbaas, A. (2009). Reconstructing the life history of querns: The case of the LBK site in Geleen-Janskamperveld (NL). In M. de Araujo Igreja & I. C. Conte (Eds.), *Recent functional studies on non-flint stone tools: Methodological improvements and archaeological inferences.* Lisbon: p. CD-ROM Publication.
Van Peer, P., Fullagar, R., Stokes, S., Bailey, R. M., Moeyersons, J., Steenhoudt, F. et al. (2003). The early to middle Stone Age transition and the emergence of modern human behaviour at site 8-B-11, Sai Island, Sudan. *Journal of Human Evolution, 45*(2), 187–193.
Vargiolu, R., Morero, E., Boleti, A., Procopiou, H., Pailler-Mattei, C., & Zahouani, H. (2007). Effects of abrasion during stone vase drilling in Bronze Age Crete. *Wear, 263*(1-6), 48–56.
Vaughan, P. C. (1981). Lithic microwear experimentation and the functional analysis of a Lower Magdalenian stone tool assemblage, Ph.D Dissertation, University of Pennsylvania, Philadelphia.
Verbaas, A., & van Gijn, A. (2008). Querns and other hard stone tools from Geleen-Janskamperveld. In P. van de Velde (Ed.), *Excavations at Geleen-Janskamperveld 1990/1991* (pp. 191–204). Leiden: University of Leiden.
Verhoeven, G. J. J. (2010). It's all about the format—unleashing the power of RAW aerial photography. *International Journal of Remote Sensing, 31*(8), 2009–2042.
Weiss, E., Wetterstrom, W., Nadel, D., & Bar-Yosef, O. (2004). The broad spectrum revisited: Evidence from plant remains, *Proceedings of the National Academy of Science 101,* 9551–9555.
Wilke, P. J., & Quintero, L. A. (1994). Naviform core-and-blade technology: Assemblage character as determined by replicative experiments. In H. G. K. Gebel & S. K. Kozlowski (Eds.), *Neolithic chipped stone industries of the Fertile Crescent, and their contemporaries in adjacent regions* (pp. 33–60). Berlin: Ex Oriente.
Wilke, P. J., & Quintero, L. A. (1996). Near Eastern Neolithic millstones production: Insights from research in the arid Southwestern United States. In S. K. Kozlowski & H. G. K. Gebel (Eds.), *Neolithic chipped stone industries of the Fertile Crescent, and their contemporaries in adjacent regions* (pp. 243–260). Berlin: Ex oriente.
Willoughby, P. R. (1985). Spheroids and battered stones in the African early Stone Age. *World Archaeology, 17*(1), 44–60.
Willoughby, P. R. (1987). *Spheroid and battered stones in the African early and middle Stone Age.* Oxford: British Archaeological Reports.
Wright, K. I. (1992a). A classification system for ground stone tools from the prehistoric Levant. *Paléorient, 18,* 53–81.
Wright, K. I. (1992b). Ground stone assemblages variation and subsistence strategies in the Levant, 22 000–5 500 BP, Ph.D Dissertation, Yale University, Department of Anthropology, Yale.
Wright, K. I. (1994). Ground-stone tools and hunter gatherer subsistence in Southwest Asia: Implications for the transition to farming. *American Antiquity, 59*(2), 238–263.
Wright, K. I. (2000). The social origins of cooking and dining in early villages of Western Asia. *Proceedings of the Prehistoric Society, 66,* 89–121.

Wright, K. I. (2008). Craft production and the organization of ground stone technologies. In Y. Rowan & J. Ebeling (Eds.), *New approaches to old stones: Recent studies of ground stone artifacts* (pp. 130–143). London: Equinox Publishing Ltd.

Wright, K. I. (2014). Domestication and inequality? Households, corporate groups and food processing tools at Neolithic Çatalhöyük. *Journal of Anthropological Archaeology, 33,* 1–33.

Wright, M. K. (1993). Simulated use of experimental maize grinding tools from Southwestern Colorado. *Kiva, 58,* 345–353.

Yamada, S. (2000). Development of the Neolithic: Lithic use-wear analysis of major tool types in the Southern Levant, Ph.D. Dissertation, Harvard University, Cambridge, Mass.

Yost, C. (2008). Protein residue analysis of clovis points and great basin points from Millard Country, Utah (Paleo Research Institute Technical Report No. 07-055). Salt Lake City, Utah: Paleo Research Institute.

Zohary, D., Hopf, M., & Weiss, E. (2012). *Domestication of plants in the old world: The origin and spread of domesticated plants in Southwest Asia, Europe, and the Mediterranean Basin* (4th ed.). Oxford: Oxford University Press.

Zurro, D., Risch, R., & Clemente-Conte, I. (2005). Analysis of an archaeological grinding tool: What to do with archaeological artefacts. In X. Terradas (Ed.), *Lithic toolkits in ethoarchaeological contexts* (pp. 57–64). Oxford: British Archaeological Reports Ltd.

Chapter 8
Use-Wear Methodology on the Analysis of Osseous Industries

Marina Almeida Évora

8.1 Introduction

Bone tool assemblages are important evidence of the material culture of prehistoric populations of hunter-gatherers. These industries encompass, in general, all objects produced from organic raw materials, i.e. the set that includes all debitage debris and equipment manufacturing.

The equipment consists of objects that had a use/function and have suffered or not a transformation. It is quite diverse and includes elements such as projectiles, intermediate pieces, awls, *lissoirs*, needles, beads, statuary, among other tools.

The osseous material industry includes objects made from mammal bone, ivory, dentine, antler, shells, horn, shell egg, shellfish, tortoise shell and baleen.

Use-wear analysis attempts to help to reconstruct how a tool was manufactured/modified and used through a microscopic analysis of traces left on the osseous surface. One important factor that should be kept in mind is that when tool morphology is identified it does not necessarily mean its function was also identified.

Their function is sometimes difficult to identify due to the fact that osseous material, such as bone or antler, were used in various states, that is dry, wet, fresh and heated. This fact influences the morphology of the traces left on the bone surface along with the mineral nature of the tools and their type, used to work and modify the bone surface. Also, some tools break during their use, and were recycled and used again in a different task. On the other hand, the active parts of a tool may deteriorate and it may have been reshaped in order to be used again.

Another important factor to keep in mind is that there are taphonomic modifications to which the osseous materials are submitted. These can alter the bone surface in different ways, to the point of creating pseudo-tools (Brain 1981; Dominguez-Rodrigo et al. 2009). That said, experimental programs and ethnographic studies are

---

M. Almeida Évora (✉)
Interdisciplinary Center for Archaeology and Evolution of Human Behaviour,
FCHS—Universidade do Algarve, Campus de Gambelas, 8005-139, Faro—Portugal
e-mail: marevora@gmail.com

important complements of the use-wear analysis of bone surfaces, because the last traces seen on the bone surface are the result of its last function.

8.2 Current Status on Use-Wear Analysis of Bone Artefacts

Use-wear research on osseous materials is mainly based on use-wear studies on stone tools.

According to Banks (1996) there are two major schools that dominate this field of research—ethnography and experimentation.

By the end of the nineteenth century and during the twentieth century some authors such as Nilsson (1838), Evans (1897), Vayson (1922) and Gould et al. (1971) (all cited in Banks 1996), examined the edges of stone tools for macroscopic damage or evidence of use. They used ethnographic analogies to explain what types of activities or tool use could have produced the edge damage that they observed.

In the twentieth century, experimentation played an important role in use-wear analysis. Photography and registering of the length of time that a tool was used was introduced by Curwen (1930). Through experimentation programs, the wear seen on the tool's surface was recognised not to always be the result of cultural activities, as noticed by Levi-Sala (1986). By using Experimentation, Levi-Sala (1986) has demonstrated that natural processes sometimes leave wear traces on tools. These traces resemble and some are even identical to wear traces left by humans on the tool's surface (Levi-Sala 1986).

Experimentation was also carried out by Bouchud (1977), Dauvois (1977), Semenov (1985), Knecht (1991), d'Errico (1993) and Christensen (1999), among others, for complementing microscopic analysis of manufacturing and polish *stigmata* on completed organic projectile points and other tools so it would provide clues to the production sequence.

Experimentation turned out to be an important factor on use-wear analysis, because the *stigmata* seen on the experimental tools allows the process of analogy and parallels with the archaeological artefacts. Simultaneously, it creates a reference collection that makes possible the understanding of tool kinematics and techniques used to manufacture and modify the tool surfaces (Christensen 1999).

According to Banks (1996), LeMoine (1997), Christensen (1999) and Gibaja Bao (2002) there are authors who identify and interpret wear features at low magnifications ($<100\times$), and others who use higher magnifications (typically $100\times$–$500\times$). Each of these methodologies presents advantages and disadvantages. Low-power magnification studies are conducted with the use of stereomicroscopes and outside light sources and usually use magnifications ranging from $10\times$–$80\times$. Their major advantage is to allow the analysis of large samples of artefacts; they also have a good depth of field in their optimal range of magnification; and finally, because they are less expensive. On the other hand, the disadvantages are the loss of resolution at magnifications above $50\times$ and having poor light-gathering capabilities. The low-power approach is not effective in identifying tools that did not suffer any edge damage during use. Also, it is difficult to interpret a sequence of tool use when the utensil edge has been used multiple times on different worked materials, because only the last phase of tool use will be readily visible on the edge.

LeMoine (1997) states that with low-power microscopes only flake scars and striations are the main features that are observable. According to Sidera and Legrand (2006) the macroscopic analysis is efficient to use on those artefacts that had volume alterations and traces of use well developed in their surface.

High-power methodologies, on the other hand, have been used on the identification and interpretation of use-generated polishes (d'Errico 1993; Christensen 1999). This method was introduced by Semenov (1985) in his book "Prehistoric Technology" first published in 1957 in the Russian version (Christensen 1999). Semenov's research described the traceology or kinematics related to tool use and accomplished this through an analysis of striations, edge damage and abrasive polishes. Polishes tend not to vary according to the manner of the tool's use. One problem is the complexity of the polishing description. High-power microscopes are very expensive and not available everywhere.

Recently, there are researchers using digital cameras to document some features. These cameras are used in conjunction with software packages that allow many attributes to be measured and quantified in a variety of ways (Banks 1996). Knecht (1991) and Christensen (1999) also used high-power magnification—Scan Electron Microscope (SEM)—for the use-wear analysis of organic artefacts and lithic artefacts used in the manufacture of organic tools. Use-wear analysis with SEM has some advantages, like increased magnification, depth of field and image quality. But some bone artefacts cannot be seen under SEM because their size is far too large to fit in the microscope chamber, and this means they would have to be cut to size or replicas would have to be made. In these instances, the artefact has to be coated with a conductive material such as gold, carbon or alloy (LeMoine 1997). The disadvantage of SEM is that some characteristic polishes are not distinctive under this high-power microscope. Some researchers also use another technique together with SEM, the X-ray analyser for detecting residues of polishes (LeMoine 1997).

8.3 Methods

I present here a methodology for the use-wear analysis of the osseous industry, based on research from previous works by Averbouh (2000), Bertrand (1999), Camps-Fabrer (1977), d'Errico et al. (1984), d'Errico and Puech (1984), d'Errico and Giacobini (1985), d'Errico and Giacobini (1986), d'Errico and Espinet-Moucadel (1986), d'Errico (1993), d'Errico and Cacho (1994), LeMoine (1997), Knecht (1991), Maigrot (1997, 2003a, 2003b), Pétillon (2006) and Tartar (2003). The methodology of use-wear analysis serves both to understand the techniques of manufacturing the tool and its possible function. It will be necessary, thus, to document the artefact as precisely as possible. To do that, it can be created a database where it will be first registered what we can verify through the naked eye observation or macroscopically. It is important that, if possible, one distinguishes the raw material (Bouchud 1974; Poplin 1974), for it may give us clues about the techniques and procedures used in blank acquisition and modification. This is due to the fact that different debitage techniques are sometimes applied to various osseous materials, because they have different mechanical properties and do not react (brake) the same way.

The observation of the bone surface's preservation state is important because it permits to identify several factors, such as the presence or absence of spongy tissue and of the cortical tissue and in what state of preservation they are. It is also possible to identify taphonomic alterations through traces left by physical-chemical agents and also by actions of natural agents such as plants and animals.

The analysis of bone surface modifications will also track vestiges of substances such as adhesives, colorants, micro-splinters of chert stuck to the bone surface, or changes caused by fire (superficially or deeply) (Behrensmeyer 1978; Blumenschine et al 1996; Lyman 1994; Manne 2010; Juana and Domínguez-Rodrigo 2011; Outram 2002; Orton 2010; Semenov 1985).

As noted by Knecht (1991) and LeMoine (1997) sometimes the preservation state of the artefact does not allow for an analysis of its surface, either caused by its deterioration or by other natural reasons. Sometimes, some artefacts are very fragile and eroded to the naked eye, not allowing a microscopic examination of its details. Others, on the other hand, seem to be well preserved but they are in fact eroded and weathered at a microscopic scale (LeMoine 1997). Knecht (1991) also refers to another problematic issue: the common practice over the last century to cover up the surface of the bone artefacts with a layer of varnish in order to prevent it from disintegrating. This method makes it quite difficult to analyse the artefact's surface because the coating does not allow the observation of *stigmata* of manufacturing and/or use with a binocular microscope (Évora 2008) or a reflected light microscope. It will also prevent the use of the Scanning Electron Microscope (Knecht 1991). Removing this varnish can also destroy the surface, and so its information will be lost.

8.3.1 Artefact Orientation

In graphical representation and photography, the artefact is always oriented with the proximal part downwards and the top surface (cortical surface) towards the observer. Except for the finished artefacts, the question of the orientation of the artefact is not simple. Since some artefacts are fragmented, others are manufactured using bone leftovers, or are either blanks or unfinished tools. This situation does not allow to define properly its future active area. So for these particular pieces, when registering their graphic orientation or photography, the artefact can be displayed following their anatomical orientation if it does not have any technical *stigmata*. For the debitage debris, the displayed orientation is either the anatomical or the technical surface always indicating, in these cases in particular, the orientation that was possible to use (Averbouh 2000).

8.3.2 Artefact Recording

For each artefact, the following list should be registered:

- Archaeological site where the artefact comes from and, whenever possible the level/stratigraphic layer;
- Identification of the raw material and respective species (and whenever possible anatomical location);
- Typology of the artefact;
- Type of contour/profile of the artefact;
- Morphological information: maximum length (proximal, mesial and distal); maximum width (proximal, mesial and distal); maximum thickness (proximal, mesial and distal);
- State of preservation (if the artefact is complete or broken, and if so which part has been preserved) and changes in the surface;
- Type of fracture and its location;
- Morphology of the distal and proximal ends;
- Type of section (proximal, mesial and distal).

After this initial macroscopic recording, we can move on to the microscopic analysis of bone surfaces, making use of various methods, some easy, others more difficult and expensive, as the case with some high power microscopes.

8.3.3 Microscopic Analysis

In the process of microscopic analysis of osseous surface several technical and use traces are recorded:

- The schematic representation of all technical *stigmata* (negative withdrawal, striations, *pan de fracture*, grooves) and use (the active regions can be located anywhere, but they are usually in the proximal and distal ends and, more rarely, in some artefacts over the cortical surface) and their location;
- The description of each *stigma*: their type; location details; their orientation in accordance with longitudinal axis of the artefact; their inclination or incidence to the surface (rough, oblique, vertical, diagonal); their extent (marginal, moderate, invasive coverage); their distribution (continuous or discontinuous); their organisation; their morphology; as to discriminate striations also its density, size and orientation relative to the longitudinal axis of the artefact.

Fig. 8.1 Manufacturing *stigma* showing the area where the lithic tool stopped on an antler projectile point from Buraca Grande site. 30× magnification (all photos by M. A. Évora)

This record, made in detail, will provide information as to any primary changes (debitage and manufacturing techniques) and secondary changes (finishing of the pieces) (LeMoine 1997) employed in the manufacture of the artefact. It will also provide information on possible functions the artefact had and, based on the analysis of the debitage debris, information on the economy of the raw material (Tartar 2003) (Figs. 8.1, 8.2, 8.3, 8.4, 8.5, 8.6, 8.7, 8.8, 8.9, 8.10, 8.11, 8.12, 8.13, 8.14, 8.15, and 8.16).

8.4 Final Remarks

Since the natural characteristics of osseous materials are very different from the characteristics of stone tools, their use-wear analysis is more difficult to interpret. Because this raw material is usually found fractured and its surface is modified by several different ways of preservation. It is the case of fresh, heated or dry states. In the case of mammal bone and antler, some tools have had more than one function, and some others, after being broken, were also recycled and gain a new function. It all depends on what specific tool the artisan wanted or needed to manufacture, for a specific task or several tasks. These working techniques and changes made during the life time of a tool have great influence on what we see under the microscope, because the traces left are not always the same. Also we have to add the fact that bone material goes through natural surface alterations due to taphonomical agents that sometimes deeply modify its surface. The basic knowledge of taphonomical alterations is, thus, fundamental when analysing bone surfaces.

From what was mentioned above, we see that the interpretation and understanding of several types of traces left on the bone surface, through use-wear analysis, is mostly based on comparisons with traces left on experimental tools. For this reason, functional studies are very important and must be complemented with ethnographic information.

Ethnographic studies of recent Hunter-Gatherers populations provide insights into the many ways an osseous raw material could be transformed and what kind of tools could be produced from it.

Fig. 8.2 Distal end of an antler tool from Buraca Grande site. 20× magnification

Fig. 8.3 Surface of an antler (?) projectile point with bevel from Buraca Grande site. 30× magnification

Fig. 8.4 Surface of a fusiform bone tool from Vale Boi site. 20× magnification

Fig. 8.5 Manufacturing *stria* on an antler projectile point from Vale Boi site. 16× magnification

Fig. 8.6 Tongue fracture on an indeterminate raw material tool from Buraca Grande site. 10× magnification COLOR

Fig. 8.7 Saw fracture on an indeterminate raw material tool from Buraca Grande site. 10× magnification

Fig. 8.8 Impact marks on a distal end of an antler tool from Vale Boi. 10× magnification

Fig. 8.9 Incisions on the lower surface of an antler massive based point from Buraca Grande Site. 10× magnification COLOR

Fig. 8.10 Incisions on the surface of a fusiform bone tool from Caldeirão Cave. 30× magnification

Fig. 8.11 Microwave pattern inside the manufacturing *stria* on the surface of a bone tool from Vale Boi site. 30× magnification

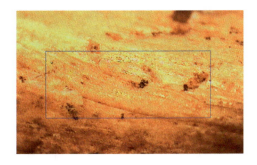

Fig. 8.12 Bumps pattern (usually left by an unretouch tool like a burin) on the surface of an antler projectile point from Vale Boi. 40× magnification

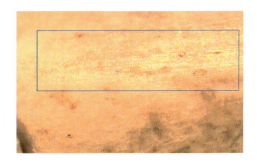

Fig. 8.13 *Stigma* on the bone surface left by a wedge used to separate, by bipartition, a metacarpus of *Cervus elaphus*. Vale Boi site. 10× magnification

Fig. 8.14 *Stigma* on the bone surface left by a wedge used to separate by bipartition a metacarpus of *Cervus elaphus*. Vale Boi site. 20× magnification

Fig. 8.15 Experimentation: scraping *stria* over an antler *spongiosa* surface showing the area where the chert tool stopped. 14× magnification

Fig. 8.16 Experimentation: scraping *stria* made with unretouched chert splinter over antler surface. 20× magnification

Acknowledgements I acknowledge João Marreiros, Nuno Bicho and Juan F. Gibaja Bao for editing a volume on this subject. Also to Fundação para a Ciência e a Tecnologia for providing me a research grant (SFRH/BD/61988/2009).

References

Averbouh, A. (2000). *Technologie de la matière osseuse travaillée et implications palethnologiques. L'exemple des chaines d'exploitation du bois de Cervidé chez les Magdaleniens des Pyrenées*. Doctoral dissertation, Université de Paris I, Vol 2.

Banks, W. E. (1996). *Toolkit structure and site use: Results of a high-power use-wear analysis of lithic assemblages from Solutré (Saône-et-Loire), France*. Doctoral dissertation, University of Kansas, USA.

Behrensmeyer, A. K. (1978). Taphonomic and ecologic information from bone weathering. *Paleobiology, 4*(2), 150–162.
Bertrand, A. (1999). *Les Armatures de sagaies magdaléniennes en matière dure animale dans les Pyrénées.* BAR international series, 773. Oxford: David Brown Book Company.
Blumenschine, R. J., Marean, C. W., & Capaldo, S. D. (1996). Blind tests of inter-analyst correspondence and accuracy in the identification of cut marks, percussion marks, and carnivore tooth marks on bone surfaces. *Journal of Archaeological Science, 23,* 493–507.
Bouchud, J. (1974). *L'origine anatomique des matériaux osseux utilisés dans les industries préhistoriques.* Premier Colloque International sur l'Industrie de l'os dans la Préhistoire, Abbaye de Sénanque, Editions de l'Université de Provence, pp. 21–26.
Bouchud, J. (1977). *Les aiguilles en os. Études comparée des traces laissées par la fabrication et l'usage sur le matériel préhistorique et les objets expérimentaux.* Méthodologie appliquée à l'industrie de l'os préhistorique. Deuxième Colloque Internationaux sur l'Industrie de l'os dans la Préhistoire, Éditions du C.N.R.S., pp. 257–267.
Brain, C. K. (1981). *The hunter or the hunted? An introduction to African cave taphonomy.* Chicago: University of Chicago Press.
Camps-Fabrer, H. (1977). *Compte rendu des travaux de la commission de nomenclature sur l'industrie de l'os préhistorique.* Méthodologie Appliquée a L'Industrie de L'Os préhistorique. Deuxième Colloque International sur l'Industrie de l'os dans la Préhistoire, Abbaye de Sénanque, Éditions du C.N.R.S., pp. 19–25.
Christensen, M. (1999). *Technologie de l'ivoire au Paléolithique supérieur. Caractérisation physico-chimique du matériau et analyse fonctionnelle des outils de transformation.* BAR international series 751 (201 p). Oxford: J and E Hedges.
Curwen, E. C. (1930). Prehistoric flint sickles. *Antiquity, 4,* 179–86.
Dauvois, M. (1977). *Stigmates d'usure présentés par des outils de silex ayant travaillé l'os. Premiers résultats. Méthodologie Appliquée a L'Industrie de L'Os préhistorique.* Deuxième Colloque International sur l'Industrie de l'os dans la Préhistoire, Abbaye de Sénanque, Éditions du C.N.R.S., pp. 275–293.
D'Errico, F. (1993). *Identification des traces de manipulation, suspension, polissage sur l'art mobilier en os, bois de cervidés, ivoire, Traces et Fonctions: les gestes retrouvés.* Colloque international de Liège, éditions ERAUL, 50, pp. 177–188.
D'Errico, F., & Cacho, C. (1994). Notation versus Decoration in the Upper Palaeolithic: A case-study from Tossal de la Roca, Alicante, Spain. *Journal of Archaeological Science, 21,* 185–200.
D'Errico, F., & Espinet-Moucadel, J. (1986). L'emploi du microscope électronique Ã balayage pour l'étude expérimentale de traces d'usure: raclage sur bois de cervidé. *Bulletin de la Société Préhistorique Française, 83*(3), 91–96.
D'Errico, F., & Giacobini, G. (1985). Approche méthodologique de l'analyse de l'outillage osseux, un exemple d'étude. *L'Anthropologie, 89*(4), 457–472 (Paris).
D'Errico, F., & Giacobini, G. (1986). L'emploi des répliques en vernis pour l'étude de surface des pseudo-instruments en os. *Artefacts, 2,* 57–68.
D'Errico, F., & Puech, P.-F. (1984). Les Répliques en vernis des surfaces osseuses façonnées: étude expérimentale. *Bulletin de la Société Préhistorique Française, 81*(6), 69–70.
D'Errico, F., Giacobini, G., & Puech, P.-F. (1984). Varnish replicas: A new method for the study of worked bone surfaces. *OSSA, 9–11,* 29–51.
Domínguez-Rodrigo, M., Juana, S., Galán, A. B., & Rodríguez, M. (2009). A new protocol to differentiate trampling marks from butchery cut marks. *Journal of Archaeological Science, 36,* 2643–2654.
Evans, J. (1897). *Ancient stone implements, weapons, and ornaments of Great Britain* (2nd ed.). London: Longmans, Green.
Évora, M. A. (2008). Artefactos em haste e em osso do Paleolítico Superior Português. *Promontória, 6,* 9–50.
Gibaja Bao, J. (2002). *La función de los instrumentos líticos como medio de aproximación socioeconómica. Comunidades neolíticas del V-IV milenio cal BC en el noreste de la Península Ibérica.* Ph. D. Thesis, Universitat Autònoma de Barcelona, 519 p.

Gould, R. A., Koster, D. A., & Sontz, A. H. (1971). The lithic assemblage of the western desert Aborigines of Australia. *Antiquity, 36,* 149–69.

Juana, S., & Domínguez-Rodrigo, M. (2011). Testing analogical taphonomic signatures in bone breaking: a comparasion between hammerstone-broken Equid and Bovid bones. *Archaeometry, 53*(5), 996–1011.

Knecht, H. (1991). *Technological innovation and design during the early upper paleolithic: A study of organic projectile technologies.* Doctoral dissertation, New York University, USA.

LeMoine, G. (1997). *Use-wear analysis on bone and antler tools of the MacKensie Inuit.* BAR international series 679. Oxford: J and E Hedges.

Levi-Sala, I. (1986). Use-wear and post-depositional surface modification: A word of caution. *Journal of Archaeological Science, 13,* 229–244.

Lyman, R. L. (1994). *Vertebrate taphonomy.* Cambridge manuals in archaeology. Cambridge: Cambridge University Press.

Maigrot, Y. (1997) Tracéologie des outils tranchants en os des V et IV millénaires av. J.-C. en Bassin parisien: essai méthodologique et application. *Bulletin de la Société préhistorique française, 94*(2), 198–216.

Maigrot, Y. (2003a). *Etude technologique et fonctionnelle de l'outillage en matières dures animales.* La station 4 de Chalain (Neólithique final, Jura, France). Thèse de Doctorat, Université de Paris I, 284 p.

Maigrot, Y. (2003b). Cycles d'utilisation et réutilisations: le cas des outils en matières dures animales de Chalain 4 (Néolithique final, Fontenu, Jura, France). *Préhistoire Anthropologie méditerranéennes, 12,* 197–207.

Manne, T. (2010). *Upper Paleolithic foraging decisions and early economic intensification at Vale Boi, Southwestern Portugal.* Unpublished doctoral dissertation, School of Anthropology, University of Arizona, USA.

Nilsson, S. (1838). *Skandinaviska Nordens Urinvanare.* Lund: Berlingska Boktryckeriet. (English edition: (1843). The primitive inhabitants of Scandinavia. 1868, London).

Outram, A. K. (2002). Bone fracture and within-bone nutrients: An experimentally based method for investigating levels of marrow extraction. In P. Miracle & N. Milner (eds.), *Consuming passions and patterns of consumption* (pp 51–64). Cambridge: McDonald Institute for Archaeological Research (Chapter 6).

Orton, D. C. (2010). Taphonomy and interpretation: An analytical framework for social zooarchaeology. *International Journal of Osteoarchaeology, 22*(3):320–337. (published online in Wiley Online Library, (wileyonlinelibrary.com) doi:10.1002/oa.1212).

Peltier, A., & Plisson, H. (1986). *Micro-tracéologie fonctionnelle sur l'os, quelques résultats expérimentaux.* Outillage peu élaboré en os et en bois de cervidés. II, Treignes, Artefacts 3, Editions du CEDARC, pp. 69–80.

Pétillon, J.-M. (2006). *Des Magdaléniens en armes. Technologie des armatures de projectile en bois de cervidé du Magdalénien Superieur de la Grotte D'Isturitz (Pyrénées-Atlantiques).* Artefacts 10, Editions du CEDARC, Treignes.

Poplin, F. (1974). *Principes de la détermination des matières dures animales.* Premier Colloque International sur l'Industrie de l'os dans la Préhistoire, Abbaye de Sénanque, Editions de l'Université de Provence, pp. 15–20.

Semenov, S. A. (1985). *Prehistoric technology, an experimental study of the oldest tools and artefacts from traces of manufacture and wear.* New Jersey: Barnes & Nobles.

Sidéra, I., & Legrand, A. (2006). Tracéologie fonctionnelle des matières osseuses: une méthode. *Bulletin de la Société préhistorique française, 103*(2), 291–304.

Tartar, E. (2003). L'analyse techno-fonctionnelle de l'industrie en matières osseuses dite " peu élaborée ": l'exemple des pièces intermédiaires en os de l'Aurignacien ancien de la grotte des Hyènes (Brassempouy, Landes). *Préhistoire Anthropologie méditerranéennes, 12,* 139–146.

Vayson, A. (1922). L'Etude Des Outillages En Pierre. *L'Anthropologie, 32*(1), 1–38.

Chapter 9
Traceology on Metal. Use-Wear Marks on Copper-Based Tools and Weapons

Carmen Gutiérrez Sáez and Ignacio Martín Lerma

9.1 Introduction

The use-wear analysis of metallic objects started late when compared to lithic use-wear studies, due to different reasons. Determining the functionality of stone implements was an early concern of most researchers (Nilsson 1868; Semenov 1964), because the morphological limitations imposed by the raw material fogged any deductions regarding functionality, apart from a few specific types. Concerning metallic objects, this issue is not so critical, as their morphologies were defined in the past, and most of them still exist. Studies on the functionality of prehistoric lithic and metallic objects are developing at different paces. Starting from the discussions of the 80s, lithic use-wear analysis has generated a huge body of knowledge on tools and weapons from different prehistoric periods. Its experimentation-based methodology provides an important frame of reference for researching metallic materials.

Traditional Archaeometallurgy sets its knowledge upon four bases. Technology addresses the point of origin and the circulation of metals, as well as the degree of technical knowledge. It is based on raw material studies, by means of mineral, metal and alloy identification through XRF, EDX, LIBS, lead isotopes or IBA techniques, while manufacturing processes can be determined by metallographic analyses (Rovira and Gómez Ramos 1998). Typology can deduce the objects' function and use from their morphologies. Finally, statistical techniques and the study of contexts complete the archaeometallurgical perspective. However, advances in these disciplines and their use of increasingly sophisticated equipments cannot hide the fact

---

C. G. Sáez (✉)
Dpt. Prehistoria y Arqueología. FF.LL., Universidad Autónoma, 28049 Madrid, Spain
e-mail: carmen.gutierrez@uam.es

I. M. Lerma
Dpt. Pehistoria, Arqueología, Hª Antigua, Hª Medieval y CC.TT. Historiográficas,
Campus de la Merced, Universidad de Murcia, 30071 Murcia, Spain
e-mail: ignacio.martin@um.es

that a sustained functional vision of prehistoric metallic implements, weapons, tools or both at the time, has barely received any attention in terms of research.

Recently though, the need for a more precise knowledge of the functionality of metallic tools started to develop, replacing functional presumptions derived solely from typology. This need is reflected by several studies on the analysis of use-wear marks on prehistoric tools and/or by experimental reconstructions, with diverse results. In any case, weapons are the type of metallic object that is getting more attention from researchers, judging from the papers on *daggers* (Wall 1987), *swords* (Bridgford 1997; Kristiansen 2002; Quilliec 2007), *spear heads* (York 2002; Appleby 2003), *halberds* (O'Flaherty 2007; Brandherm 2004), *Palmela points* (Gutiérrez et al. 2010; Gutiérrez et al. in press), shields (Coles 1979; Malloy 2004) or the technology and functionality of Bronze Age weaponry documented in the recent edition by Uckelmann and Mödlinger (2011). Attention has been paid to *axes* as well (Kienlin and Ottaway 1998; Roberts and Ottaway 2003; Moyler 2008; Dolfini 2011). An experimental approach to marks left on different materials by such tools as punches, saws and knifes/daggers was carried out in recent years (Gutiérrez Sáez et al. 2008; Gutiérrez and Soriano 2008).

Other works have focused on the comparative study of metallic implements and their lithic counterparts (Greenfield 1999, 2002; Matthieu and Meyer 1997; Skak-Nielsen 2009) or on finding contrasts between the different marks left by both materials on bone (Olsen 1988; Sands 1997; Liesau 1998; Greenfield 1999), aiming at determining the use of metallic implements in archaeological assemblages.

9.2 Copper-Based Raw Materials and their Production

Copper (Cu) is a relatively abundant, reddish mineral with a metallic luster. Copper can occur in native form but also in various minerals as oxides (tenorite and cuprite), carbonates (azurite and malaquite) and sulphides. Impurities may occur in low concentrations after extracting copper from ore. The melting point of pure copper reaches 1083 °C. Among the main properties of copper, the more relevant are its tenacity, ductility and malleability, which provide it with plasticity, i.e., the ability to deform without breaking, in response to an applied force.

Despite its tenacity, copper is a relatively soft metal, with a hardness of 3.0 on Mohs scale. That is why, so early in prehistoric metallurgy, it appears mixed with other elements such as tin (producing bronze) or arsenic (arsenical coppers) that provide hardness. This mixture can be deliberate or not. When these elements appear in low percentages it is probably not a deliberate alloy. Actually, alloys in which the minority metals are less than 1 % or 2 % are often called natural alloys. This happens with arsenical coppers and some low-tin bronzes from Bell Beaker and ancient Bronze Age contexts (Montero Ruiz 2010, pp. 162–172).

Arsenic (As) is a semimetal with a hardness of 3.5 on the Mohs scale and a melting point of 817 °C. It commonly occurs as sulfur but it can be found in nature as a mineral component together with other elements such as copper. It is toxic and easily volatilized during the processes of reduction and smelting.

Tin (Sn) is a silvery metal with a hardness of 1.5 and a low melting point of 232 °C. It is quite malleable and resistant to corrosion. Its presence as a native metal is scarce; its common mineral form is cassiterite, which melts at 1000 °C. The addition of tin improves the qualities of copper, such as hardness, thus providing weapons and tools that are more resistant to deformation. Tin also lowers the melting point and improves the fluidity of the alloy, which facilitates distribution in the mould.

Metal working processes are laborious and require several stages. The first stage is reduction, i.e. the process of extracting metals from ores. Reduction is achieved by heating in a furnace or smelting crucible where metal will be separated from gangue. This stage is not required for native coppers but it is necessary for other copper minerals, even for sulphides.

Once the metal has been obtained, casting is the next step. Tin is usually added during casting, in mineral or metallic form. Still, experimentation has shown that both materials can be combined in mineral form during reduction (Rovira 2007). Gases should be allowed to escape during casting to avoid the formation of bubbles in the metal. Once the melting point is reached, the metal is immediately poured into moulds and left to cool down. Different types of moulds can be used: single-piece open or closed, bivalve or multiple, made of stone, clay or metal (Renzi 2010). The simpler, single-piece open molds can also be made from sand.

At this point, different post-casting treatments can be applied to achieve optimal results. Possible treatments are cold hammering and annealing. The former provides hardness but also brittleness to the material. Annealing softens the metal and reduces hardness, but grain recrystallisation returns plasticity and uniformity to the structure. The best treatment is forging, which combines both of these processes, i.e. red-hot forging produces the required shape and hardness without risking breakage. The use of hot forging in prehistory is debated due to the absence in the archaeological record of any tongs to hold the hot pieces during hammering (Montero 2010, p. 181). According to Rovira and Gómez Ramos (2003), treatments applied to copper-based metals in Prehistoric times show the use of various operational chains that combine cold hammering and annealing in different ways.

Forging is carried out using a hammer, the object resting on an anvil. Both hammer and anvil can leave imprints on the surface of the tools. Post-casting processes such as cold hammering and annealing modify the metallic structure in varying degrees and, consequently, the mechanical properties of the objects. In this sense, each type of object requires a specific treatment, for example, producing a bracelet does not require the same operational chain as a halberd or a sword.

Furthermore, finishing involves other processes, like whetting by means of an abrasive element to sharpen the edges of cutting implements or shearing, when required, e.g. by saws and several other objects. Besides, filing the whole surface is quite common, to eliminate roughness and the opaque color resulting from casting and annealing, and thus obtain a polished and shinny metallic surface. Whetting and filing, both generate important fields of striations, the former on edges and adjacent areas and the latter over the entire surface. The orientation of striations in relation to the major axis of the object indicates the direction followed by the abrasive element. In terms of use-wear analysis, metal objects are similar to those made on bone and polished stone, as all of them require finishing by means of intense polishment, which originates a field of marks prior to use. Knapped stone objects are different, as their production techniques generate fewer marks, over limited areas. Finally, other tasks such as attaching a blade to its haft may require further processes, including drilling holes for rivets, amongst other. Decoration can also be applied, but until late Bronze Age, this is mostly limited to ornaments.

Copper and bronze are plastic materials that are deformable rather than breakable. This property is one of the main features that distinguish copper-based from lithic materials, particularly the siliceous ones, as the latter are fragile materials which, under the same strain, will break with scarce deformation only. The set of mechanical marks which can be found on the working edge of flint/obsidian or copper/bronze implements, used for the same action, will be very different. The former will show dulling and various types of scars, while metallic surfaces will show a range of plastic deformations but scarce breakage.

On the other hand, the degree of plasticity varies in relation to the proportion of tin in the alloy. A recent study (Soriano and Gutiérrez 2007), aiming at assessing the influence of different copper-based raw materials on use-wear marks, showed that copper has a tendency to feature more plastic deformations, while bronzes with a greater proportion of tin (15–17%) show deformations and small breakage. Low-tin bronzes (5% tin) show less marks than the former metals and no breakage, and feature less damage from technological processes and use.

Determining Functionality: Experimentation
Defining the function of implements is more than just interpreting use-wear marks. It involves knowing their social value, their role in the economy and the technological processes. Therefore, context must be taken into account, and the operational chain must be studied, as thoroughly as possible. The latter should cover the four fundamental stages: raw material type and procurement, production, consumption/sharpening and recycling/abandonment or deposit (hoards). The study of consumption is directly related to the specific use of a particular implement, trying to address the basic issues: on which material, which kinematics, for how long or how intensely. This is the field of work of use-wear or traceology, based upon experimentation and providing a reference collection that can be compared to the marks found on archaeological objects.

The circumstances in which a certain type of object was used may vary significantly both in chronological and geographical terms, namely due to raw material availability and each group's own cultural forms. Trying to reproduce those circumstances requires a deep knowledge of contexts and putting into practice the widest possible range of original situations. Furthermore, during experimentation one learns about the effectiveness of the implement itself regarding a specific task. Such a close contact with the tool or weapon provides an understanding that includes and goes beyond the strictly technical and typological data.

Different experimentations on metallic objects have been carried out so far, with varying quality degrees. Kienlin and Ottaway (1998) and Roberts and Ottaway (2003) studies on flanged and socketed axes are amongst the more consistent pioneer works. Other authors mostly base themselves on an extremely undersized experimental sample, generally limited to producing a few implements to test their effectiveness on a pre-determined task. Such a narrow starting basis produces only partial results, hardly applicable to archaeological materials. Often, but not always, tool use is followed by an examination of marks. Sometimes, marks found on prehistoric objects are interpreted directly, without the support of an experimental reference corpus. A comprehensive discussion on the need and validity of different experimental approaches can be found in Kamphaus (2007).

Use-wear experimentation methodology has been well established in studies on the use-wear marks of lithic tools (Keeley 1980; González and Ibáñez 1994). As far as metal is concerned, the main variables are raw materials and production techniques, as an implement's hardness and resistance to strain depends on these two factors. A small, specifically designed experimental program has shown how different raw materials—pure copper and 5 and 17% tin bronzes—have an effect on the variability of use-wear marks (Soriano and Gutiérrez 2007). The authors also determined that post-casting technical processes, combining cold hammering and annealing, did not seem to add any variation to the patterns of use-wear marks. However, the metallographic analysis concluded that neither hammering nor annealing had significantly affected the objects, so this issue still needs to be addressed. A broader approach, combining different raw materials, post-casting processes, types of actions and worked materials, should be the common base of an experimental corpus.

Furthermore, some elements directly related to use must also be taken into account: the design of implements and working edges, as well as hafting, worked material, tasks and time of work. The combinations of each of these aspects or independent variables generate a specific pattern of marks. This is how one can build up an experimental basis that may establish relationships between different types of marks and the causes that produce them.

Archaeological objects feature different types of marks, which are not always use-related. Some may result from technological processes and from a range of post-depositional events. Concerning metal, the latter are critical due to corrosion, which affects materials with varying degrees of intensity. Cleaning and restoration treatments are another major issue, as they can obliterate or add marks without keeping a proper record of such procedures.

Undertaking comprehensive experimentation to include all these aspects is seldom possible, due to the high infrastructure costs and investment in terms of the time and effort required to produce metallic objects. Still, it can be achieved; starting from limited samples whereby crosschecking variables and object response is done at a small scale, using an explicit method of variable and experimentation control.

9.3 The Marks

The catalogue of marks resulting from experiments is extensive and it is expected to be further extended as new experiments are developed. In fact, since the table proposed in 2002 (Gutiérrez 2002) new marks have been identified and are still being researched.

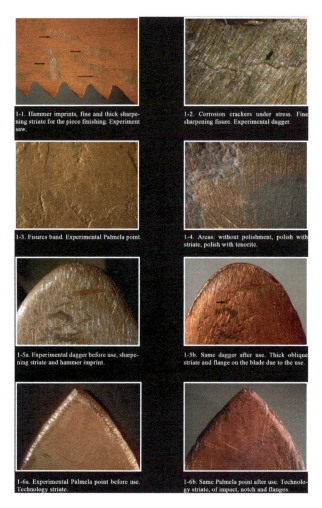

Fig. 9.1 Technological (1-1 to 1-4) and functional (1-5a to 1-6b) plastic deformations

9.3.1 Plastic Deformations

They are due to the tenacity of metal and its plastic deformation range, that is, its ability to deform once a strong enough force is applied, without returning to its original shape. Some of these marks are visible to the naked eye; in other cases, a stereo microscope is required, generally at magnifications not higher than 30×. In any case, these ought to be considered macro-traces as they do not require microscopic examination, with the exception of polish and some types of very small striations.

Massive Depressions Varied imprints: indentations, generally wide and shallow that may appear throughout the whole surface and may have varied morphologies. They usually correspond to hammer (Fig. 9.1: 1-1) and anvil marks made during forging, but they may also result from other impacts, due to different causes, accidental or not, during use or deposition. They may occur isolated or grouped, mainly along the central part of both sides of the object. Determining their exact origin is rather difficult. Some of the marks that Quilliec (2007, p. 104) calls blow impacts on sword blades could be included in this paragraph; their morphology cannot be typified.

Lineal Depression Fissures: Isolated cracks, featuring a V-shaped bottom and an irregular outline, resulting from corrosion under strain. Their length, width and depth are variable. They are more common in cases of intense forging, in pieces bent by hammering and in bronzes with a high tin content; in this last case the malleability of the metal is lower than in pure copper (Fig. 9.1: 1-2).

Band of fissures: A set of multiple tiny, parallel fissures that form a band (Fig. 9.1: 1-3). They have been detected experimentally after hammer-flattening items bent during use. These fissures occur on the inner surface of the curvature once the object has been flattened. The bands are barely perceptible in experimental objects, both to the naked eye and under the stereo microscope, and hardly detectable in archaeological materials.

Incisions: The term refers to decorative elements or technical gestures. Incisions are grooves of variable width, thickness and regularity, which can form simple or complex motifs, usually made with a chisel or burin (Montero Ruiz 2010, p. 187). These grooves can be extremely shallow due to intensive use, as shown by the study of a set of bracelets from the *Depósito de Miedes* (Lucas et al. 2005-6). Incisions not related to decorative motifs can be considered technical gestures, e.g. near the handle to facilitate its attachment or, in other cases, aiming at modifying or destroying the item.

Striations: Striations appear as regular, straight or curved grooves on the metal surface. The bottom is generally U-shaped and they are difficult to classify due to their high numbers and morphological variety. Striations can be detected by the naked eye or with a stereo microscope; microscopes with higher magnification are required for the smallest ones. Different causes may account for striations. The most abundant striations on experimental objects result from polishing and sharpening. A lesser amount is due to object use. Both types of striations are hard to tell apart in the absence of a pictorial record – magnified photographs or moulds - taken before and after use, for comparison purposes. Striations may occur isolated or in clusters of parallel striations. The former can be due to use, accidental causes or to the use of a scalpel. When they are found in clusters, they ought to be considered the result of sharpening, filing or a consequence of using such elements as glass fibber during cleaning. Their location and orientation are equally diverse. A brief classification has been proposed in Gutiérrez (2002).

Experimentation has shown that striations, either technological or caused by use, disappear gradually under the layer of tenorite that appears when metal is exposed to the elements. This may explain why they are so rare on archaeological materials and draws attention to the fact that many striations may result from restoration and cleaning processes, using such elements as glass fibber (Fig. 9.2: 2-2b), scalpels or

Fig. 9.2 Main types of deformations due to usage on archaeological (2-2b and 2-4) and experimental (2-1 a and b, 2-2a, 2-3, 2-5a and b) tools

a mechanical lathe. The main criterion to establish their origin is their relationship with the tenorite layer. If striations cover or cut the tenorite film, they are due to post-depositional processes.

Rounding Dulling: Rounding of the working edge and of the protuberant parts (Figs. 9.2: 2-2a, 2-2b). It is hard to assess on the edges, as prehistoric edges are not extremely sharp, and also over the surface, due to filling processes. Dulling caused by use is easier to identify on decorative incisions or on items that lost a significant part of their apex in result of intensive use.

Edge Deformation Marks located along an item's edge, either active or passive, or on the hafting zone.

Breakage: Edge deformation of irregular morphology due to loss of material or tearing. In some cases, it's the far end of a fissure originated inside the item, which spreads easily during intense forging. Unlike chipping in lithic industry, which also involves loss of material, breakage in metallic items does not feature clear patterns.

   Notch: A concavity on a continuous edge that does not involve breakage or loss of material, but a displacement instead. The morphology of a notch is usually semi-circular and more or less regular. A type of deep notch with an angular bottom has been related to the clash of weapon edges or "edge on edge" (Kristiansen 2002; Fig. 4A and b). Notches are caused by a plastic displacement of the metal and can be associated to other marks, such as thickening on one or both sides or a ridge. Notches are formed in response to pressure against a hard element, for instance a file, during production or against the handle and the worked material during use, or due to accidental causes. Along with ridges, notches are one of the most frequent plastic marks, and typical of working edges (Figs. 1-6b, 2-1a, 2-1b, 2-3).

   On rare occasions, notches start from the edge and are located on one of the sides; their shape is usually triangular. Under those circumstances, they might be associated to percussion events.

   Ridge: A small metal chip either on vertical position on the edge or over one side (Figs. 1-5b, 1-6b, 2-1b, 2-3, 2-4). Its morphology can be regular or irregular and it is, in fact, a result of metal overrunning in response to pressure. Ridges resulting from technological processes are vertical and their edges are irregular. Should the item be used, the ridge will fold over one of the sides of the working edge. Ridges caused by use may occur in vertical position on the edge or, more often, folded over one side, but their shape is always regular. They may be associated with other plastic marks, such as notches and flattening.

   Flattening: A flat or slightly curved surface is produced when metal is pushed back by a strong impact that removes the apex. It is typical of weapons such as arrows, spears or javelins (Fig. 9.2: 2-5a, 2-5b). It may occur on the active apex after hitting a hard element and be located on the tip, or start at the tip and extend slightly over one surface, or be located laterally, much like a burin blow. Its position depends upon a point's penetration angle during impact. A less common position is at the apex of the tang, caused by a backlash against the handle. Thus, it may occur on any hafted implement. The surface can be smooth, striated or coarse, as it is a micro-breakage of the metallic surface caused by increased cold-shortness when metal deforms and overflows. This particular mark is hardly perceptible to the naked eye and sometimes requires magnifications of up to 20× to be identified. The apices of throwing weapons may show more than one flattening.

Thickening: A small, roughly semicircular protuberance, caused by a displacement of the metal (Fig. 9.2: 2-5a). It occurs below notches and flattening, on one or both sides of the edge. It is equivalent to the bulb on the ventral face of knapped lithics. Notches or flattening do not always cause thickening as metal overflows; sometimes the result may be a ridge.

Edge asymmetry: This particular mark has been identified and described by Kienlyn and Ottaway (1998, p. 275), on the edges of experimental and archaeological socketed axes. Asymmetry is caused by sharpening only one side of the working edge, to keep the instrument sharp.

Deformation of the Profile Folding: An easily identifiable mark, as one side of the implement folds over the other. This may occur with varying degrees of intensity, up to the point that one side completely folds over the other. Folding is frequent on the blades of knifes and points, on the junction between blades and hafting tangs or on the lower end of tangs. Folds located on the lower third of the blade or on the blade/tang junction are related to the upper limit of the hafting zone or handle (Fig. 9.3: 3-1). A particular form of folding is the S-profile, a series of soft folds along the blade. A number of folds have been identified by the authors on archaeological and experimental Palmela points, associated to other impact marks (Gutiérrez et al. in press). Kristiansen (2002, p. 323) also found this mark on the tips of Bronze Age swords; according to the author, these folds result from clashes against a shield.

Lateral folding: A bending towards one of the sides, which can occur, with varying intensity, at any spot along the profile, but more commonly on the tang (Fig. 9.3: 3-2).

Micro-folding: Bending of a pointed edge over one of the sides (Fig. 9.3: 3-5a, 3-5b). The authors have identified this mark on the distal apex of throwing weapons, and occasionally, on the tip of the tang (Fig. 9.4: 4-1). It is not always evident to the naked eye.

Torsion: A soft, helicoidal folding. It may occur at the distal end or along the profile, especially on the weakest points like the junction between blade and tang (Fig. 9.4: 4-2).

Morphological asymmetry: Two metal points from the Late Bronze deposits found in the cave sites of Carritx and Mussol (Menorca, Spain) featured a strongly asymmetrical configuration. This asymmetry, along with the presence of striations on one lateral edge only, was interpreted by the excavation team as evidence for the preferential use of a single edge (Lull et al. 1999, pp. 119–120 and 221–222; Table 9.1).

9.3.2 *Physical and Chemical Deformations*

Physical and Chemical Alterations Corrosion: Corrosion is part of a metal's nature and starts just as it comes out of the mould and is exposed to the elements. Atmospheric oxygen, water and mineral salts from sedimentary environments are the main agents of corrosion. The contact of metal objects with organic matter also fosters corrosion.

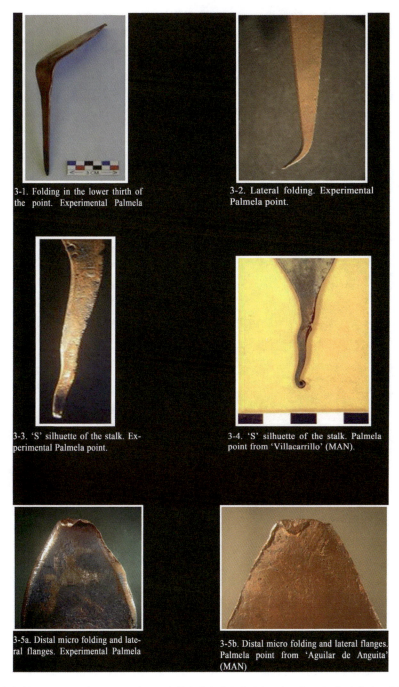

Fig. 9.3 Use-wear marks on experimental (3-1, 3.2, 3-3, 3-5a) and archaeological (3-4 and 3-5b) Palmela points

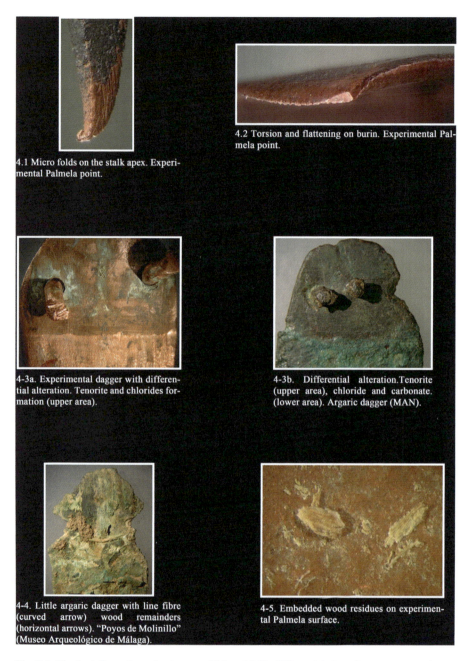

4.1 Micro folds on the stalk apex. Experimental Palmela point.

4.2 Torsion and flattening on burin. Experimental Palmela point.

4-3a. Experimental dagger with differential alteration. Tenorite and chlorides formation (upper area).

4-3b. Differential alteration. Tenorite (upper area), chloride and carbonate. (lower area). Argaric dagger (MAN).

4-4. Little argaric dagger with line fibre (curved arrow) wood remainders (horizontal arrows). "Poyos de Molinillo" (Museo Arqueológico de Málaga).

4-5. Embedded wood residues on experimental Palmela surface.

Fig. 9.4 Plastic deformations due to usage (4-1 and 4-2), differential alterations on an experimental (4-3a) tool and an archaeological (4-3b) tool, and adhering residues on a archaeological metal tool (4-4) and an experimental metal tool (4-5)

Table 9.1 All types of marks

Category	Description	Type of marks	Causes
Plastic deformations	Massive depressions	Varied imprints	Technological processes
			Use/handle
			Post-depositional alterations
	Lineal depressions	Incisions	Technological process/decoration
		Striations	Use/Handle/Resharpening
		Fissures	Post-depositional alterations
		Band of fissures	Mechanical cleaning
	Rounding	Dulling	Technological processes
			Use/Handle
			Post-depositional alterations
	Edge deformation	Breakage	Technological processes
		Notch	Use/Handle/Resharpening
		Ridge	Mechanical cleaning
		Flattening	Post-depositional alterations
		Thickening	
		Edge asymmetry	
	Deformation of the profile	Folding	Technological processes
		Lateral folding	Use/Handle/ Resharpening
		Micro-folding	
		Torsion	
		Morphological asymmetry	
Physical and chemical deformations	Physical and chemical alterations	Corrosion	Technological processes
		Polishment	Use/Handle
		Luster bands	Post-depositional alterations
		Differential alterations	
Added elements	Adhering materials	Residues	Use/Handle
			Post-depositional alterations

Different types of corrosion affect metal in different ways. The so-called copper patina, which tends to protect the metal, consists of cuprous oxide or cuprite, of reddish colour, or cupric oxide or tenorite (Fig. 9.1: 1-4) of blackish color. Copper sulphates and sulphides (antlerite, covellite and chalcocite) are of green-bluish color. Other bluish or greenish corrosions are copper salts or carbonates: azurite and malachite. Chlorine hydroxides or halides like green atacamite and paratacamite are more harmful to artifact preservation. All these alterations cover use-wear marks to the point of partly or completely hiding them. Furthermore, they can deteriorate the artifact and even destroy it in the worst cases.

Polish: Despite being an important mark in lithic use-wear analysis, for identifying worked materials, it has only a limited use in studies on metallic artifacts. During experimentation, the authors have found examples of polishment on the edge of used implements (Gutiérrez and Soriano 2008), but they were always scarce and only occur on those rare spots where corrosions like cuprite and tenorite were not present. Corrosion hides polishment. In addition, restoration treatments that use waxes prevent observation under the microscope, even if thorough cleaning didn't obliterate marks before.

Luster band: Areas of shinier metal forming bands along the used edge were observed by the authors on experimental materials (Fig. 9.2: 2-2a). These bands are produced by friction between metal and the worked material and obliterate the layer of alteration that formed since the implement was produced. It is a hardly recognizable mark on archaeological material, as corrosion forms well developed layers that cover-up these differences.

Differential alterations: An assemblage of archaeological objects will show different degrees of corrosion along each item. This is common in elements such as knives/daggers, between the hafting zone and the blade (Figs. 9.4: 4-3a, 4-3b). After experimental butchery, the authors observed the same phenomenon when the wooden handle was removed for use-wear analysis. Differential alteration is due to contact with diverse organic materials along the implement's length. Tenorite will be eliminated by friction during use, while part of the organic residues such as fat, flesh, hair and skin find its way under the handle, leaving small deposits that cause more intense corrosion. If archaeological artifacts were deposited at the sites with their organic handles still attached, one may consider that the latter would protect the hafting zone from some external aggressions, but its turn would also lead to other alterations, caused by contact with the handle.

9.3.3 Added Elements

Adhering Materials
Residues: It is not uncommon to find small organic residues adhered to metallic archaeological objects, as the former become impregnated with copper oxide. A small notched dagger showed a flax fibber rolled between head and blade, as well as remains of *Quercus* sp. wood, perhaps from a sheath, adhering to both sides of the blade (Badal et al. 2005; Figs. 9.4: 4-4, 4-5). These residues can help in the determination of materials used in hafting and of other elements used to assemble the artifact.

The above is a catalogue of marks identified during the authors' experimental work (Gutiérrez and Soriano 2008). It is by no means the ultimate list of all the marks resulting from technology or use. Apart from some of the marks included here, some authors have forwarded other evidence of use, such as edge asymmetry (Kienlyn and Ottaway 1998, p. 275) or morphological asymmetry (Lull et al. 1999, pp. 119–120), which would indicate successive resharpening events on a specific part of the implement. There are also some comprehensive sets of technological, use or destruction marks related to Late Bronze Atlantic swords (Quilliec 2007) or to a Chalcolithic metallic assemblage (Dolfini 2011) The plastic capacity of metal to deform generates a significant morphological diversity of marks.

9.4 Working Procedures

Items should be cleaned prior to examination, in order to facilitate the detection of marks. Cleaning is more urgent in experimental objects because residues from worked materials must be removed quickly, before organic matter generates corrosion spots. Cleaning may be carried out by means of a soft brush and a solution of water and alcohol (deionised water and 50 % alcohol) followed by chemical drying in a bath of pure alcohol for 1 min, and then acetone for another minute. Finally, items are left to air dry.

Regarding archaeological materials, procedures are similar, if cleaning is at all possible. A higher percentage of alcohol in the water-alcohol solution is required (about 80 %) and brushing should be replaced by a bath in an ultrasonic tank. Should artifacts feature strong corrosion, a wooden punch or a laser may be used, but the latter should be handled by a professional restorer. In any case, it is convenient to take pictures under the stereo microscope before cleaning, and to keep a photographic record of the whole process.

Most of the observations were carried out using a Leica Wild M3C stereo microscope with two wide angle eyepieces 10×/21Ba, magnification intervals at 0.64×, 10×, 16×, 25× and 40× and a 2–40× work range, featuring a micrometer on the eyepieces. For polishes and small striations a Leitz DMRX transmitted/reflected light microscope with revolving nose and magnifications from 50 to 400× was used. Both were equipped with a Canon Eox450 digital camera connected to a computer; ZoomBrowser EX 4.0 and Helicon-Focus 4.48 software was used as well. This must be stressed because out of the realm of Traceology, mentions of unused metalwork based upon simple, naked eye observation only are commonplace.

9.5 Conclusions

Metal Traceology started its development in the last decade but is still undergoing the inherent problems of a developing discipline. The experimental corpus is scarce; experimentation often lack structured designs. In addition, the definition and typification of marks is insufficient and there is a lack of relationship between the marks and the use variables. Thus, it is important to consolidate a proper methodology that sets conclusions and enables the application of results to broader assemblages.

The examination of archaeological artifacts also has significant limitations, sometimes impossible to overcome. Corrosion hides many of the marks, to the point of invalidating use-wear analysis. Besides, obliteration of the original marks and their replacement by new ones is commonplace during restoration. Roberts and Ottaway (2003, pp. 119–120) also point out that artifact sharpening and recycling add potential limitations to the use-wear analysis of metallic objects. Concerning resharpening, the problem is the same as when the worn out edges of lithic implements are rejuvenated by retouch. If the implement has been further used, one can observe its last function, otherwise there will be no use-wear marks. Therefore, lithic use-wear analysis shows that absence of marks does not always mean absence of use. The same authors argue that the diversity of uses with the same instrument leaves unclear or hardly identifiable patterns. Both are, indeed, limitations inherent to the study of marks on any raw material.

A first approach at evaluating the potential of metal traceology can be achieved, based upon the results obtained so far. By comparing the results with those obtained in the analysis of lithic industry, the contributions of metal traceology are rather poor. The lack of access to such marks as polishment or, quite often, striations, deprives us of important criteria to interpret aspects like worked materials or actions performed.

The most important corpus of marks on metalwork concerns the plastic deformations on the edges or other parts of the artifact. There is a whole range of deformations and in many cases it is difficult to relate them with variables such as material or action. Most deformations have limited diagnostic capabilities. They will only allow for generic interpretations on whether the artifact has been used and in which specific zone. On the basis of sound experimentation, results might be extended as far as determining aspects like the hardness of worked materials or whether marks were caused by percussion or pressure—much like chippings in lithic industry.

Fortunately, these data are important by themselves as far as interpreting the functions of prehistoric metalwork is concerned. Thorough research can provide an assessment of functional effectiveness and relate it to issues like raw materials, work processes and morphological design; these issues are not limited to tools only, as they can also apply to ornaments. The latter, together with tools and weapons such as saws, halberds, swords, shields and several other items found in domestic, funerary or deposit contexts, have very specific morphologies and are scarcely susceptible of a diversified use. Evidence on whether or not they have been used can help reinterpreting some aspects of technological, social, economic and even ideological nature.

Acknowledgements The authors wish to express their gratitude to the staff from the Laboratorio de Prehistoria y Arqueología of UAM University and to all graduate and post-graduate students who participated in the experimentation program. We are especially grateful to Armando Lucena, Laura Llorente, Elena Sanz, Anabel Pardo, Charles Bashore, Alba López, Pedro Muñoz, Álvaro Simón, Olga de Miguel, Jorge Chamón and Ignacio Soriano.

References

Appleby, G. A. (2003). *Warfare or use-wear: Conflicts in interpretation*. An analysis of damage pattern in Bronze Age spears held in the Cambridge University Museum of Archaeology and Anthropology. Unpublished BA Dissertation, University of Cambridge (Magdalene College).

Badal, E., Gutiérrez, C., Cabrera, A., Cortés, M., Simón, M. D., Pardo, A. I., Sánchez, A., & Gómez, M. J. (2005). Evidencias de materias orgánicas en instrumentos metálicos del Calcolítico y Edad del Bronce andaluces. In J. Molera, J. Farjás, P. Roura, & T. Pradell (Eds.), *Avances en Arqueometría*. Actas del VI Congreso Ibérico de Arqueometría (pp. 229–239). Fundació Privada: Girona, Universitat i Futur.

Brandherm, D. (2004). Porteurs de hallebardes? Überlegungenzur Herkunft, Entwicklung und Funktion der bronzezeitlichen Stabklingen. *Varia Neolithica, 3,* 279–334.

Bridgford, S. (1997). Mightier than the pen? An edgewise look at Irish Bronze Age swords. In J. Carman (Ed.), *Material harm: Archaeological studies of war and violence* (pp. 95–115). Glasgow: Cruithne Press.

Coles, J. (1979). *Experimental archaeology*. London: Academic.

Dolfini, A. (2011). The function of Chalcolithic metalwork in Italy: An assessment based on use-wear analysis. *Journal of Archaeological Science, 38*(5), 1037–1049.
González, J. E., & Ibáñez, J. J. (1994). *Metodología del análisis funcional de instrumentos en sílex*. Bilbao: Universidad de Deusto.
Greenfield, H. J. (1999). The origins of metallurgy: Distinguishing stone from metal cut-marks on bones from archaeological sites. *Journal of Archaeological Science, 26*, 797–808.
Greenfield, H. J. (2002). Distinguishing metal (steel and low-tin bronze) from stone (flint and obsidian) tool cut marks on bone: An experimental approach. In J. R. Mathieu (Ed.), *Experimental archaeology. Replicating past objects, behaviours and processes*. BAR International Series 1035, pp. 35–54.
Gutiérrez Sáez, C. (2002). Traceología aplicada al material metálico: límites y posibilidades. *Análisis funcional. Su aplicación al estudio de las sociedades prehistóricas*. I Congreso Peninsular de Análisis Funcional. Barcelona. BAR International Series 1073, pp. 261–272.
Gutiérrez Sáez, C., & Soriano Llopis, I. (2008). La funcionalidad sobre material metálico. Bases y aplicaciones de estudio. In S. Rovira, M. García Heras, M. Gener, & I. Montero Ruiz (Eds.), *Actas del VII Congreso Ibérico de Arqueometría* (pp. 432–447). Madrid: CSIC.
Gutierrez Saéz, C., García Moldes, A., Jiménez Arés, E., Márquez González, R., & Campayo García, C. (2008). *Microwear analysis and metal tools. The study of use wear traces and the contribution to the understanding of protohistoric societies*. "Prehistoric Technology" 40 years later: functional studies and the Russian Legacy. BAR International Series 1783, pp. 471–474.
Gutiérrez Sáez, C., López del Estal, A., Simón Martín, A., Muñoz Moro, P., Bashore Acero, Ch., Chamón Fernández, J., Martín Lerma, I., Sanz Salas, E., pardo Naranjo, A. I., & Marín de Espinosa, J. A. (2010). Puntas de Palmela: procesos tecnológicos y experimentación. *Trabajos de Prehistoria, 67*(2), 405–428.
Gutiérrez Sáez, C., Martín Lerma, I., López Del Estal, A., & Bashore Acero, Ch. (In press). *The functionality of Palmela points as throwing weapons and projectiles. Use-wear marks*. Paper presented to Use-Wear 2012. International Conference on Use-Wear analysis, 10–12 October, Faro, Portugal.
Kamphaus, B. (2007). Use-wear and functional analysis of bronze weapons and armor. *Journal of World Anthropology, III*(1), 113–38.
Keeley, L. H. (1980). *Experimental determination of stone tools uses: A microwear analysis*. Chicago: University of Chicago Press.
Kienlin, T. L., & Ottaway, B. S. (1998). Flanged axes of the north-alpine region: An assessment of the possibilities of use-wear analysis on metal artefacts. In C. Mordant, M. Perno, & V. Rychner (Eds.), *L'Atelier du bronzier en Europe du XX au VIII siècle avant notre ère*, (Vol. II, pp. 271-286). Paris: Comité des travaux historiques et scientifiques.
Kristiansen, K. (2002). The tale of the sword—swords and swordfighters in Bronze Age Europe. *Oxford Journal of Archaeology, 21*(4), 319–332.
Liesau, C. (1998). El Soto de Medinilla: Faunas de mamíferos de la Edad del Hierro en el Valle del Duero (Valladolid, España). *Archaeofauna, 7*, 25–62.
Lucas, R. †, Gutiérrez, C., Blasco, C., & Rovira, S. (2005-6). El depósito de Miedes y otros materiales metálicos (Bronce Final/Hierro I) procedentes de la provincia de Guadalajara. Homenaje a Dña Rosario Lucas Pellicer y D. Vicente Viñas. *Boletín de la Asociación de Amigos de la Arqueología, 44*, 129–160, Madrid.
Lull, V., Micó, R., Rihuete, C., & Risch, R. (1999). *Ideología y sociedad en la prehistoria de Menoría. La Cova des Càrritx y la Cova des Mussol*. Islas Baleares: Consell Insular de Menorca.
Malloy, B. (2004). Experimental combat with Bronze Age weapons. *Archaeology Ireland, 18*(1), 32–34.
Matthieu, J. R., & Meyer, D. A. (1997). Comparing axe heads of Stone, Bronze and steel: Studies in experimental archaeology. *Journal of Field Archaeology, 24*(3), 333–351.
Montero Ruiz, I. (2010). Tecnología de la metalurgia de base cobre. I. Montero Ruiz (Coord.), *Manual de arqueometalurgia* (pp. 159–188). Madrid: Museo Arqueológico Regional, Comunidad de Madrid.

Moyler, S. (2008). Doing away with Dichotomies? Comparative use-wear analysis of early Bronze age axes from Scotland. In C. Hamon & B. Quilliec (Eds.), *Hoards from the neolithic to the metal ages: Technical and codified practices*. BAR International Series 1758, pp. 79–90.

Nilsson, S. (1868). *The primitive inhabitants of Scandinavia*. London: General Books LLC.

O'Flaherty, R. (2007). A weapon of choice: experiments with a replica Irish Early Bronze Age halberd. *Antiquity, 81,* 423–434.

Olsen, S. L. (1988). The identification of stone and metal tool marks on bone artefacts. In S.L. Olsen (Ed.), *Scanning electron microscopy in archaeology.* BAR International Series 452, pp. 337–360.

Quilliec, B. T. (2007). Vida y muerte de una espada atlántica del Bronce final en Europa: Reconstrucción de los procesos de fabricación, uso y destrucción. *Complutum, 18,* 93–107.

Renzi, M. (2010). Vasijas de uso metalúrgico, toberas y moldes. In Ruiz, M. (ed.) Manual de arqueometalurgia, pp.123–158.

Rovira, S. & Gomez Ramos, P. (1998). Metalurgia calcolítica en Carmona (Sevilla). SPAL 7, 69–79.

Roberts, B., & Ottaway, B. S. (2003). The use and significance of socketed axes during the Late Bronze Age. *EuropeanJournal of Archaeology, 6*(2), 119–140.

Rovira, S. (2007). La producción de bronces en la Prehistoria. Avances en Arqueometría 2005. Actas del VI Congreso Ibérico de Arqueometría (Girona 2005). Girona, pp. 21–35

Rovira, S., & Gómez Ramos, P. (2003). *Las Primeras Etapas Metalúrgicas en la Península Ibérica III. Estudios metalográficos.* Madrid: Instituto Universitario Ortega y Gasset.

Sands, R. (1997). *Prehistoric woodworking. The analysis and interpretation of Bronze and Iron Age toolmarks.* London: Institute of Archaeology, University college of London.

Semenov, S. A. (1964). *Prehistoric technology. An experimental study of the oldest tools and artifacts from traces of manufacture and wear.* London: Cory, Adams and Mackay Ltd.

Skak-Nielsen, N. V. (2009). Flint and metal daggers in Scandinavia and other parts of Europe: a reinterpretation of their function in the late Neolithic and early Copper and Bronze Age. *Antiquity, 83,* 349–358.

Soriano, I., & Gutiérrez, C. (2007*). Use-wear analysis on metal: the influence of raw material and metallurgical production processes. Archaeometallurgy in Europe* (pp. 115–124). Milano: Associazione Italiana di Metallurgia.

Uckelmann, M., & Mödlinger, M. (Eds.). (2011). *Warfare in Bronze Age Europe: Manufacture and use of weaponry.* BAR International Series 2255.

Wall, J. (1987). The role of daggers in Early Bronze Age Britain: the evidence of wear analysis. *Oxford Journal of Archaeology, 6*(1), 115–118.

York, J. (2002). The life cycle of Bronze Age metalwork from the Thames. *Oxford Journal of Archaeology, 21*(1), 77–92.

Chapter 10
Pottery Use-Alteration Analysis

James M. Skibo

10.1 Introduction

My interest in pottery use-alteration analysis is now in its third decade. A series of experiments (O'Brien 1990; Schiffer and Skibo 1989; Skibo et al. 1997; Vaz Pinto et al. 1987) and ethnoarchaeological work among the Kalinga, (Longacre 1974, 1981, 1985, 1991; Longacre and Skibo 1994; Stark and Skibo 2007) culminated in my book (Skibo 1992) that developed the method and theory for understanding how pottery was used based upon three use-alteration traces: attrition, residue, and carbonization. This initial work was developed further in *Understanding Pottery Function* (Skibo 2013), which is a manual for conducting use-alteration analysis. Interested readers should refer to this book for a full description for not only how to conduct a use-alteration study but also how to complete examination of pottery function. In this chapter I briefly review the methods for analyzing pottery use-alteration traces.

10.2 An Approach to Pottery Analysis

Any analysis of pottery should start with the notion that all pots are designed to be used—that is to perform some function. My notion of function, however, is a bit wider than one used most typically, as it includes not just utilitarian function (techno-function in our terms) but also social and symbolic functions as well (socio-, ideo and emotive functions) (see Schiffer and Skibo 1987; Skibo and Schiffer 2008). To isolate these functions one can speak in terms of performance characteristics, which are the capabilities any technology must possess in order to perform its functions in an activity. Any potter has at their disposal a series of technical choices when making a pot. Thus they could add more temper to increase

---

J. M. Skibo (✉)
4640 Anthropology, Illinois State University, Normal, IL 61790-4640 USA
e-mail: jmskibo@ilstu.edu

thermal shock resistance (an important techno-functional performance characteristic for cooking pots) or alter the angle of the shoulder profile to perform an important social performance characteristic (e.g., Pauketat and Emerson 1991). The point is that pottery, being an extremely malleable medium, gives potters many choices when designing and making a pot to suit a particular *intended function*. One goal of ceramic analysis is to tease out these functional performance characteristics. So we measure a host of technical properties, like size, thickness of the wall, temper attributes, and firing temperature to try and understand why these vessels were made—their intended function.

There are a number of reasons, however, why a reconstruction of intended function is insufficient and, consequently, an exploration of *actual pottery function* is important. Actual function does not always follow intended function. A potter may design a pot to perform specific functions but the vessel user may choose to use the pot in a very different way. Pots can also be designed to be multifunctional, performing a number of roles at an acceptable level—cooking, storing, brewing beer, etc. So an exploration of actual function is necessary to determine how the vessels were used. Pots can also be recycled and reused, and these functions are lost if one looks only at the intended function. Finally, everyday cooking pots can become ritual containers under some circumstances and it is important to develop strategies to infer these secondary functions as well.

10.3 Use-Alteration Traces

10.3.1 *Carbonization*

Carbonization on vessels occurs in two forms, internal carbonization of food and external deposition of soot from the smoke of a cooking fire. Soot is the product of the pyrolysis of wood from a cook fire and it consists of various products including tars and resins. Beginning with Hally (1983), experiments have shown that there are three types of soot patches on the exterior of vessels. The first type is flat black and fluffy and is deposited over any part of the vessel that impacts rising smoke and is deposited immediately after the pot is put over the fire. This type of soot is easily rubbed off and can be removed by simply rinsing with water. This transient layer of soot would not likely survive the various effects of cultural (washing) and noncultural processes and thus is not particularly useful in use-alteration analysis.

The second type of soot is more permanently affixed to the ceramic surface because it contains resin droplets, which are drawn up with the rising smoke and are solidified once they come in contact with cooler surfaces. Once the resin cools, it can produce a hard, waterproof soot layer that is very resistant to breakdown. The oldest pottery in North America from the southeastern USA has evidence of this type of soot suggesting that it is very resistant to various forms of bioturbation (Beck et al. 2002; Sassaman 1993; Skibo 2013).

The third patch on the exterior of vessels is really the absence of soot, which occurs because soot cannot form on surfaces as they approach 400 °C. If soot was deposited in an early cooking episode, it will burn away when subject to high temperatures. This patch can vary from a light gray area to an area that is completely oxidized.

The temperature of the ceramic surface is the key variable in the deposition of the different types and patches of exterior soot. There are a number of factors that can control the temperature of the ceramic surface that include the distance of the vessel above the flames, presence of water in the vessel, type of wood, and hearth design. The presence of water in the vessel is especially an important factor as it can, in many types of cooking, keep the temperature of the ceramic surface cool enough, so that soot can be deposited. Consequently, with many types of low-fired wares water will permeate into the vessel wall and keep the ceramic surface relatively cool so that soot can be deposited. Thus pots used for boiling, for example, may be sooted on the base, whereas pots used in the absence of water, as in roasting or cases in which water is boiled off, the ceramic surface will get to temperatures approaching 400 °C and no soot will be deposited.

Carbonization on the interior of vessels is caused by the charring of food. Charred food can either lay on the surface as encrustations, or carbonize within the ceramic surface itself. Encrustations of charred food often times extend to the exterior of the vessels as a result of boil-overs. Although both types of internal carbonizations are important and can be useful for inferring vessel function, encrustations are far less common and much more prone to removal in the depositional environment. Nonetheless, when encrustations are found they can be important as they can be useful for inferring cooking behavior and can be linked to what was being cooked (see Malainey 2011). The processes that form internal carbonizations, however, are the same whether they are found within the vessel wall or laying on the surface as encrustations.

The temperature of the ceramic surface is the primary factor controlling the deposition of internal carbonization as the vessel wall must reach between 300 and 400 °C for food particles to char. If cooking is done in the wet mode (boiling) carbonization will not occur below the water line as the temperature of the interior surface will not go much beyond 100 °C. But just above the water line, where food particles and fats can adhere to the vessel wall, the temperatures will exceed 300 °C and carbonization will occur. If the pots are permeable, which often occurs in low-fired cooking pots, food particles and fats can be transported into the vessel wall where they will be carbonized. This type of internal carbonization has great permanence as it becomes part of the vessel wall. A ring of carbonization at the water line is a signature trace of vessels used to cook in the wet mode.

In the dry cooking mode, as in roasting or in cases where water is completely removed from the contents, the surface temperatures on the interior of the vessel will exceed 300 °C and carbonization will occur. This type of carbonization, however, will not penetrate the surface as described above.

10.3.2 Recording External and Internal Carbonization

There is certainly a great deal of ceramic diversity in prehistory and no analytic strategy can be devised that could accommodate this diversity. Consequently, each ceramic analyst must devise a strategy unique to their collections and research questions. With that said, there are some common factors that should be employed when conducting an analysis of carbonization traces.

The first important point for recording carbonization patterns is that the analysis should start with whole vessels if possible. Whole and reconstructable vessels are often a rare commodity in a region, so I do not mean to imply that this analysis can only be done with such collections. The point here is that these vessels should be consulted if available and partially reconstructable vessels or large sherds should be analyzed first. The analysis should start with the largest fragments in the collection preferably from each size and morphological class.

There can be a great deal of variability in internal carbonization and sooting traces. The good news for the analyst is that we are concerned not with idiosyncratic sooting patches but rather general patterns. I have found that sketches are the best way to quickly and accurately record carbonization on whole vessels. There is a long tradition in archaeology of scientific and technical drawing that can make a detailed recording of ceramic variability, but in most cases such drawings are not necessary for initial data recording. The strategy I found most effective to record the general use-alteration traces are roughly measured sketches that can be recorded by any lab analyst with just a small amount of instruction.

Many ceramic analysts are left with piles of small sherds to record. In these cases the presence and absence of interior and exterior carbonization can be recorded. These data can be combined with the whole or partially reconstructed vessel data to help infer vessel use activity. Even in cases where no whole vessel data are available, some important information can still be retrieved from sherd data. For example, Sassaman (1993) was able to infer with only sherd data that some of the Late Archaic pottery from the southeastern USA was used for direct heating over a fire while other vessels were used for indirect heating with hot rocks.

Cooking over a fire, however, is not the only reason that carbonization patterns can occur on ceramic surfaces. For example, during the firing process fuel or gas can come in contact with the vessel and create fire clouds (Rye 1981, pp. 120–121). These fire clouds can mimic carbonization created while cooking. In addition, the purposeful darkening of a pot in a reducing environment during firing (smudging) can create a surface that is completely carbonized. Finally, carbonization or oxidation of surfaces can happen if a vessel is subject to great heat such as in a house or a room fire. Fire clouds, smudging, and postdepositional burning, however, can be easily discriminated from use-related carbonization by the patterning of the patches. Smudging will usually cover an entire surface and fire clouds will occur randomly, whereas use-related carbonization will occur in patches that are usually repeated in each size and morphological class.

Carbonization data can be used by the researcher to draw a number of inferences about cooking activity, such as mode of cooking (wet or dry), direct or indirect heating, or hearth design. There are a number of scholars who have successfully analyzed carbonization patterns and made inferences about vessel function. Hally (1983, 1986) was the first to systematically examine carbonization from late prehistoric sites from the northwestern portion of Georgia in the USA. Based on exterior sooting patterns, he was able to determine the hearth designs and the way the pots were suspended over a fire. He also noted that two different sizes of morphologically identical pots were used differently.

Also from the southeastern USA, Sassaman (1993) examined exterior sooting patterns on Late Archaic vessels, the first pottery containers in North America. The most important finding of his study was that pottery from interior sites had very little evidence of sooting while sooting was found on a high percentage of sherds excavated from sites on the coast. Sassaman argued that the people on the coast were using the pots for direct heating over a fire whereas the Late Archaic cooks from interior villages were using the vessels for indirect heating—hot rock cooking.

10.3.3 Attrition

Pottery surface attrition is the removal or deformation of the ceramic that occurs throughout a vessel's life history and thus is created by a number of use and nonuse related processes. Use attrition is created by a number of processes during cooking, cleaning, storage of liquids, and other activities as a vessel is used for its primary function. But attrition is a very instructive trace for informing on a vessel's life history beyond its primary function where it can be used in a secondary function or even recycled. Broken sherds are often used as scrapers, scoops, and other tools that can leave attritional traces indicative of a particular use. And once sherds are deposited, attrition can also be used to infer a vessel's postdepositional life history as it may be impacted by wind, water, or freezing and thawing.

There are a number of abrasive and nonabrasive processes that can cause ceramic attrition. Abrasive processes create traces like scratches, gouges, and nicks that grow into patches as an abrasive activity is repeated. The principles of ceramic abrasion (Schiffer and Skibo 1989) include the characteristics of the ceramic, characteristics of the abrader, and the nature of the ceramic-abrader contact.

There are also several common forms of nonabrasive attritional processes: spalling as a result of fermentation, vaporization of water, and salt crystallization. When fermentation is done in low-fired pottery that permits some liquid permeation, spalling can occur as expanding gases within the vessel wall remove some of the interior surface. Arthur (2002, 2003, 2006) noted this trace on ethnographic vessels and it has subsequently been noted on a number of prehistoric collections (Skibo and Blinman 1999).

Exterior spalls often occur in low-fired water storage jars in arid environments (O'Brien 1990). Water permeates the wall and evaporates, which creates a cooling effect, but the crystallization of salts just beneath the surface can create spalling. Finally, spalling can occur in some cooking situations. This was noted in Kalinga rice cooking pots during their final stage of cooking when they are taken off the fire and placed next to the flames to remove the last of the water in the rice. In this situation, the water in the vessel wall turns to steam and escapes through the interior surface, which creates spalls.

10.3.4 Recording Attritional Traces

Attritional traces can be recorded on sherds or vessels. If recorded on vessels, I recommend the same strategy as described above for recording carbonization—sketch attritional traces on a vessel profile template. Attritional traces on sherds are also very instructive as they are often used as tools (e.g., López Varela et al. 2002) or the abrasion can also inform on important postdepositional processes. Use-attrition is described by two terms (Schiffer and Skibo 1989): marks and patches. A mark is created by a single attritional event, such as a spall, nick, chip, or scratch. In some cases the direction, angle, and force applied can be inferred from the attributes of this mark. Use-activities create repeated marks that grow into patches. Patches sometimes have the entire exterior surface removed so individual marks of this use-activity are not apparent in the center. But at the periphery, individual marks can often be identified. Together, the attributes of marks and patches can provide important clues to vessel use activities.

A number of scholars have used attritional traces to infer ceramic use throughout a vessel's life history. The production of alcoholic beverages through the fermentation of food is found throughout the world and in many areas it is a practice that has been going on for thousands of years (Dietler 2006; McGovern 2003; McGovern et al. 2004). Chemical residue analysis would seem like the most direct way to find evidence of fermentation in ceramic vessels, but for a number of reasons this is not easily done (McGovern et al. 2004). Consequently, I would predict that the practice of fermentation and alcohol consumption in prehistory is more common than we have been able to confirm. But there is an abrasive trace, interior pitting, which often is formed in ceramic vessels used for alcohol fermentation.

I did a study of the earliest pottery on the Colorado Plateau in the American Southwest. The first pottery in this region was globular, neckless, jars referred to as "seed jars" in the local taxonomy because they are similar to forms used in the historic period to store seeds. My analysis, however, discovered that many of the pots were used over a fire, based on sooting, and that they were used to cook foods in both the wet and dry modes (Skibo and Blinman 1999; Skibo and Schiffer 2008). Besides being used as cooking pots, these vessels had tell-tale traces of fermentation—interior spalling. As noted above, the fermenting liquid can penetrate the vessel wall and spall the interior surface as expanding gases rise to the surface.

Finally, attritional traces have also been used to infer how recycled sherds are used as tools (Sullivan et al. 1991). López Varela et al. (2002) found extensive evidence of sherd tools at K'axob, the Late Classic Period site in northern Belize. By examining the attritional traces on these tools they were able to classify them into smoothing, scraping, incising, polishing, and boring tools.

10.3.5 Residue

Pots are designed to hold contents and they have a number of unique characteristics that permit them to perform differently than other containers such as baskets, skins, and wooden bowls. Among the benefits of pottery is that they can be put directly over a fire so that they can be used in direct heat cooking. Additionally, ceramic containers make good storage containers, especially if you want to keep the contents safe from rodents or you have a liquid that needs a sturdy container. Since the primary function of pottery is to serve as a container, it is certainly important for archaeologists to determine what was stored, cooked, processed, or transferred in these vessels.

The chemical analysis of residues that are left behind in these vessels has become an extremely active area of research (e.g., Evershed 1993; Heron and Evershed 1993, Malainey 2007). Although a variety of different chemical compounds can be used to identify past contents, I have preferred to focus on fatty acids in my work for a number of reasons. First, every living thing has different types and combinations of fatty acids, so it is at least theoretical possible to link residues to foods once stored or cooked in a vessel. Second, fatty acids are quite resistant to breakdown in the depositional environment, especially if one focuses on the fatty acids that have been absorbed in the vessel walls. Third and finally, if one does focus on the absorbed lipids then there is far less chance of contamination from the depositional environment or from handling the sherds.

I once tried to do lipid analysis but have learned that unless one is familiar with lipid chemistry and gas chromatography/mass spectroscopy or other analytical techniques, the lab work should be left to those who have the training to conduct it. Below I describe some of the most useful techniques and how archaeologists can use it to identify the former contents of their vessels (see Evershed 1993; Malainey 2007 for a detailed description of these techniques).

A number of labs will conduct residue analysis and they should also be consulted regarding the protocol for the process of selecting and caring for sherd samples. The techniques used and the sampling procedure will depend in large part on the researcher's questions and the types of vessels being sampled. For example, to identify the contents of storage pots it would be best to collect a sample from the base of a vessel. Cooking pot samples, however, should be recovered from the area that corresponds to the maximum capacity as heat can break down some of the compounds of interest (Charters et al. 1993; Malainey 2007). The zone of maximum capacity on vessels can often be identified by a patch of internal carbonization.

To avoid contamination, either from the depositional environment or handling by archaeologists, it is best to extract the lipids from within the vessel wall. A number of researchers have demonstrated that lipids within the vessel wall not only occur in greater amounts (Condamin et al. 1976) but they are also far less likely to be contaminated by the migration of lipids from the soil (Heron et al. 1991). Avoiding the lipids on the exterior surface also reduces the possibility that handling of the sherds may have introduced lipids (Evershed 1993). Although lipids have been successfully extracted from curated samples and washing sherds in water does not seem to have a significant impact, it is best to select samples in the field and not only handle them with clean tools and hands but also to leave them unwashed (Oudemans and Boon 1991). Because plasticizers, likely the result of storage in plastic bags, are often found in archaeological residues (Oudemans and Boon 1991, p. 223), it is also best to place the samples in aluminum foil while in the field.

To date there have been a number of successful attempts at identification of contents of vessels through the analysis of fatty acids. For example, Malainey et al. (2001; 1999a, b, and c) did an extensive study of pottery lipids extracted from the Late Pre-contact Period in Western Canada. They investigated changes in diet, as represented by what was cooked in the vessels, at sites from four different environmental settings that ranged from open grassland to boreal forest. Using gas chromatography they determined the contents of the vessels based upon the relative percentages of ten fatty acids. Among their findings is that the residue from the grassland sites was dominated by large herbivore products. Evidence of herbivores in the residue decreased in the transition zones between the grassland and forest and were not found at all in the boreal forest zone. This type of information is important for reconstructing the hunter-gatherer mobility and subsistence strategy in this region.

In North American prehistory the appearance and spread of maize across the continent and the impact of domesticated plants on the communities is of considerable interest. Reber and Evershed (2004a, b; see also and Reber et al. 2004) have explored this question with the investigation of pottery residue. If corn was processed in pots then it should leave behind residue evidence. For a number of reasons, however, finding a unique biomarker of corn processing in pottery residue has been a challenge. They have found that a strong case for maize processing can be made if the residue contains a long chain alcohol (*n*-dotricontanola) along with fatty acids common to C_4 plants. One of most interesting findings is that lower status individuals at Late Emergent Mississippian sites consumed proportionately more maize than high status individuals.

10.4 Summary and Conclusion

The analysis of use-alteration traces is now becoming routine part of ceramic analysis (e.g., Garraty 2011; Hally 1983; Hardin and Mills 2000; López Varela et al. 2002 Sassaman 1993). These types of studies have shown that use-alteration traces can provide much more specific information about pottery function that include what was stored or cooked in vessels, whether it was used over a fire, the method of cooking used, and also the reuse and recycling of ceramic material.

References

Arthur, J. W. (2002). Pottery use-alteration as an indicator of socioeconomic status: An ethnoarchaeological study of the gamo of Ethiopia. *Journal of Archaeological Method & Theory, 9*(4), 331–355.

Arthur, J. W. (2003). Brewing beer: Status, wealth and ceramic use alteration among the gamo of south-western Ethiopia. *World Archaeology, 34*(3), 516–528.

Arthur, J. W. (2006). *Living with pottery: Ethnoarchaeology among the Gamo of southwest Ethiopia*. Salt Lake City: University of Utah Press.

Beck, M. E., Skibo, J. M., Hally, D. J., & Yang, P. (2002). Sample selection for ceramic use-alteration analysis: The effects of abrasion on soot. *Journal of Archaeological Science, 29*(1), 1–15.

Charters, S., Evershed, R. P., Goad, L. J., Leyden, A., Blinkhorn, P. W., & Denham, V. (1993). Quantification and distribution of lipid in archaeological ceramics: Implications for sampling potsherds for organic analysis and the classification of vessel. *Archaeometry, 35*(2), 211–223.

Condamin, J., Formmenti, F., Metais, M. O., Michel, M., & Blond, P. (1976). The application of gas chromatography to the tracing of oil in ancient amphorae. *Archaeometry, 18*(2), 195–201.

Dietler, M. (2006). Alcohol: Anthropological/archaeological perspectives. *Annual Review of Anthropology, 35*(1), 229–249.

Evershed, R. P. (1993). Biomolecular archaeology and lipids. *World Archaeology, 25*(1), 74–93.

Garraty, C. P. (2011). The origins of pottery as a practical domestic technology: Evidence from the middle Queen Creek area, Arizona. *Journal of Anthropological Archaeology, 30*, 220–234.

Hally, D. J. (1983). Use alternation of pottery vessel surfaces: An important source of evidence for the identification of vessel function. *North American Archaeologist, 4*, 3–26.

Hally, D. J. (1986). The identification of vessel function: A case study from northwest Georgia. *American Antiquity, 51*(2), 267–295.

Hardin, M. A., & Mills, B. J. (2000). The social and historical context of short-term stylistic replacement: A Zuni case study. *Journal of Archaeological Method & Theory, 7*(3), 139–163.

Heron, C., & Evershed, R. P. (1993). The analysis of organic residues and the study of pottery use. *Journal of Archaeological Method and Theory, 5*, 247–284.

Heron, C., Evershed, R. P., & Goad, L. J. (1991). Effects of migration of soil lipids on organic residues associated with buried potsherds. *Journal of Archaeological Science, 18*(6), 641–659.

Longacre, W. A. (1974). Kalinga pottery making: The evolution of a research design. In M. J. Leaf (Ed.), *Frontiers of anthropology* (pp. 51–67). New York: Van Nostrand.

Longacre, W. A. (1981). Kalinga pottery: An ethnoarchaeological study. In I. Hodder, G. Issac, & N. Hammond (Eds.), *Pattern of the past: Studies in honour of David Clarke* (pp. 49–66). London: Cambridge University Press.

Longacre, W. A. (1985). Pottery use-life among the Kalinga, Northern Luzon, the Philippines. In B. Nelson (Ed.), *Decoding prehistoric ceramics* (pp. 334–346). Carbondale: Southern Illinois University Press.

Longacre, W. A. (1991). *Ceramic ethnoarchaeology*. Tucson: University of Arizona Press.

Longacre, W. A., & Skibo, J. M. (1994). *Kalinga ethnoarchaeology: Expanding archaeological method and theory*. Washington, DC: Smithsonian Institution Press.

López Varela, S., Van Gijn, A., & Jacobs, L. (2002). De-mystifying pottery production in the Maya Lowlands: Detection of traces of use-wear on pottery sherds through microscopic analysis and experimental replication. *Journal of Archaeological Science, 29*(10), 1133–1147.

Malainey, M. E. (2007). Fatty acid analysis of archaeological residues: Procedures and possibilities. In H. Barnard & J. W. Eerkens (Eds.), *Theory and practice of archaeological residue analysis* (pp. 77–89). Oxford: British Archaeological Reports International Series 1650.

Malainey, M. E. (2011). *A consumer's guide to archaeological science*. New York: Springer.

Malainey, M. E., Przybylski, R., & Sherriff, B. L. (1999a). The effects of thermal and oxidative degradation on the fatty acid composition of food plants and animals of Western Canada: Implications for the identification of archaeological vessel residues. *Journal of Archaeological Science, 26*(1), 95–103.

Malainey, M. E., Przybylski, R., & Sherriff, B. L. (1999b). The fatty acid composition of native food plants and animals of Western Canada. *Journal of Archaeological Science, 26*(1), 83–94.

Malainey, M. E., Przybylski, R., & Sherriff, B. L. (1999c). Identifying the former contents of late precontact period pottery vessels from Western Canada using gas chromatography. *Journal of Archaeological Science, 26*(4), 425–438.

Malainey, M. E., Przybylski, R., & Sherriff, B. L. (2001). One person's food: How and why fish avoidance may affect the settlement and subsistence patterns of hunter-gatherers. *American Antiquity, 66*(1), 141–161.

McGovern, P. E. (2003). *Ancient wine: The search for the origins of viniculture.* Princeton: Princeton University Press.

McGovern, P. E., Zhang, J., Tang, J., Zhang, Z., Hall, G. R., Moreau, R. A., et al. (2004). Fermented beverages of pre- and proto-historic China. *Proceedings of the National Academy of Sciences of the United States of America, 101*(51), 17593–17598.

O'Brien, P. (1990). An experimental study of the effects of salt erosion on pottery. *Journal of Archaeological Science, 17,* 393–401.

Oudemans, T. F. M., & Boon, J. J. (1991). Molecular archaeology: Analysis of charred (food) remains from prehistoric pottery by pyrolysis-gas chromatography/mass spectrometry. *Journal of Analytical and Applied Pyrolysis, 20,* 197–227.

Pauketat, T. R., & Emerson, T. E. (1991). The ideology of authority and the power of the pot. *American Anthropologist, 93*(4), 919–941.

Reber, E. A., & Evershed, R. P. (2004a). How did Mississippians prepare maize? The application of compound specific carbon isotope analysis to absorbed pottery residues from several Mississippi valley sites. *Archaeometry, 46,* 19–33.

Reber, E. A., & Evershed, R. P. (2004b). Identification of maize in absorbed organic residues: A cautionary tale. *Journal of Archaeological Science, 31*(4), 399–410.

Reber, E. A., Dudd, S. N., van der Merwe, N. J., & Evershed, R. P. (2004). Direct detection of maize processing in archaeological pottery through compound-specific stable isotope analysis of n-dotriacontanol in absorbed organic residues. *Antiquity, 78,* 682–691.

Rye, O. S. (1981). *Pottery technology: Principles and reconstruction.* Washington, DC: Taraxacum.

Sassaman, K. E. (1993). *Early pottery in the southeast: Tradition and innovation in cooking technology.* Tuscaloosa: University of Alabama Press.

Schiffer, M. B., & Skibo, J. M. (1987). Theory and experiment in the study of technological change. *Current Anthropology, 28,* 595–622.

Schiffer, M. B., & Skibo, J. M. (1989). A provisional theory of ceramic abrasion. *American Anthropologist, 91*(1), 101–115.

Skibo, J. M. (1992). *Pottery function: A use-alteration perspective.* New York: Plenum.

Skibo, J. M. (2013). *Understanding pottery function.* New York: Springer.

Skibo, J. M., & Blinman, E. (1999). Exploring the origins of pottery on the Colorado Plateau. In J. M. Skibo & G. M. Feinman (Eds.), *Pottery and people: A dynamic interaction* (pp. 171–183). Salt Lake City: University of Utah Press.

Skibo, J. M., & Schiffer, M. B. (2008). *People and things: A behavioral approach to material culture.* New York: Springer.

Skibo, J. M., Schiffer, M. B., & Butts, T. C. (1997). Ceramic surface treatment and abrasion resistance: An experimental study. *Journal of Archaeological Science, 24*(4), 311–317.

Stark, M. T., & Skibo, J. M. (2007). A history of the Kalinga ethnoarchaeological project. In J. M. Skibo, M. W. Graves, & M. T. Stark (Eds.), *Archaeological anthropology: Perspectives on method and theory* (pp. 93–110). Tucson: University of Arizona Press.

Sullivan, A. P., Skibo, J. M., & VanBuren, M. (1991). Sherds as tools: The roles of vessel fragments in prehistoric succulent plant processing. *North American Archaeologist, 12*(3), 243–255.

Vaz Pinto, I., & Schiffer, M. B., Smith, S., & Skibo, J. M. (1987). Effects of temper on ceramic abrasion resistance: A preliminary investigation. *Archaeomaterials, 1,* 119–134.

Chapter 11
About Small Things and Bigger Pictures: An Introduction to the Morphological Identification of Micro-residues on Stone Tools

Geeske H. J. Langejans and Marlize Lombard

11.1 Introduction

On what and how were stone tools used in the past? This seems an obvious question, but often proves hard or even impossible to answer. Sometimes, we find points embedded in prey (Boëda et al. 1999; Milo 1998), or visible glue remains on tools (Deacon and Deacon 1980). Such rare finds give direct insight into prehistoric tool use and technology, but most often no obvious clues remain. The morphological identification and analysis of micro-residues is one way to investigate processed materials and aspects of tool function and technology. Depending on the research question, the method is best applied in combination with other approaches (e.g., Akerman et al. 2002; Fullagar et al. 2006; Hardy and Garufi 1998). For example, investigating early use or domestication of certain plant materials can be augmented by detailed starch grain analysis (e.g. Piperno et al. 2009), or reconstructing Stone Age hunting technologies is best combined with macro-fracture and micro-wear analyses (e.g. Lombard 2011).

As a subdivision of use-trace or functional studies, most micro-residue analysts base their interpretations on replication, experimental or ethnographic work (e.g., Lombard et al. 2004; Rots and Williamson 2004). By recording these micro-residues similarly to those on archaeological tools, modern reference collections are established and functional hypotheses can be assessed. We promote an all-round

G. H. J. Langejans (✉)
Centre for Anthropological Research, University of Johannesburg, Private Bag 524, Auckland Park, 2006, South Africa
e-mail: geeske.langejans@gmail.com

Faculty of Archaeology, Leiden University, PO box 9515, 2300 RA, Leiden, The Netherlands

M. Lombard
Department of Anthropology and Development Studies, University of Johannesburg, PO Box 524, Auckland Park, 2006, South Africa

approach where archaeological interpretation is regularly assessed or tested with replication or ethnographic work, and where combinations of use-trace techniques are applied, refined, or developed to specifically and best address the question at hand. Here we focus on the morphological identification of micro-residues, their documentation and interpretation—also highlighting some of the "bigger questions" the approach can address. Other supporting methods are discussed elsewhere in this book.

Once an analyst is familiar with the morphological characteristics of replicated comparative micro-residues, a variety of plant, animal, and mineral remains can be recognized on archaeological tools from contexts with good preservation. The discipline has a long and lively history and as early as 1849 it was recognized that the optical properties of starch grains can be used to identify them to species level (Schleiden 1849). However, this knowledge was not used in archaeology until much later (Ungent et al. 1981, 1982). In addition, in 1938 the preservation of organic micro-residues on European prehistoric artifacts was presented (Von Stokar 1938), and in 1973 the discovery of red blood cells on a 2000-year-old mummy was announced (Zimmerman 1973). During the 1970s, large-scale micro-residue analyses on stone tools were conducted (Bruier 1976; Shafer and Holloway 1979). A decade later, the method drew attention due to the interest in blood remains, and later DNA analysis (Hardy et al. 1997; Loy 1983, 1993). The feasibility of these focus areas was heavily debated (compare Eisele et al. 1995; Newman et al. 1996, for an overview see Smith 2001). The most recent work, in which morphological analysis of residues was combined with a non-destructive chemiluminescence technique, again demonstrated that, under favorable conditions, blood residues can preserve on stone tools dated to more than 60 000 years old (Lombard 2014).

Presently, as a result of long-term dedication, replication, and development of new techniques and interpretative frameworks, the approach is used to address a wide variety of research interests, for example: the identification of early crop plants and horticulture (Piperno et al. 2009; Summerhayes et al. 2010), variability in Neanderthal subsistence (Hardy and Moncel 2011; Henry et al. 2011), and the reconstruction of hunting and hafting technologies (Barton et al. 2009; Lombard 2011). There are different levels of study where the results obtained from micro-residue analysis can be applied or fed into, these include:

1. Investigating aspects of old and rare artifacts (e.g., Barton 2007; Loy 1998).
2. DNA analysis and dating (e.g., Milanesi et al. 2011; Zarrillo et al. 2008).
3. Determining the function of particular tools or tool types and assessing viability in functional typologies (e.g., Hardy et al. 2008; Langejans 2012a, b).
4. Assessing site function, mobility, and the range of activities undertaken at particular places (e.g., Fullagar and Jones 2004; Piperno et al. 2004).
5. Reconstructing and/or evaluating behavioral hypotheses, such as cognitive evolution (e.g., Lombard and Haidle 2012; Wadley et al. 2009); developing and/or assessing archaeological explanations of (cultural) change and stability, (e.g., Fullagar and Field 1997; Lombard and Phillipson 2010).

11.2 Site and Sample Selection

An important criterion for sample selection is the preservation of micro-residues on archaeological tools. We suggest that sites are assessed for suitability before large-scale micro-residue projects are initiated, as not all are appropriate for this method, and open-air sites are considered problematic. The decay of micro-remains is generally similar to that of macro-remains. Archaeological contexts with good organic preservation are, therefore, good candidates for micro-residue studies (Langejans 2010). Different materials will decay differently, for example, muscle tissue preserves well in waterlogged, acidic deposits (Borsheim et al. 2001; Painter 1991), but bone only preserves when the waterlogged environment is not acidic (Child 1995; Gernaey et al. 2001). On a very general level, muscle tissue and starch are more susceptible to decay than bone and plant tissue (Langejans 2010). Decay can be biological (caused by bacteria and fungi), chemical (such as crystal growth and leaching), and mechanical (erosion) (Kars 2003; Langejans 2010 and references therein).

Sites with good preservation are usually dry and have stable in situ deposits, such as caves or rock shelters. In general, acidic ($pH < 6.5$) and alkaline ($pH > 7.5$) conditions are both good for preservation. Desiccated, waterlogged, and oxygen deprived environments also prevent decay. Very low temperatures ($< 0\,°C$) can ensure preservation, but high ones ($> 25\,°C$) ensure preservation only when deposits are dry. The presence of heavy metals can prevent decay, but UV light will enhance decay of residues such as muscle and woody tissue. Corrosive soils generally consist of large aggregates, such as sand, and are permeable and acidic (Langejans 2010).

Tracing the life history of a sample is similarly important—not all curated tools/assemblages are suitable for micro-residue analysis (e.g. Langejans 2012a, b). The best results are achieved from samples that are specifically excavated and curated for micro-residue studies (e.g., Lombard 2007), because cleaning, handling, transportation, and storage conditions may all negatively affect the integrity of micro-residue results. Contaminants (and the absence of remains) can confuse and complicate a study (Wadley et al. 2004), but this can be overcome to an extent by applying a multi-stranded approach, which we discuss below.

Meaningful results are mostly obtained when research questions guide sample selection. For example, to understand how stone points were used over time and space, samples of comparable artifacts from various contexts are studied. If a study focuses on site function, a variety of tools from a single context is needed. We found it useful to analyze relatively large samples of morphologically comparable tools so that outcomes can be statistically assessed (Lombard 2005, 2007).

11.3 Hardware and Methods

Morphologically identified micro-residues are recorded with thorough observation notes, spatial plotting on photographs or line drawings of tools (see Fig. 11.1 for a simplified example), and through detailed photographic records (e.g., Fullagar

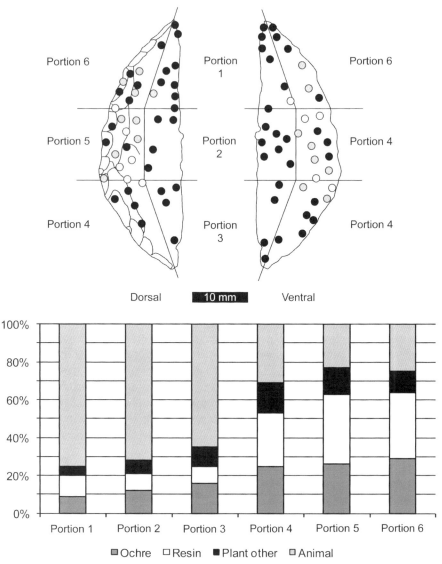

Fig. 11.1 The top is a simplified residue distribution map for a Middle Stone Age stone segment from Sibudu Cave, South Africa (adapted from Lombard 2008, Fig. 3). The segment is divided in six portions and here the general residue groups are indicated by the following symbols: *black circle* = animal type remains (muscle tissue, bone, collagen, blood, and hair); *open circle* = plant type remains (plant tissue/fibers, starch); *grey circle* = ochre and resin micro-residues. The lower part of the figure is a graph with the combined and quantified results of an assemblage of segments ($n=53$) (from Lombard 2007, 2008). Note that plant remains, ochre, and resin are most abundant on portions with steep retouch (the backed side, portions 4–6). Animal type remains are dominant on the sharp edged portions 1–3. Lombard (2007, 2008) interpreted these patterns as evidence for the hafting of the segments using mixed ochre and resin adhesives, and their use as hunting weapons

2006; Lombard 2011; Wadley and Lombard 2007). Detailed analyses are time-consuming and require expensive, specialized equipment. It is thus wise to test a sample for feasibility by scanning a few tools using low-power microscopy (magnification<100). In doing so, larger parts of the tool surface are in focus and this highlights potential micro-residue preservation and distribution patterns. Accurate identification of micro-residue types, however, often requires high magnifications (200–1000), using reflected light microscopes.

Based on the research question, some micro-residues can be isolated from the tools on which they occur and mounted on microscope slides. For the study of these samples, direct or transmitted light microscopes are used where samples and slides are illuminated from below (Artioli 2010; Murphy 2001). The generally very clear image achieved with direct light can be further improved with image enhancing techniques, such as differential interface contrast (DIC) (Murphy 2001). The identification of some residue types, such as starch grains or phytoliths is better facilitated using this technique than when observed in situ using a reflected light microscope (e.g., Fullagar 2006).

However, and again subject to the research question, the associations between micro-residues, other use-traces and their orientations and distribution patterns on the tools can be critical. First, where good preservation prevails, the amount of information is amplified; enabling detailed functional and technological interpretations (Lombard 2008; Lombard and Wadley 2007). Also, the study and interpretation of in situ micro-residues can help distinguish use-related from non use-related remains (Langejans 2011; Lombard and Wadley 2007; Wadley and Lombard 2007).

Stone tools are usually opaque and irregular, requiring the use of a reflected light microscope fitted with long working distance lenses. Here, light is projected onto the sample and reflected back into the lens. Polarizing filters help to identify micro-residues using their optically anisotropic (directional property of light) characteristics. The result of cross-polarization (where the two polarizing filters are aligned) is that micro-residues with birefringent characteristics become brighter compared to other materials (Murphy 2001; Rost and Oldfield 2000). In polarized light (using only the east–west filter), some organic remains with crystalline structures are birefringent (refracted light gives a "rainbow shimmer") (Murphy 2001). Different materials respond differently to polarized and cross-polarized light and the intensity or brightness of materials can be used to identify different micro-residue types.

Microscopes with a fluorescent option may also add to the quality of information. Unlike conventional microscopy and other contrast enhancing technologies, the sample does not reflect light, but reemits light (Artioli 2010; Lakowicz 2006). Depending on their chemical composition, some remains have a characteristic autofluorescence, for example, when using the UV filter, many organic materials emit a weak yellow fluorescent light, and many recent contaminant fibers are strongly fluorescent (blue).

11.4 Guidelines for the Morphological Identification of Micro-Residues on Tools

The morphological identification of micro-residues is based on their visual characteristics including shape, color, size, texture, and their original nature; for example, were they, during deposition, hard or soft, liquid, dry, or viscous? Modern comparative collections are used to establish these characteristics and interpret aspects of tool function and technology (Lombard 2007; Lombard and Wadley 2007, 2009). Reference samples can be replicated, experimental, or ethnographic; as long as the mode of handling, use, and processed materials are known (Fullagar 2006; Rots and Williamson 2004). Below we provide an overview of the morphological characteristics of different micro-residue types. This is a general list, partly based on our own work so far, and we recommend that analysts create their own experimental reference collections, aimed at resolving specific research questions. For example, previously, micro-residues were interpreted as plant types if they displayed birefringence and if starch grains were present. However, this did not always make sense when compared to tool morphology, other related use-traces or the associated faunal assemblages. Only after extensive experimentation, blind testing, and reading on animal histology, did ML establish that some animal micro-residues are also birefringent (Lombard and Wadley 2007, compare their Fig. 1; 2009; Wadley and Lombard 2007).

11.4.1 Plant Micro-Residues

11.4.1.1 Plant Tissue and Fibers

Plant cells can be recognized by their double cell walls, large vacuoles, and chloroplast organelles (Devlin and Witham 1983; Mauseth 1988). Plant cell walls are composed of cellulose fibers that are embedded in hemicelluloses and lignin, and other polysaccharides and proteins (Campbell 1990), making them rather robust and very suitable for preservation. The rigid organization of plant tissue gives plant residues a characteristic stiff and angular appearance (Lombard and Wadley 2007, Fig. 3a). Although, it is seldom possible to differentiate between specific cell types or tissues on archaeological tools, some distinctions can be made. For example, elongated vessels are different from brick-like epidermal tissue (Wadley et al. 2004, Fig. 3a, 3c), and the latter can have a waxy top layer and hairs (Devlin and Witham 1983; Mauseth 1988).

Plant tissue is often birefringent and bright in cross-polarized light (Langejans 2012a, b, Fig. S11), and can appear translucent under high-power magnification (Lombard 2008, also see Fullagar 2006). Plant or cellulose fibers usually consist of long, slender cells that commonly occur in ribbon-like strands or fibrous bundles. The cellulose strands often appear as broken twisted fibers, with shattered ends. Such breaks can seem straight and abrupt (Lombard 2008). Fibers are likely to be sclerenchyma tissue (a supporting tissue), which may develop in any or all parts of the primary and secondary plant bodies (Raven et al. 1992). Other plant micro-residues, such as starch grains and resin, often accompany plant tissues and fibers (Fullagar 2006; Lombard 2008).

Ancient micro-residues tend to lose color and brightness, sometimes taking on colors from the sediment, and they generally appear more faded than fresh micro-residues. When preserved, cellular structures are often warped and fragmented. Post-depositional and post-excavational plant remains are mostly exceptionally birefringent with bright colors and intact cellular structures. In fresh green plant tissue, chlorophyll can be observed, which does generally not preserve over time (Langejans 2012a, b).

11.4.2 Degraded Plant Tissue and Charcoal

When microbes attack a plant cell they focus on the nutrients inside the cell, leaving the tough cellulose in the cell walls; thus, archaeological plant tissue generally only consists of a silica skeleton, compared to fresh tissue. Degraded plant tissue can be white or light yellow, but frequently appears dark brown. Degraded wood is often fragmented (Langejans 2012a, b).

Charcoal or burnt plant tissue varies in color between brown and black, depending on the temperature and burning process. The plant cells carbonize during burning and this leaves a carbon skeleton behind. Degraded plant tissue and charcoal may appear similar, and burnt plant tissue can have a fatty gloss. Both degraded and burnt plant tissue can be birefringent, but this is not always the case (Langejans 2012a, b).

11.4.3 Starch Grains

Starch grains are specialized cells in which plants store energy in the form of sugars. Large grains are most abundant in storage organs, such as roots, tubers, and seeds, but smaller ones can also be found in smaller quantities in other plant parts (Haslam 2004). As a grain grows, two types of sugars are alternately deposited (Gott et al. 2006; Lillford and Morrison 1997) and these are visible as concentric (growth) rings or lamella (Donald et al. 2001). Inside the grains, the sugars form a crystalline structure that, under cross-polarized light, creates the distinctive polarization cross (Gidley 2001): Two discrete dark bands that cross more or less in the middle of the granule (Torrence 2006).

Starch grains can vary in size from 1 to 175 µm; they can be circular, elliptical, or triangular. The shapes, sizes, lamella, position and nature of the hilum or grain core, and polarization crosses can be specific for different plant species (Gott et al. 2006; Langejans 2006, compare Figs. 3.1–3.10; Torrence 2006). Identification of starch grains to species level requires extraction of the residue and direct light microscopy. Starch grains are birefringent and translucent, but when damaged, they may lose their distinctive shape and become opaque (Barton and Matthews 2006; Gott et al. 2006). On staining extracted samples with Congo red dye or iodine, or on applying an iodine–potassium–iodine test, (damaged) starch grains and cellulose change color. Other remains, such as proteins, are unaffected by this staining (Lamb and Loy 2005; Torrence 2006).

Small (<5 μm) starch grains are ubiquitous in most sediments, and other remains, such as fungal spores, spherulites, and diatoms have similar, though weaker, optical properties and might be mistaken for starch (Haslam 2006; Loy 2006). Therefore, without the association of other plant micro-residues and repeated spatial clustering on a representative sample of tools, starch cannot be considered use-related (Lombard 2008).

11.4.4 Resin

Resin is a general term for plant secretions that includes pitch, waxy oils, gums and latex, and is sometimes confused with petroleum-based materials, such as bitumen. Pristine resins are not processed, whereas tar and pitch are the by-products of the distillation of resinous wood (Connan and Nissenbaum 2003; Font et al. 2007). Pitch, tar, and resin mixes are difficult to distinguish visually and only spectrographic analysis can reveal the nature of an archaeological substance (Font et al. 2007); therefore, we use the word resin here for a suite of different materials.

Resin or gum films can have a glassy transparent appearance and their color can range from brown to yellow (Lombard and Wadley 2007, Fig. 2). The deposit indicates the fluid or viscous nature of the residue and can appear like small smooth droplets or have a cracked appearance (Langejans 2012a, b, Fig. S3). The cracks are usually straight-edged and clear (Lombard 2008). Resin might also appear birefringent, and starch grains, woody residue, plant fibers, epidermal cells, and other plant cells are often recorded within a resinous deposit (Fullagar 2006; Lombard and Wadley 2007). Tar and pitch are darker than pristine resins; ranging from brown to black. Degraded resinous residues can have a granular appearance with more visible starch grains around the edges of deposits (Lombard 2008, Fig. 8). Resin mixes generally lose their glassy and transparent characteristics. They appear more organic with globular shapes; they become more gummy and sticky, and less brittle. Breaks appear more rounded and fluid than pristine and fresh resins.

Plant exudates are much less viscous than resins, and quickly dry on exposure, often only leaving a stain (Langejans 2012a, b, Fig. S7). Depending on the thickness of the exudate, the stain can be a simple dark spot or a thin deposit. Often the deposit resembles a mud cracked surface with straight, but smooth edges. Sometimes starch grains are present inside the deposit. Thicker plant exudate deposits are birefringent and semi-translucent (Langejans 2012a, b).

11.4.5 Animal Micro-Residues

Animal cells are made from proteins, are less rigid than plant cells, and only contain small vacuoles that are not clearly visible when using reflected light microscopy. Animal residues often become dull or opaque when the light polarizer is rotated, and nuclei are sometimes visible although obvious cell structure is seldom observed (Lombard 2008). Of the four types of animal tissue, supporting/connective and muscle tissue are most common on archaeological tools.

11.4.6 Supporting and Connective Tissues

Supporting or connective tissues include bone, sinew, and cartilage and they bind and support other tissues. They all consist of an extracellular matrix with scattered cells and collagen fibers. Collagen refers to a group of proteins that is abundant in these supporting tissues, but is also present in, for example, epithelial and muscle tissue. The parallel collagen fibrils are arranged into strong bundles of 2–10 mm in diameter (Young and Heath 2002). In loose connective tissue, such as the tissue layers that connect skin to muscle tissue, the limited collagen fibers have a loose weave and the (fat) cells have no rigid organization. Fibrous connective tissue, such as tendons, on the other hand, is dense because it contains many collagen fibers. Bone is a mineralized supporting tissue, and cartilage is a specialized type of fibrous connective tissue, where collagen fibers are imbedded in a rubbery chondrin matrix (Campbell 1990; Moran and Rowley 2005).

Because collagen consists of parallel bundles, divided in to fibrils, the fibers often have the appearance of rope and the ends may appear unraveled (Lombard 2011, Fig. 6d; Wadley and Lombard 2007, Fig. 3a). The orientation of the elongated tropocollagen molecules in collagen fibers makes them birefringent, but under polarized light they often appear opaque. Some collagen bundles may display structured layers (Junqueira et al. 1998). Certain collagen types do not form fibrils but rather have a mesh-like structure (Young and Heath 2002), sometimes described as sheet collagen (see Lombard 2005, 2008). Due to its positioning between other tissues and connecting function, loose connective tissue can have a mixed appearance of fat, bone, and muscle tissue.

Cartilage is organic, or flowing and fibrous, but less than loose connective tissue; cartilage can be birefringent. Bone and fatty bone often appear as amorphous, opaque deposits on archaeological tools (Lombard 2008, Figs. 13 and 14). They have a greasy appearance with no characterizing structure, and they are generally not birefringent. Bone flakes can be angular and rigid (Langejans 2012a, b, Fig. S10) and can sometimes have small perforations under magnifications of ≥ 200. Bone deposits are usually white to light yellow; when extremely fatty, they can appear bluish in cross-polarized light. Degraded non-fatty bone can be translucent (Lombard 2008). Burnt bone is similar to unburnt bone, but often varies in color from deep yellow to orange and can appear more granular (Langejans 2012a, b, Fig. S1). In a recent study, using non-destructive Fourier transform infrared (FTIR) spectroscopy, we were able to verify the micro-morphological identification of bone (Prinsloo et al. 2013).

11.4.7 Blood

Mammalian red blood cells or erythrocytes lack nuclei and are thus recognized by their biconcave disc shape with an average diameter of 7.2 µm (Young and Heath 2002). On drying, they may be smaller (3–5 µm) and the edges of the cells may become crenated or ruffled (Lombard 2008, 2014). Because red blood cells are so small, they are usually only visible at $\geq 500 \times$. Amphibian, avian, and reptile blood cells have nuclei and these cells have elongated shapes; the cell sizes vary between orders and species (Gulliver 1875). Chemstrip or Hemastix© tests can be used to test an extracted micro-residue for blood (e.g., Loy 1983; Newman et al. 1997), but these and similar tests are known to give false positives and their reliability is debated (for an overview see Smith and Wilson 2001). An enhanced, non-destructive luminol product that can be used directly on the surfaces of stone tools to reveal blood distribution patterns, however, withstood the rigour of blind testing and it was demonstrated that false positives could be distinguished from true blood residues (Gundy et al. 2008; Lombard 2014).

Blood residues on archaeological tools are often associated with other animal residues, and indicated by the characteristic mud-cracking of thick films, the color and/or the presence of red blood cells (Wadley et al. 2004, Figs. 3c, d, Lombard 2014). Blood films are relatively reflective and may range in color from yellow, for thin films to red or black, for thicker deposits. (Lombard 2008, also see Lombard 2011).

11.4.8 Muscle Tissue

Muscle tissue is composed of long cells, which are capable of contraction. In skeletal tissue or striated muscle tissue, the muscle cells or fibers are subdivided into many longitudinally oriented units, myofibrils, which are again divided into sarcomeres. This alignment forms dark and light bands, and gives the tissue a striped appearance (Wadley et al. 2004, Fig. 3d). Visceral or smooth muscle tissue does not have striations; visceral cells are spindle shaped and can be much smaller than other muscle cells. In longitudinal section, striated tissue appears as very elongated and parallel fibers, and in cross-section the cells are circular (Campbell 1990; Moran and Rowley 2005).

The darker bands in the tissue are anisotropic and therefore birefringent under cross-polarized light (Junqueira et al. 1998; Lombard 2008). Sometimes, animal tissue on replicated stone tools used for hunting or butchering is soft, organic and flowing with associated gelatinous strands; very unlike any plant tissue (Lombard and Wadley 2007, Fig. 4a, b; Wadley et al. 2004, Fig. 3a). Muscle tissue varies in color from pale to yellow, orange and brown (Lombard 2008). Muscle tissue is generally not as translucent as plant tissue. The ends of fibers can appear like unraveled ropes or twisted. When muscle tissue dries out, it shrinks, discolors, and can become stiff causing it to crack, sometimes resembling woody fibers, but it is usually much darker brown or orange. When rehydrated it can regain its flowing nature, although the change in color is permanent (Zimmerman 2001).

11.4.9 Fat and Marrow

Fat (adipose tissue) and marrow cells have distinctive globular or ovoid shapes (Lombard and Wadley 2007, Figs. 4c, d). When crushed or smeared, the tissue becomes amorphous but the smear itself can be detected (Lombard 2008). Unilocular (common or yellow) adipose tissue is composed of cells that contain one large central droplet of yellow fat in their cytoplasm. Multilocular (or brown) adipose tissue is limited in mammalian adults and composed of cells that contain numerous lipid droplets and abundant brown mitochondria (Junqueira et al. 1998). In some marrow deposits, bright red erythrocytes occur, which are responsible for platelet formation (Young and Heath 2002). In archaeological samples these brown and red spots can sometimes be detected within a whitish deposit and indicate the faunal origin of the residue. Fat and marrow can appear birefringent on the surface, but often become opaque when the polarizer is rotated. These residues are sometimes bluish under cross-polarized light (Lombard 2008; Wadley and Lombard 2007, Fig. 3e). This blue haze is caused by the secondary mineral vivianite that is present in fat (Fullagar 2006). FTIR spectroscopy conducted on replicated artefacts demonstrated that the morphological identification of microscopic fat residues using microscopy can be assessed without destruction of the sample or interfering with the distribution of micro-residues on an artefact (Prinsloo et al. 2013).

11.4.10 Hair

Animal hairs are formed in the deeper layers of the skin and they are made from long keratin proteins. Hairs are cylindrical and consist of three layers. The outer layer is the cuticula and it displays cuticular scales. Moving inwards is the cortex that contains amorphous dry cells and pigment granules; these are not clearly visible under the microscope. The centre of the hair is the medulla and consists of tightly packed dry cells. The medulla is clearly visible under the microscope as a dark core; the cells are so packed that the cell structure is not visible (Bonnichsen et al. 2001; Teerink 1991). The scales and medulla of different mammal species have characteristic patterns and hairs can be used to identity species (e.g., Teerink 1991, and Figs 56–284 therein).

11.4.11 Fish Micro-residues

The tissue of fish has similar properties as that of mammals. Some tissue has similar banded skeletal muscle tissue and fish muscle tissue can also be birefringent. In general it appears oilier than mammalian tissue, but this can differ between species. The red blood cells of fish are about the same size as those of mammals (6–8 μm), but they are elliptical instead of round. More characteristic, however, are fish scales. The skin of most bony and cartilaginous fish is covered with scaly plates. Scales are produced by the dermis and mainly consist of collagen. The degree of mineralization varies between species, as does the shape; for example, they can be round, diamond shaped, or teethed. Most have clear concentric growth lines (Helfman et al. 2009, and Fig. 3.18 therein). The growth rings and cells within can be birefringent and in polarized light the surface of the scales is translucent, but in cross-polarized light it is opaque. The size and shape of scales is diagnostic for species; however, one species can have different types of scales and there can be differences between sexes (Helfman et al. 2009).

11.4.12 Ochre

Ochre is a red iron oxide (Fe_2O_3) or yellow hydroxide (FeOOH). Heating dehydrates the hydroxide, turning it into red ochre (Wadley 2009). These deposits are granular. Polarized light enhances the color and in cross-polarized light ochre is dull. Ochre is sometimes mixed with other materials like fat or resin, and as it is absorbed it may lose its granular properties. Fat and ochre mixes generally appear as (bright) red fat deposits, but without the blue haze in cross-polarized light (Langejans 2012a, b, Figs. S2, 3; Lombard 2006a, Figs. 1, 2).

11.4.13 Non-use Related Remains

Archaeological soil can be a source of micro-residues that are not related to use. Site sediments can contain organic remains such as ash, bone, pollen, insect remains, plastic bits, and charcoal amongst sand, clay and other particles. To ensure that "dirt" is not confused with use-related micro-residues, it is good practice to analyze soil samples from the contexts associated with the artifact samples (Fullagar 2006; Fullagar et al. 1996). One way to do this is to take double-sided tape and attach it to a microscope slide; the other sticky side is dipped in the soil sample until the sediment covers the tape. The "soil" particles can then be analyzed and recorded under the same lighting and magnification conditions as used during micro-residue analysis (c.f. Wadley and Lombard 2007). Once excavated, non use-related micro-residues can also contaminate a sample by air or through handling. Dust consists of starch, pollen, fibers, hairs and so on; a way to test what dust particles can be expected is by setting out dust catchers (c.f. Wadley and Lombard 2007, also see their Fig. 1). Remains from handling are generally fat or oily deposits (Wadley et al. 2004, Fig. 1) and skin flakes; the latter can resemble bone flakes. Generally, non use-related remains can be recognized by their random distribution on a tool's surface. If they are recent, they often are "fresh" looking and can have bright colors.

11.5 Analysis of the Results: A Multi-stranded Approach

We follow a multi-stranded approach when analyzing and interpreting micro-residues recorded on archaeological stone tools (for a discussion of the method see Langejans 2011; Lombard and Wadley 2007; Wadley and Lombard 2007, and for archaeological applications see Langejans 2012a, b; Lombard 2008, 2011; Wadley and Langejans 2014). This approach combines different contextual factors to inform on the origin of the observed remains. First, micro-residues are identified, recorded and carefully plotted in relation to tool morphology (as in the distribution map in Fig. 11.1). The different types are then quantified and appraised according to their distribution patterns, their association with other micro-residue types, and mechanical use-traces (Fig. 11.1). Some non use-related micro-residues may be recognized as remains from the site sediment and dust. Although, they can appear similar to use-related residues, they tend to have random and less concentrated distribution patterns. Additionally, they lack repeated association with other micro-residue types or use-wear. Use-related micro-residues generally appear in more abundant concentrations than incidental remains, usually reoccurring in specific combinations (e.g., the resin, ochre, and plant remains in Fig. 11.1), and they often have meaningful repeated associations with micro-wear or macro-fracture traces. In addition, on morphologically similar artifacts, the use-related micro-residues commonly display recurring distribution patterns (see the graph in Fig. 11.1). This patterning indicates which portions were used or hafted, and the micro-residue types reveal processed or contact materials (Lombard 2011; Lombard and Wadley 2007; Wadley and Lombard 2007).

Quantification of micro-residue observations remains a challenge, but progress is being made. For example, in Fig. 11.1, the surfaces of similar morphology tools were divided into portions and the micro-residues types per portion were counted; in doing so micro-residue occurrences could be quantified and interpreted (c.f. Lombard 2008). The number and position of the portions used depend on the tool type and size, and the research question. The tool portions are similar throughout the sample to ensure comparability of the results across the assemblage (Langejans 2011; Lombard 2004, 2005). Different research questions may, however, require different quantification systems.

After quantification, the number and types of micro-residues per portion and across samples can be compared. This may lead to the identification of general patterns; for example, some remains will always be found together, in particular suites, or on similar portions and others not (e.g., in Fig. 11.1, the ochre and animal type remains are not often found together) (e.g. Lombard 2008). If the tool samples are large enough and if preservation is good (ensuring a generous dataset), statistical tests such as T-tests and Chi-square tests, can be used to assess the probability of use-related or coincidental distribution patterns (e.g., Langejans 2011; Lombard 2004, 2005, 2007). When tool and recorded micro-residue samples are too small, low-level statistics, such as percentages, can be used (c.f. Langejans 2012a, b; Lombard 2011).

11.6 Addressing the Bigger Questions

Getting bogged down with the microscopic details as described above is tedious, and may appear inconsequential. However, depending on scope and approach, results can contribute meaningfully to the larger arena of anthropological discourse, and even stimulate paradigm shifts. To illustrate such potential, we use a very brief and simplified account of the global debate around the early use of stone-tipped, hand-delivered spears and mechanically-projected arrows (e.g., Barton et al. 2009; Lombard 2011; Sisk and Shea 2011; Villa and Soriano 2010). Initially, it was assumed that Neanderthals were "primitive scavengers" (e.g., Binford 1985; Stiner 1994), yet, Shea (1989, 1993) suggested that fracture patterns on Levantine Middle Paleolithic stone tools indicated their use as spear tips. Others were unable to reproduce similar results and questioned this outcome; they instead proposed that the tools were convergent scrapers or had multiple functions (e.g., Holdaway 1989; Plisson and Beyries 1998; Roler and Clark 1997). Subsequently, however, Shea's notion of Neanderthals as effective, well-equipped hunters was reinforced with micro-residue analysis. A study conducted on stone points associated with the Neanderthals in the Crimea, demonstrated that some were hafted and probably used to tip hunting weapons (Hardy 1999; Hardy et al. 2001).

More recent use-trace work on South African tools showed that since about 100,000 years ago modern humans used stone-tipped hunting weapons (Lombard 2011; Villa and Soriano 2010). The micro-residue suites on the hafted tools from about 70,000 years ago include resin, plant tissue, fibers, ochre, and animal remains such as fat and muscle tissue (Lombard 2006a, b, 2008, also see our Fig. 11.1). Use and hafting interpretations, based on the multi-stranded approach presented above, have now culminated in what can be called "the spear vs bow-and-arrow debate" (e.g., Lombard and Parson 2011; Sisk and Shea 2009; Villa and Soriano 2010; Wadley and Mohapi 2008); with direct evidence now established for the use of stone-tipped arrows at 64,000 years ago in South Africa (Backwell et al. 2008; Lombard 2011; Lombard and Phillipson 2010). Early use of bow-and-arrow technology may also inform on levels of cognitive complexity (Lombard and Haidle 2012). Thus, as with the "hunting vs scavenging debate", knowing how weapons were delivered can help to understand early human behavior and cognition (c.f. Wadley 2010; Wadley et al. 2009).

11.7 Concluding Thoughts: From an Observation to a Change in Paradigm

For many years, micro-residue analysis was a contested method (Grace 1996; Smith and Wilson 2001, and see the debate in Fullagar et al. 1996), but with rigorous testing much criticism has and will be overcome. Blind tests demonstrated the merit of the morphological approach to identify micro-residue types (e.g., Lombard and Wadley 2007; Wadley and Lombard 2007; Monnier et al. 2012; Wadley et al. 2004). The preservation of micro-residues has been addressed (e.g., Barton 2009; Haslam 2004; Langejans 2010; Lu 2006), and it is generally accepted that although not all sites are suitable, in many contexts micro-residues are preserved.

Contaminants, such as spores can be distinguished from use-related remains based on their optical properties (Haslam 2006; Loy 2006); contaminants have random distribution patterns and less concentrated deposits and frequencies (Barton et al. 1998; Williamson 2006). By scrutinizing soil and dust samples, and by working in a controlled and clean lab environment (Crowther et al. 2014; Loy and Barton 2006; Wadley and Lombard 2007), and by applying the multi-stranded approach (Hardy and Garufi 1998; Langejans 2011; Wadley and Lombard 2007), use-related remains can be distinguished from non use-related micro-residues. Moreover, micro-residues have been directly dated, proving their age (Zarrillo et al. 2008). The cumulative efforts of many researchers indicate that micro-residue analyses, conducted on appropriate samples of archaeological stone tools, are successful because use-related remains are notably (and sometimes statistically significantly) different in terms of their distribution patterns, numbers, contexts, and optical properties, compared to non use-related remains.

Micro-residue analysis is a growing discipline. Here we only covered morphological identification of micro-residues using reflected light microscopy as it is the method we have been using and developing for our particular research aims over the past decade. Yet, new techniques, technologies and quantification methods will no doubt refine and improve future work. Most importantly, when approaches are developed and tested with pertinent research questions in mind, the results can provide detailed insight into past human behavior and ways of thinking, on a scale and quality previously inconceivable.

Acknowledgements We thank the editors João Marreiros, Juan F. Gibaja, and Nuno Bicho for inviting us to write a chapter for this volume, and colleagues and friends who took the time to comment on, and review the draft manuscript. We also acknowledge Lyn Wadley for her continued support to the micro-residue work in South Africa, and Thea de Wet for housing the micro-TRACKS laboratory in the Centre for Language and Culture at the University of Johannesburg. GL's research is sponsored by Netherlands Organisation for Scientific Research with a Veni grant (the Netherlands). The research of ML is funded by the African Origins Platform of the National Research Foundation of South Africa. Opinions and mistakes, however, remain our own.

References

Akerman, K., Fullagar, R., & Van Gijn, A. (2002). Weapons and Wunan: Production, function and exchange of Kimberley points. *Australian Aboriginal Studies, 22,* 13–42.

Artioli, G. (2010). *Scientific methods and cultural heritage: An introduction to the application of materials science to archaeometry and conservational science.* Oxford: Oxford University Press.

Backwell, L., d'Errico, F., & Wadley, L. (2008). Middle Stone Age bone tools from the Howiesons Poort layers, Sibudu Cave, South Africa. *Journal of Archaeological Science, 35,* 1566–1580.

Barton, H. (2007). Starch residues on museum artefacts: Implications for determining tool use. *Journal of Archaeological Science, 34,* 1752–1762.

Barton, H. (2009). Starch granule taphonomy: The results of a two year field experiment. In M. Haslam, G. Robertson, A. Crowther, S. Nugent, & L. Kirkwood (Eds.), *Archaeological science under a microscope: Studies in residue and ancient DNA analysis in honour of Thomas H. Loy* (pp. 129–140). Canberra: ANU E press.

Barton, H., & Matthews, P. J. (2006). Taphonomy. In R. Torrence & H. Barton (Eds.), *Ancient starch research* (pp. 75–94). Walnut Creek: Left Coast.

Barton, H., Torrence, R., & Fullagar, R. (1998). Clues to stone tool function re-examined: Comparing starch grain frequencies on used and unused obsidian artefacts. *Journal of Archaeological Science, 25,* 1231–1238.

Barton, H., Piper, P. J., Rabett, R., & Reeds, I. (2009). Composite hunting technologies from the terminal Pleistocene and early Holocene, Niah Cave, Borneo. *Journal of Archaeological Science, 36,* 1708–1714.

Binford, L. R. (1985). Human ancestors: Changing views of their behavior. *Journal of Anthropological Archaeology, 4,* 292–327.

Boëda, E., Geneste, J. M., Griggo, C., Mercier, N., Muhesen, S., Reyss, J. L., Taha, A., & Valladas, H. (1999). A Levallois point embedded in the vertebra of a wild ass (*Equus africanus*): Hafting, projectiles and Mousterian hunting. *Antiquity, 73,* 394–402.

Bonnichsen, R., Hodges, L., Ream, W., Field, K. G., Kirner, D. L., Selsor, K., & Taylor, R. E. (2001). Methods for the study of ancient hair: Radiocarbon dates and gene sequences from individual hairs. *Journal of Archaeological Science, 28,* 775–785.

Borsheim, K. Y., Christensen, B. E., & Painter, T. J. (2001). Preservation of fish by embedment in *Sphagnum* moss, peat or holocellulose: Experimental proof of the oxopolysaccharidic nature of the preservative substance and of its antimicrobial and tanning action. *Innovative Food Science & Emerging Technologies, 2,* 63–74.

Bruier, F. L. (1976). New clues to stone tool function: Plant and animal residues. *American Antiquity, 41,* 478–484.

Campbell, N. A. (1990). *Biology* (2nd ed.). Redwood City: Benjamin/Cummings.

Child, A. M. (1995). Towards an understanding of the microbial decomposition of archaeological bone in the burial environment. *Journal of Archaeological Science, 22,* 165–174.

Connan, J., & Nissenbaum, A. (2003). Conifer tar on the keel and hull planking of the Ma'agan Mikhael Ship (Israel, 5th century BC): Identification and comparison with natural products and artefacts employed in boat construction. *Journal of Archaeological Science, 30,* 709–719.

Crowther, A., Haslam, M., Oakden, N., Walde, D., & Mercader, J. (2014). Documenting contamination in ancient starch laboratories. *Journal of Archaeological Science, 49,* 90–104.

Deacon, H. J., & Deacon, J. (1980). The hafting, function and distribution of small convex scrapers with an example from Boomplaas Cave. *The South African Archaeological Bulletin, 35,* 31–37.

Devlin, R. M., & Witham, F. H. (1983). *Plant physiology* (4th ed.). Belmont: Wadsworth.

Donald, A. M., Perry, P. A., & Waigh, T. A. (2001). The impact of internal granule structure on processing and properties. In T. L. Barsby, A. M. Donald, & P. J. Frazier (Eds.), *Starch: Advances in structure and function* (pp. 45–52). Cambridge: Royal Society of Chemistry.

Eisele, J. A., Fowler, D. D., Haynes, G., & Lewis, R. A. (1995). Survival and detection of blood residues on stone tools. *Antiquity, 69,* 36–46.

Font, J., Salvado, N., Buti, S., & Enrich, J. (2007). Fourier transform infrared spectroscopy as a suitable technique in the study of the materials used in waterproofing of archaeological amphorae. *Analytica Chimica Acta, 598,* 119–127.
Fullagar, R. (2006). Residues and usewear. In J. Balme & A. Paterson (Eds.), *Archaeology in practice: A student guide to archaeological analysis* (pp. 207–233). Oxford: Blackwell.
Fullagar, R., & Field, J. (1997). Pleistocene seed grinding implements from the Australian arid zone. *Antiquity, 71,* 300–307.
Fullagar, R., & Jones, R. (2004). Usewear and residue analysis of stone artefacts from the Enclosed Chamber, Rocky Cape, Tasmania. *Archaeology in Oceania, 39,* 79–93.
Fullagar, R., Furby, J., & Hardy, B. L. (1996). Residues on stone artefacts: State of a scientific art. *Antiquity, 70,* 740–745.
Fullagar, R., Field, J., Denham, T., & Lentfer, C. (2006). Early and mid Holocene tool-use and processing of taro (*Colocasia esculenta*), yam (*Dioscorea sp.*) and other plants at Kuk Swamp in the highlands of Papua New Guinea. *Journal of Archaeological Science, 33,* 595–614.
Gernaey, A. M., Waite, E. R., Collins, M. J., Craig, O. E., & Sokol, R. J. (2001). Survival and interpretation of archaeological proteins. In D. R. Brothwell & A. M. Pollard (Eds.), *Handbook of archaeological sciences* (pp. 323–329). Chichester: Wiley.
Gidley, M. J. (2001). Starch structure/function relationships: Achievements and challenges. In T. L. Barsby, A. M. Donald, & P. J. Frazier (Eds.), *Starch: Advances in structure and function* (pp. 1–7). Cambridge: Royal Society of Chemistry.
Gott, B., Barton, H., Samuel, D., & Torrence, R. (2006). Biology of starch. In R. Torrence & H. Barton (Eds.), *Ancient starch research* (pp. 35–45). Walnut Creek: Left Coast.
Grace, R. (1996). Use-wear analysis: The state of the art. *Archaeometry, 38,* 209–229.
Gulliver, G. (1875). On the size and shape of red corpuscles of the blood of vertebrates, with drawings of them to a uniform scale, and extended and revised tables of measurements. *Proceedings of the Zoological Society of London, 1875,* 474–495.
Gundy, B. J., Mohney, K. W., Espenshade, C. T., Vish, A. T., & Sams, M. G. (2008). A few hours in the Piedmont: archaeological investigations of the site 7NC-B-54 (Ronald McDonald House). Unpublished report for the State of Delaware Department of Transportation, submitted by Skelly and Loy, Inc. Engineers-Consultants.
Hardy, B. L. (1999). Microscopic residue analsys of stone tools from the Middle Paleolithic site of Starosele. In K. Monigal & V. Chabai (Eds.), *The Middle Paleolithic of the Western Crimea* (Vol. 2, pp. 197–209). Liegè: Liegè University Press.
Hardy, B. L., & Garufi, G. T. (1998). Identification of woodworking on stone tools through residue and use-wear analyses: Experimental results. *Journal of Archaeological Science, 25,* 177–184.
Hardy, B. L., & Moncel, M.-H. (2011). Neanderthal use of fish, mammals, birds, starchy plants and wood 125–250,000 years ago. *PLoS ONE, 6,* e23768.
Hardy, B. L., Raff, R. A., & Raman, V. (1997). Recovery of mammalian DNA from Middle Paleolithic stone tools. *Journal of Archaeological Science, 24,* 601–611.
Hardy, B. L., Kay, M., Marks, A. E., & Monigal, K. (2001). Stone tool function at the Paleolithic sites of Starosele en Buran Kaya III, Crimea: Behavioral implications. *Proceedings of the National Academy of Sciences, 98,* 10972–10977.
Hardy, B. L., Bolus, M., & Conard, N. J. (2008). Hammer or crescent wrench? Stone-tool form and function in the Aurignacian of southwest Germany. *Journal of Human Evolution, 54,* 648–662.
Haslam, M. (2004). The decomposition of starch grains in soils: Implications for archaeological residue analyses. *Journal of Archaeological Science, 31,* 1715–1734.
Haslam, M. (2006). Potential misidentification of in situ archaeological tool-residues: Starch and conidia. *Journal of Archaeological Science, 33,* 114–121.
Helfman, G. S., Collette, B. B., Facey, D. E., & Bowen, B. W. (2009). *The diversity of fishes: Biology, Evolution, and Ecology* (2nd ed.). Chichester: Wiley-Backwell.
Henry, A. G., Brooks, A. S., & Piperno, D. R. (2011). Microfossils in calculus demonstrate consumption of plants and cooked foods in Neanderthal diets (Shanidar III, Iraq; Spy I and II, Belgium). *Proceedings of the National Academy of Sciences, 108,* 486–491.

Holdaway, S. (1989). Were there hafted projectile points in the Mousterian? *Journal of Field Archeology, 16,* 79–85.

Junqueira, L. C., Carniero, J., Kelly, R. O. (1998). *Basic histology* (9th ed.). New York: Lange Medical Books.

Kars, H. (2003). Het bodemarchief is kwetsbaar. In H. Kars & A. Smit (Eds.), *Handleiding fysiek behoud archeologisch erfgoed* (pp. 1–6). Amsterdam: Vrije Universiteit.

Lakowicz, J. R. (2006). *Principles of fluorescence spectroscopy* (3rd ed.). New York: Springer.

Lamb, J., & Loy, T. (2005). Seeing red: The use of Congo Red dye to identify cooked and damaged starch grains in the archaeological residues. *Journals of Archaeological Science, 32,* 1433–1440.

Langejans, G. H. J. (2006). Starch grain analysis on Late Iron Age grindstones from South Africa. *Southern African Humanities, 18,* 71–91.

Langejans, G. H. J. (2010). Remains of the day-preservation of organic micro-residues on stone tools. *Journal of Archaeological Science, 37,* 971–985.

Langejans, G. H. J. (2011). Discerning use-related micro-residues on tools. Testing the multi-stranded approach for archaeological studies. *Journal of Archaeological Science, 38,* 985–1000.

Langejans, G. H. J. (2012a). Middle Stone Age *pièces esquillées* from Sibidu Cave, South Africa: An initial micro-residue study. *Journal of Archaeological Science, 39,* 1694–1704.

Langejans, G. H. J. (2012b). Micro-residue analysis on Early Stone Age tools from Sterkfontein South Africa: A Methodological enquiry. *South African Archaeological Bulletin, 67,* 120–144.

Lillford, P. J., & Morrison, A. (1997). Structure/function relationship of starches in food. In P. J. Frazier, P. Richmond, & A. M. Donald (Eds.), *Starch: Structure and functionality* (pp. 1–8). Cambridge: Royal Society of Chemistry.

Lombard, M. (2004). Distribution patterns of organic residues on Middle Stone Age points from Sibudu Cave, Kwazulu-Natal, South Africa. *South African Archaeological Bulletin, 59,* 37–44.

Lombard, M. (2005). Evidence of hunting and hafting during the Middle Stone Age at Sibidu Cave, KwaZulu-Natal, South Africa: A multianalytical approach. *Journal of Human Evolution, 48,* 279–300.

Lombard, M. (2006a). Direct evidence for the use of ochre in the hafting technology of Middle Stone Age tools from Sibudu Cave. *Southern Africa Humanities, 18,* 57–67.

Lombard, M. (2006b). First impressions of the functions and hafting technology of Still Bay pointed artefacts from Sibudu Cave. *Southern Africa Humanities, 18,* 27–41.

Lombard, M. (2007). The gripping nature of ochre: The association of ochre with Howiesons Poort adhesives and Later Stone Age mastics from South Africa. *Journal of Human Evolution, 53,* 406–419.

Lombard, M. (2008). Finding resolution for the Howiesons Poort through the microscope: Micro-residue analysis of segments from Sibudu Cave, South Africa. Including Appendix A. *Journal of Archaeological Science, 35,* 26–41.

Lombard, M. (2011). Quartz-tipped arrows older than 60 ka: Further use-trace evidence from Sibudu, KwaZulu-Natal, South Africa. *Journal of Archaeological Science, 38,* 1918–1930.

Lombard, M. (2014). In situ presumptive test for blood residues applied to 62 000-year-old stone tools. *South African Archaeological Bulletin 69,* 80–86.

Lombard, M., & Haidle, M. N. (2012). Thinking a bow-and-arrow set: Cognitive implications of Middle Stone Age bow and stone-tipped arrow technology. *Cambridge Archaeological Journal, 22,* 237–264.

Lombard, M., & Parson, I. (2011). What happened to the human mind after the Howiesons Poort? *Antiquity, 85,* 1433–1443.

Lombard, M., & Phillipson, L. (2010). Indications of bow and stone-tipped arrow use 64,000 years ago in KwaZulu-Natal, South Africa. *Antiquity, 84,* 1–14.

Lombard, M., & Wadley, L. (2007). The morphological identification of micro-residues on stone tools using light microscopy: Progress and difficulties based on blind tests. *Journal of Archaeological Science, 34,* 155–165.

Lombard, M., & Wadley, L. (2009). The impact of micro-residue studies on South African Middle Stone Age research. In M. Haslam, G. Robertson, A. Crowther, S. Nugent, & L. Kirkwood (Eds.), *Archaeological science under a microscope: Studies in residue and ancient DNA analysis in honour of Thomas H. Loy* (pp. 11–28). Canberra: ANU E press.

Lombard, M., Parsons, I., & Van der Rijst, M. M. (2004). Middle Stone Age lithic point experimentation for macro-fracture and residue analyses: The first set of experiments and preliminary results with reference to Sibudu Cave points. *South African Journal of Science, 100,* 159–166.

Loy, T. H. (1983). Prehistoric blood residues: Detection on tool surfaces and identification of species of origin. *Science, 220,* 1269–1271.

Loy, T. H. (1993). The artifact as site: An example of the biomolecular analysis of organic residues on prehistoric tools. *World Archaeology, 25,* 44–63.

Loy, T. H. (1998). Blood on the axe. *New Scientist, 159,* 40–43.

Loy, T. (2006). Optical properties of potential look-alikes. In R. Torrence & H. Barton (Eds.), *Ancient starch research* (pp. 123–124). Walnut Creek: Left Coast.

Loy, T., & Barton, H. (2006). Post-excavation contamination and measures for prevention. In R. Torrence & H. Barton (Eds.), *Ancient starch research* (pp. 165–167). Walnut Creek: Left Coast.

Lu, T. (2006). The survival of starch residues in a subtropical environment. In R. Torrence & H. Barton (Eds.), *Ancient starch research* (pp. 80–81). Walnut Creek: Left Coast.

Mauseth, J. D. (1988). *Plant anatomy*. Menlo Park: Benjamin/Cummings.

Milanesi, C., Bigliazzi, I., Faleri, C., Caterina, B., & Cresti, M. (2011). Microscope observations and DNA analysis of wine residues from Roman amphorae found in Ukraine and from bottles of recent Tuscan wines. *Journal of Archaeological Science, 38,* 3675–3680.

Milo, R. G. (1998). Evidence for hominid predation at Klasies River Mouth, South Africa, and its implications for the behaviour of early modern humans. *Journal of Archaeological Science, 25,* 99–133.

Monnier, G. F., Ladwig, J. L., & Porter, S. T. (2012). Swept under the rug: The problem of unacknowledged ambiguity in lithic residue identification. *Journal of Archaeological Science, 39,* 3284–3300.

Moran, D. T., & Rowley, J. C. (2005). *Visual Histology.com*. http://www.visualhistology.com/products/atlas/index.html. Accessed 21 Mar 2008.

Murphy, D. B. (2001). *Fundamentals of light microscopy and electronic imaging*. New York: Wiley.

Newman, M. E., Ceri, H., & Kooyman, B. (1996). The use of immunological techniques in the analysis of archaeological materials—a response to Eisele; with report of studies at Head-Smashed-In Buffalo Jump. *Antiquity, 70,* 677–682.

Newman, M. E., Yohe Ii, R. M., Kooyman, B., & Ceri, H. (1997). "Blood" from stones? Probably: A response to Fiedel. *Journal of Archaeological Science, 24,* 1023–1027.

Painter, T. J. (1991). Lindow man, Tollund man and other peat-bog bodies: The preservative and antimicrobial action of *Sphagnan*, a reactive glycuronoglycan with tanning and sequestering properties. *Carbohydrate Polymers, 15,* 123–142.

Piperno, D. R., Weiss, E., Holst, I., & Nadel, D. (2004). Processing of wild cereal grains in the Upper Palaeolithic revealed by starch grain analysis. *Nature, 430,* 670–673.

Piperno, D. R., Ranere, A. J., Holst, I., Iriarted, J., & Dickauc, R. (2009). Starch grain and phytolith evidence for early ninth millennium B.P. maize from the Central Balsas River Valley, Mexico. *Proceedings of the National Academy of Sciences, 106,* 5019–5024.

Plisson, H., & Beyries, S. (1998). Pointes ou outils triangulaires? Données fonctionnelles dans le Mousterian Levantin. *Paléorient, 24,* 5–24.

Prinsloo, L. C., Wadley, L., & Lombard, M. (2013). Infrared reflectance spectroscopy as an analytical technique for the study of residues on stone tools: potential and challenges. *Journal of Archaeological Science 41,* 732–739.

Raven, P. H., Evert, R. F., & Eichhorn, S. E. (1992). *Biology of plants* (5th ed.). New York: Worth Publishers.

Roler, K. L., & Clark, G. A. (1997). Use-wear analysis of Levallois Points from the 'Ain Difla Rockshelter, West-Central Jordan. In H. G. K. Gebel, Z. Kafafi, & G. O. Rollefson (Eds.), *The prehistory of Jordan II, perspectives from 1997* (pp. 101–109). Berlin: Ex Oriente.

Rost, F., & Oldfield, R. (2000). *Photography with a microscope*. Cambridge: Cambridge University Press.

Rots, V., & Williamson, B. S. (2004). Microwear and residue analyses in perspective: The contribution of ethnoarchaeological evidence. *Journal of Archaeological Science, 31*, 1287–1299.

Schleiden, M. J. (1849). *Principles of scientific botany*. London: Longman, Brown, Green and Longmans.

Shafer, H. J., & Holloway, R. G. (1979). Organic residue analysis in determining stone tool function. In B. Hayden (Ed.), *Lithic use-wear analysis* (pp. 385–399). New York: Academic Press.

Shea, J. J. (1989). A functional study of the lithic industries associated with hominid fossils in the Kebara and Qafzeh caves, Israel. In P. Mellars & C. Stringer (Eds.), *The human revolution, behavioural and biological perspectives on the origin of modern humans* (pp. 612–625). Edinburgh: Edinburgh University Press.

Shea, J. J. (1993). Lithic use-wear evidence for hunting in the Levantine Middle Paleolithic. In P. Anderson, S. Beyries, M. Otte, & H. Plisson (Eds.), *Traces et fonction: Les gestes retrouvés* (pp. 21–30). Liège: Université de Liège Press.

Sisk, M. L., & Shea, J. J. (2009). Experimental use and quantitative performance analysis of triangular flakes (Levallois points) used as arrowheads. *Journal of Archaeological Science, 36*, 2039–2047.

Sisk, M. L., & Shea, J. J. (2011). The African origin of complex projectile technology: An analysis using tip cross-sectional area and perimeter. *International Journal of Evolutionary Biology, 2011*, Article ID 968012, 1–8.

Smith, P. R., & Wilson, M. T. (2001). Blood residues in archaeology. In D. R. Brothwell & A. M. Pollard (Eds.), *Handbook of archaeological sciences* (pp. 313–322). Chichester: Wiley.

Stiner, M. C. (1994). *Honor among thieves, a zooarchaeological study of Neanderthal ecology*. Princeton: Princeton University Press.

Summerhayes, G. R., Leavesley, M., Fairbairn, A., Mandui, H., Field, J., Ford, A., & Fullagar, R. (2010). Human adaptation and plant use in highland New Guinea 49,000–44,000 years ago. *Science, 330*, 78–81.

Teerink, B. J. (1991). *Hair of West European mammals. Atlas and identification key*. Cambridge: Cambridge University Press.

Torrence, R. (2006). Description, classification and identification. In R. Torrence & H. Barton (Eds.), *Ancient starch research* (pp. 115–143). Walnut Creek: Left Coast.

Ungent, D., Pozorski, S., & Pozorski, T. (1981). Prehistoric remains from the sweet potato from the Casma Valley, Peru. *Phytologia, 49*, 401–415.

Ungent, D., Pozorski, S., & Pozorski, T. (1982). Archaeological potato tuber remains from the Casma Valley of Peru. *Economic Botany, 36*, 182–192.

Villa, P., & Soriano, S. (2010). Hunting weapons of Neanderthals and early modern humans in South Africa: Similarities and differences. *Journal of Anthropological Research, 66*, 5–38.

Von Stokar, W. (1938). Prehistoric organic remains. *Antiquity, 12*, 82–86.

Wadley, L. (2009). Post-depositional heating may cause over-representation of red coloured ochre in Stone Age sites. *South African Archaeological Bulletin, 64*, 166–171.

Wadley, L. (2010). Were snares and traps used in the Middle Stone Age and does it matter? A review and a case study from Sibudu, South Africa. *Journal of Human Evolution, 58*, 179–192.

Wadley, L., & Lombard, M. (2007). Small things in perspective: The contribution of our blind tests to micro-residue studies on archaeological stone tools. *Journal of Archaeological Science, 34*, 1001–1010.

Wadley, L., & Mohapi, M. (2008). A Segment is not a monolith: Evidence from the Howiesons Poort of Sibudu, South Africa. *Journal of Archaeological Science, 35*, 2594–2605.

Wadley, L., Lombard, M., & Williamson, B. (2004). The first residue analysis blind tests: Results and lessons learnt. *Journal of Archaeological Science, 31*, 1491–1501.

Wadley, L., Hodgskiss, T., & Grant, M. (2009). Implications for complex cognition from the hafting of tools with compound adhesives in the Middle Stone Age, South Africa. *Proceedings of the National Academy of Sciences, 106,* 9590–9594.

Wadley, L., & Langejans, G. H. J. (2014). Preliminary study of scrapers around combustion features in layer SS, Sibudu, 58 000 years ago. *South African Archaeological Bulletin, 69,* 19–53.

Williamson, B. S. (2006). Investigation of potential contamination on stone tools. In R. Torrence & H. Barton (Eds.), *Ancient starch research* (pp. 89–90). Walnut Creek: Left Coast.

Young, B., & Heath, J. W. (2002). *Wheather's functional histology: A text and colour Atlas* (4th ed.). London: Churchill Livingstone.

Zarrillo, S., Pearsall, D. M., Raymond, J. S., Tisdale, M. A., & Quon, D. J. (2008). Directly dated starch residues document early formative maize (*Zea mays* L.) in tropical Ecuador. *Proceedings of the National Academy of Sciences, 105,* 5006–5011.

Zimmerman, M. R. (1973). Blood cells preserved in a mummy 2000 years old. *Science, 180,* 303–304.

Zimmerman, M. R. (2001). The study of preserved human tissue. In D. R. Brothwell & A. M. Pollard (Eds.), *Handbook of archaeological sciences* (pp. 249–257). Chichester: Wiley.

Index

A
Abrasion, 43, 61, 73, 194
Acheulean, 46
Alps, 56
Alyawara, 33
Andalucía, 53
Antler, 8, 9, 13, 33, 60, 61, 73, 159
Arrow, 44, 55
Association of Archaeological Wear and Residue Analysts. (AWRANA), 1, 9
Asturias
 province of, 30
Atlatl, 55
Attrition, 73, 189, 193, 194
Auriac, 50

B
Barcelona, 49, 50
Basalt, 63, 71
Bédoulien, 49, 50
Behavior, 3
 socio-cultural, 18
Belize, 195
Binocular
 microscope, 162
Blind test, 6, 41, 213
Bòbila Madurell, 49, 50, 55
Bone tools, 5, 56
Bow, 55, 212
Butchering, 13, 46, 56, 208

C
Camera, 161
Canary islands, 28, 32, 75
Carbonization, 189–191
 exterior, 192
 internal, 195

Ceramic, 1, 4, 7, 8, 190, 193, 195
Chaîne opératoire, 32, 43
Chalain, 55
Chalcolithic, 75
Chasséen, 44, 46
Chert, 4, 8, 10
China, 63
Cleaning, 18, 61, 193, 201
Colorado plateau, 194
Combe Saunière, 54
Confocal microscope, 60
Cova Eirós, 63
Cyrus, 55

D
Débitage, 49
Diagnostic impact fractures, 10, 12, 14
Digital cameras, 161

E
Edge damage, 6, 9, 12, 13, 17, 160, 161
Edge rounding, 15, 42, 43
El Kown, 46
Ethiopia, 31, 33, 34
Ethnoarchaeology, 3, 27, 28, 35
Ethnographic, 2, 3, 6, 16, 27–29, 31, 33, 34, 36, 159, 164, 204
Experimental, 2, 6, 13, 15
 data, 44, 55
 programmes, 61, 73
 programs, 159

F
Farming, 34, 56
Fast expert system, 11, 16
Flint, 50, 60–62, 64, 73
 tools, 41, 43

Focus, 3, 14, 17, 54, 200
Fourneau du Diable, 54
Fractures, 5, 6, 12, 13, 60
   diagnostic, 9
France, 43, 48–50
François Bordes, 7
French Jura, 46
Friction, 16
Function, 2, 6, 50, 159, 207
   artifacts, 8
   primary, 193, 195
Functional, 1
   analysis, 3
   interpretation, 2, 6, 10, 16, 35
Funerary deposits, 57

G
Girona, 49
Gravettian, 63
Greece, 48
Grooves, 14, 62, 66, 163
Grotte de l'Église, 48
Ground stone tools, 4

H
Hafting, 15, 33
   traces, 16
Handle, 15
Hide, 9, 28, 31, 56
High-power approach, 9
Howiesons Poort, 63
Hunter-gatherers, 33, 159, 164

I
Iberian Peninsula, 34, 47, 53
Image processing software, 11
Ivory, 8, 159

J
Jbala, 34

K
Khirokitia *See* Cyrus, 55
Kinematics, 6, 32, 64, 70, 161
   indicator marks, 66
Knapping, 46, 60
Konso, 33, 34

L
La Draga, 53
Languedoc, 50
Lapa do Anecrial, 63

Laser Scanning Confocal Microscope
   (LSCM), 11, 12, 19
Le Baratin, 46
Levallois, 46
Lipids, 17, 195, 196
Lithics, 1, 7
Low-power approach, 9, 161
Luster, 18

M
Macroscopic, 10–12, 74, 161
Macro traces, 6, 13
Magnification, 64, 210
   high, 9, 11
Mastic, 14
Mediterranean, 53, 75
Meso-American, 75
Mesolithic, 33
Metal, 1, 4
Metallic tools, 8
Micro-fractures, 61
Microliths, 30
Micropolish, 42, 59, 60, 66
Micro-residue, 4, 199–201, 203, 204,
      211, 212
   animal, 207
   fish, 210
   plant, 204, 205
Micro-scarring, 66
Microscopy, 10, 17, 41, 205, 213
Micro traces, 10
Middle Palaeolithic, 46
Montbolo, 49
Morocco, 30, 34
Morph-types, 8
Motte aux Magnins, 46
Mousterian, 46

N
Neolithic, 33, 43, 44, 48, 53, 55, 62, 75
New Archeology, 6
Non-siliceous, 3
North American
   prehistory, 196
Nunamiut, 33

O
Obsidian, 8, 10, 30, 41, 60, 63, 73, 74
Oceania, 63
Olduvai, 63
Orinoco Valley, 30
Osseous, 3, 159, 162

Index

P
Palau-Savardera, 49
Paleolithic, 4, 7, 75
Paleotechnology, 7
Payre, 63
Pech de la Boissière, 54
Phonolith, 71
Photograph, 201
    technique, 3
Phytoliths, 17, 203
Placard, 54
Plants, 28, 31, 34, 61
    non-woody, 43
    silica-rich, 44
    siliceous, 74
Polish, 11, 12, 14, 15, 17, 42, 74, 160
    formation, 9, 10, 14
Post-depositional alterations, 17
Postdepositional alterations, 62
Pottery, 43, 50, 189, 194
Prehension, 4, 16
Projectiles, 2, 54–56, 159
Provence, 44, 46, 49

Q
Quantitative methods, 3
Quartz, 8, 10, 13, 30, 41, 60–63
Quartzite, 8, 10, 13, 41, 60, 62, 63, 69

R
Raw materials, 2, 4, 6, 8, 10, 48, 64, 75
Residues, 8, 14, 16, 29, 73
    analysis, 17, 195
Resin, 15, 190, 205, 206, 210
Rhyolite, 64
Rock crystal, 60, 63
Rounding, 42
Roussillon, 50
Russian archeology, 6

S
Sant Quirze del Vallès, 49
Sardinia, 56
Scanning Electron microscope (SEM), 11, 12, 60, 61
Scarring, 60, 66, 68, 73–75
Scars
    edge-damage, 42

Seasonality, 29, 36
Sepulcros de Fosa, 49
Sergei Semenov, 5
Shell, 7, 8, 61, 73, 159
Sibudu Cave, 63
Sickle, 30, 34
Siliceous, 3
Smoothing, 73–75, 195
Software, 8, 10, 15
Solutrean, 54
South Africa, 63, 212
South America, 30
Spain, 43
State of art, 162
Stereomicroscopy, 9
Stone tools, 4, 59, 199
Striations, 10, 12, 14, 15, 17, 42, 59, 163
Subsistence strategies, 4
Syria, 46

T
Terminology, 2, 8, 10
Tierra del Fuego, 30
Tool-kit, 63
Traceology, 4, 8, 59, 161
Tribology, 74

U
Upper Palaeolithic, 47, 54
Use-wear, 1–4, 6, 8, 10–12, 18, 42, 62, 159

V
Valencia, 53
Vanuatu, 63
Vessels, 190, 191, 194, 196
    ceramic, 44, 56, 194

W
Western Europe, 6, 48
Wolayta, 34

X
X-Ray, 161

Y
Yamada, S., 10, 16

Printed by Printforce, the Netherlands